85,–

Völkerrecht

'19

MAX-PLANCK-INSTITUT
FÜR AUSLÄNDISCHES ÖFFENTLICHES RECHT
UND VÖLKERRECHT

Beiträge zum ausländischen
öffentlichen Recht und Völkerrecht

Begründet von Viktor Bruns

Herausgegeben von
Armin von Bogdandy · Anne Peters

Band 273

Matthias Goldmann · Silvia Steininger (eds.)

Democracy and Financial Order: Legal Perspectives

Springer

ISSN 0172-4770 ISSN 2197-7135 (electronic)
Beiträge zum ausländischen öffentlichen Recht und Völkerrecht

ISBN 978-3-662-55567-5 ISBN 978-3-662-55568-2 (eBook)
https://doi.org/10.1007/978-3-662-55568-2

Library of Congress Control Number: 2018936368

Springer

Printed on acid-free paper

This Springer imprint is published by the registered company Springer-Verlag GmbH, DE part of Springer Nature.
The registered company address is: Heidelberger Platz 3, 14197 Berlin, Germany

Contents

Introduction: Democracy and Financial Order – Legal Perspectives

Matthias Goldmann and Silvia Steininger

This volume assembles nine articles on the relationship between democracy and the financial order from various legal perspectives. Each contribution adopts a unique perspective on the legal and political challenges brought to the fore by the Global Financial Crisis. This crisis and the ensuing sovereign debt crisis in Europe are only the latest in a long series of financial crises in the last decades all over the world. By their very existence, but also by the political turmoil they have created, these financial crises testify to the well-known tensions between democracy and a market-based economic and financial order.

Revised version of the original published article "Introduction: Democracy and Financial Order – Legal Perspectives" by Matthias Goldmann and Silvia Steininger, German Law Journal 17(5):705–708

M. Goldmann (✉)
Goethe University Frankfurt, Frankfurt a.M., Germany
e-mail: goldmann@jur.uni-frankfurt.de

S. Steininger
Max Planck Institute for Comparative Public Law and International Law, Heidelberg, Germany
e-mail: steininger@mpil.de

M. Goldmann, S. Steininger (Eds.), *Democracy and Financial Order: Legal Perspectives*, Beiträge zum ausländischen öffentlichen Recht und Völkerrecht,
https://doi.org/10.1007/978-3-662-55568-2_1

To explain these tensions, two basic positions emerge: On one hand, some scholars fear that the interests of the market will harm democracy. The accumulation of capital will not remain without political repercussions. Rather, if economic power is concentrated in the hands of few people, it might equip that minority with disproportionate political clout. The result might be policies favoring the interests of the wealthy at the expense of the democratic majority, endangering equality and social rights. On the other hand, there is the belief that democratic decision-making would undermine the economy. Majority voting might compromise the adoption of burdensome, but economically efficient or sustainable solutions. It might entice popular policies that are beneficial only in the short term, not in the long term. At worst, majority voting might lead to policies that cater to the special interests of whichever group happens to be in power, to the detriment of the common interest. Naturally, these arguments appear in as many varieties as there are varieties of capitalism and democracy.

Yet, there is one factor that remains often ignored in these debates—law. Only a few studies put the concept of law center stage.[1] This is quite surprising. Both theories of democracy and political economy regularly assign a central role to law. Law is the conveyor of the popular will and keeps it in check at the same time. Law delineates the spheres of freedom of different economic actors, establishes the institutions that keep the economy running, and entrenches private economic interests against state intervention. Our surprise derives from the fact that the concept of law is all but uncontroversial in legal theory, not least because of Weber's ground-breaking work on the role of law in the emergence of capitalist societies.[2]

This volume attempts to fill this lacuna. It focuses on the controversy surrounding the concept of law, thereby adding another variable to the debate about the relation between democracy and capitalism. Each chapter engages with the concept of law from a particular theoretical angle, be it a full-grown legal theory or an approach in political economy that has a particular view of the law. We have arranged the volume in order to reflect certain debates. Thus, the volume begins with a debate between two contemporary German theories of law by Jürgen Habermas (*Goldmann and Steininger*) and Niklas Luhmann (*Viellechner*). Next is a transatlantic debate between rational choice conceptions of law (*Towfigh*) and ideas of constitutional pluralism (*Avbelj*). Different traditions of mostly Anglo-Saxon liberalism are reflected in the contribution by *Suttle*, while *Goldmann* focuses on Amartya Sen's non-Western take of liberalism. Eventually, three contributions engage with conceptions of law in neoliberalism and ordoliberalism and the way they have shaped our perceptions of public finance, including budgetary rules, taxes, and money (*Biebricher, Saffie, Feichtner*). Of course, this list by no means reflects the entire spectrum of available legal theories, but rather attempts to strike a balance between a plurality of approaches and the need to keep the project manageable. Notable lacunae therefore exist, for example French poststructuralism.[3]

---

[1] Most notably, *see* Pistor (2013).

[2] Weber (1972 [1922]).

[3] In that respect, we refer the reader to Hunt (1992).

Each contribution elaborates its salient theoretical points by using an example of a particular case study or issue area that faces challenges in the aftermath of the financial crisis. Thus, while the articles all concern the law's capacity to accommodate both democracy and capitalism, each individually contributes to the development of law and policy in a particular issue area. Topics range from sovereign debt issues (*Goldmann and Steininger, Viellechner, Suttle*) to budgetary restrictions (*Biebricher*), banking regulation (*Avbelj and Goldmann*), money and the ECB (*Towfigh and Feichtner*), and taxes (*Saffie*).

The selected articles do not account for universality. The authors neither claim to present the most fitting theory nor to provide an all-encompassing analysis of the financial order; instead, each author aims to scrutinize the currently accepted ideas on the relationship between democracy and capitalism. They generally argue that the current frameworks are not without alternatives and prompt us to rethink and reimagine the relationship between democracy and a market-based financial order along the lines of their chosen approach. In this respect, the articles composing this special issue highlight the imperative of legal scholarship to go beyond the black letter of the legal measures adopted in the aftermath of a financial crisis and theorize about them with an awareness of the tensions between democracy and capitalism.

Specifically, *Matthias Goldmann and Silvia Steininger* argue that Habermas' theory of social integration assigns certain properties to the law, such as centralized governmental enforcement, a distinction between law-making and law-application, and a definition of the public as opposed to the private. Current sovereign debt restructuring practice calls each of these properties into question. The article shows that a contemporary conceptualization of international public authority, a democratization of international courts and tribunals, and the development of legitimate articulations of public interest that accounts for the different sides of emerging transnational cleavages might vindicate the discursive theoretical version of the relationship between democracy and capitalism.

In contrast, *Lars Viellechner* adopts a systems theoretical perspective on the Eurozone debt crisis. He finds that the current sovereign debt restructuring framework challenges and partly contradicts Luhmann's description of the performance, the relevance, and the function of law. Apart from explaining the limits of law in dealing with sovereign debt crises, a systems theoretical perspective also highlights the potential of the politicization, contestation, and debate surrounding the crisis for improving the legitimacy of European integration.

By applying insights of rational choice, *Emanuel Towfigh* claims—in opposition to theories like those by Habermas and Rawls—that actors in a democracy behave according to an economic logic. He argues that the discussion about a conflict between democracy and the economy is therefore misleading; it is the primarily economic structure of democratic decision-making itself which puts the economy at risk. The economic interests of democratic actors endanger financial stability and economic welfare. To remedy these institutional flaws, Towfigh looks to independent, expert-driven institutions such as the ECB.

Matej Avbelj analyzes the European banking union from the perspective of constitutional pluralism. While this approach has been extraordinarily successful in making sense of European integration in the last decades, it is hard-pressed to accommodate the complex and rapidly developing framework of EU banking supervision. EU banking supervision features a plurality of regimes, constituencies, regulatory levels, and institutions—and it often acts on a sub-constitutional level. With this in mind, Avbelj proposes thinking of the banking union in terms of administrative pluralism to describe, explain, and normatively guide the current, multilevel framework.

Oisin Suttle juxtaposes two varieties of liberalism: (1) a Humean, contextual one which dominates debates about domestic private debt, with (2) a Lockean, decontextualized one which permeates discourse about sovereign debt. He argues that the difference cannot be reconciled in terms of a coherent account of global justice. Instead, he advocates adopting a Humean approach to sovereign debt restructuring and elaborates the consequences of this approach for the duties of debtors and creditors. *Goldmann* adds another variant of liberalism with Amartya Sen's theory of justice. He argues that if democracy is understood on Sen's terms, one cannot blame an irredeemable conflict between capitalism and democracy for the failure to prevent the financial crisis, but rather a remediable lack of public reasoning as the material core of democracy according to Sen.

Neoliberalism is undeniably the most prominent and controversial theoretical approach. *Thomas Biebricher* opens the debate on neoliberalism by providing an extensive account on the development of neoliberal thought and practice. He analyzes the role of juridical neoliberalism; in other words, he looks at how judicial norms contribute to the success of neoliberal economic activities. Paradigmatic for this debate is Buchanan's idea of a balanced-budget amendment, which finds its real life counterpart in the European fiscal compact. *Francisco Saffie Gatica* and *Isabel Feichtner* analyze how current law and practice in various jurisdictions is framed by neoliberal ideas of taxation (Saffie) and ordoliberal ideas of money (Feichter). Saffie, in an analysis based on the work of Wolfgang Streeck and Colin Crouch, shows how neoliberalism has decoupled the idea of taxation from notions of solidarity. He is skeptical about the potential of the OECD's 2015 recommendations on Base Erosion and Profit Sharing to remedy this problem. Feichtner explores how the ordoliberal idea of money prevalent in the European Monetary Union has been called in question by the European sovereign debt crisis, especially by the ECB's Outright Monetary Transactions Program and the court decisions it entailed. She shows the contingency of this debate by contrasting it with the alternative theory of money devised by Abba Lerner.

Most of the contributions in this volume were published as part of a special issue of the German Law Journal in 2016 (vol. 17 issue 5). The idea behind this volume is to provide a more durable platform for this unique project. Most of the chapters have been updated for publication in this volume, and we would like to thank the team of Springer for their thorough editorial work. We are very grateful to Armin von Bogdandy and the Max Planck Institute for Comparative Public Law and International Law for supporting this project over the course of several years, to the DFG-funded Cluster of Excellence "The Formation of Normative Orders" at Goethe University Frankfurt for hosting, and the Bundesbank for generously funding a workshop in

September 2015 which allowed for an exchange of views on draft contributions. Emilios Avgouleas, Francesco Costamagna, Henrik Enderlein, Cristina Fasone, Bernd Goller, Agnieszka Janczuk-Gorywoda, Jennifer Hendry, Robert Howse, Stefan Magen, and Frank Schorkopf provided valuable talks and comments at this occasion. Last but not least, we want to express our warmest thanks to the authors whose contributions make this volume a unique scholarly endeavor.

References

Weber M (1972 [1922]) Wirtschaft und Gesellschaft 503 et seq., 5th edn. Mohr Siebeck, Tübingen
Goldmann M, Steininger S (2016) Introduction: democracy and financial order – legal perspectives. German LJ 17(5):705–708
Hunt A (1992) Foucault's expulsion of law: toward a retrieval. Law Soc Inq 17(1):1–38
Pistor K (2013) A legal theory of finance. J Comp Econ 41:315

Matthias Goldmann is Junior Professor for International Public Law and Financial Law at Goethe University Frankfurt and Senior Research Affiliate at the Max Planck Institute for Comparative Public Law and International Law, Heidelberg.

Silvia Steininger is a Research Fellow at the Max Planck Institute for Comparative Public Law and International Law, Heidelberg.

A Discourse Theoretical Approach to Sovereign Debt Restructuring: Towards a Democratic Financial Order

Matthias Goldmann and Silvia Steininger

Abstract This chapter studies the role of law for aligning democracy with a market-based financial order. Jürgen Habermas's discourse theoretical understanding of the role of law in the welfare state establishes a structure for exploring this issue. According to this approach, law needs to be enforceable, law-making and law-application need to be institutionally separated, and public law needs to be distinguishable from private law. The contemporary practice of sovereign debt restructuring reveals some empirical and normative challenges to this understanding of the law. Based on these findings, this chapter proposes several conceptual and institutional improvements that might lead to a more stable relationship between democracy and financial order. In particular, we argue that sovereign debt restructuring should tap the legitimating potential of existing transnational discourses that are characterized by cross-border cleavages in public discourse.

Revised version of the original published article "A Discourse Theoretical Approach to Sovereign Debt Restructuring: Towards a Democratic Financial Order" by Matthias Goldmann and Silvia Steininger, German Law Journal 17(5):709–746

While both authors assume responsibility for the entire text, Sects. 3.3 and 4.3 were mainly drafted by Silvia Steininger, and the rest of the text by Matthias Goldmann.

M. Goldmann (✉)
Goethe University Frankfurt, Frankfurt a.M., Germany
e-mail: goldmann@jur.uni-frankfurt.de

S. Steininger
Max Planck Institute for Comparative Public Law and International Law, Heidelberg, Germany.
e-mail: steininger@mpil.de

M. Goldmann, S. Steininger (Eds.), *Democracy and Financial Order: Legal Perspectives*, Beiträge zum ausländischen öffentlichen Recht und Völkerrecht,
https://doi.org/10.1007/978-3-662-55568-2_2

1 Democracy and Financial Order as a Challenge for Legal Theory

The financial crisis, which began in 2008, triggered an extensive debate—both public and academic—about the impact of a globalized financial order on democracy. Is it possible to match the power of the former by democratic institutions?[1] In many respects, this debate rehashes and further develops earlier controversies about the relationship between democracy and capitalism. One position in the controversy fears that the economic powers unleashed by capitalism will endanger equality and democratic sovereignty, whereas a counter-position suspects that democratic decision-making will unduly restrict liberty and hinder individuals from unfolding their economic potential.[2]

The debate has been ongoing for centuries. Scholars adapted the basic positions described above to the particular challenges of their time. Alexis de Tocqueville observed a highly egalitarian, pre-industrial society in the United States, which he believed would endanger political freedom, prompting him to send a warning message about the authoritarian potential of the quest for equality to his native France.[3] In contrast, Karl Marx and Friedrich Engels believed that the capitalist mode of production relied on, and reproduced, economic inequalities.[4] They concluded that only revolutionary change would bring about a democratic economic order in a post-capitalist society.[5] The development of the modern welfare state since the late nineteenth century has juxtaposed writers like Karl Polanyi, who cautioned that a market-based society would require a strong nation-state to curb market forces,[6] and Friedrich August von Hayek, who claimed that a free-market economy was a precondition of democracy.[7]

Contemporary contributions to this debate are abundant, but traditional left-right distinctions provide little orientation. Some theorists perceive democracy as being irreversibly dismantled by financial markets,[8] while others believe that a return to the nation-state or the democratization of international institutions are the only options for democracy.[9] Still others imply that technocratic policy-making guided by benchmarks will achieve outputs that overcome problems of democratic input.[10] Finally, some authors propose measures to increase economic equality in

---

[1] *See generally* Rodrik (2011); Avgouleas (2012), p. 110; von Weizsäcker et al. (2013).

[2] *See* Suttle, chapter "Debt, Sovereign Default, and Two Liberal Theories of Justice", for varieties within the liberal tradition.

[3] *See* de Tocqueville (1838), Ch. 1–2.

[4] *See* Marx and Engels (1974), p. 474.

[5] *See id.*

[6] *See* Polanyi (1944).

[7] *See* von Hayek (1960). For more on this debate, *see* von Weizsäcker (2014).

[8] *See, e.g.*, Sassen (2012); Streeck (2013).

[9] *See* Boutros Ghali (2009); Rodrik (2011).

[10] *See* Reinhart and Rogoff (2010).

the developed world,[11] while others recommend emancipating the developing world from its economic dependence.[12]

Yet, what is underrepresented in the recent debate about the complicated relationship between democracy and the financial order is any reflection on the role of law. Despite Weber's legacy,[13] scholarship theorizing about the role of law in this relationship remains in an infant stage.[14] This is especially surprising because both democracy and a market-based financial order heavily rely on the law—in practice as well as in theory. Democratic decision-making manifests itself in law-making, while financial orders require a legal infrastructure for the regulation of financial markets as well as for aspects that are government controlled such as public spending, taxes, and money.[15] It is thus fair to suppose that the perceived relationship between democracy and the financial order hinges on a person's particular concept of law. Just as there are "varieties of capitalism"[16] and different theoretical approaches to democratic governance, the role attributed to law—and the understanding of its capacity and limits—varies with the particular legal theory adopted. Often, however, the underlying concept of law seems to be implicit rather than explicit.

This is aggravated by the fact that developments in the globalized financial order during the last decades have called into question legal theories that were mostly developed with a view to the nation-state. These theories face several obstacles when addressing the aforementioned problems associated with aligning democracy and financial order. On the one hand, the current financial order lacks some of the structures and institutional requirements presupposed by concepts of law developed for democratic states. On the other hand, legal theory falls short of providing a satisfactory conceptual framework for capturing the inherent problems of financial order. Structural-institutional deficits and conceptual shortcomings mutually reinforce each other. This impairs the search for a viable solution to the democracy-capitalism conundrum for a globalized financial order.

This chapter seeks to remedy this problem by recasting the interaction of democracy and the financial order in the light of a legal theory perspective. As there is no universally accepted legal theory, we approach this research question from one particular understanding of the law: Jürgen Habermas's discourse theory of law and democracy.[17] Discourse theory lends itself to this analysis because it has arguably provided one of the most widely referred-to and enlightening reconstructions of the role of law for the politics and economy of Western post-war welfare states. Sect. 2 of the chapter elaborates upon how Habermasian discourse theory views the

[11] *See* Piketty (2014), pp. 471 f.

[12] *See* Haque (2002).

[13] Weber (1972 [1922]), pp. 503 f.

[14] There are certain remarkable publications, though, *see* Kirchhof (2010), § 169; Pistor (2013), pp. 315–330; in the context of world trade law, *see* Lang (2013).

[15] *See, e.g.*, Friedman (1962), p. 22.

[16] *See generally* Hall and Soskice (2001).

[17] *See* Habermas (1992).

relationship between democracy and the financial order. It develops the underlying concept of law, both in the original setting of the post-war welfare state and in today's globalized environment. Sect. 3 applies this theoretical approach to the contemporary legal framework for sovereign debt restructuring. Notably, three essential elements and preconditions of the discourse theoretical understanding of the law are absent in this context: first, soft law is much more effective than discourse theory assumes; second, there is no clear functional separation between law-making and law-applying institutions; and third, the distinction between public and private interests and law is not straightforward. In line with the normative and reconstructive character of discourse theory, Sect. 4 makes tentative proposals which comprise both modifications to the discourse theoretical understanding of law and democracy, and to the structural-institutional framework for sovereign debt restructuring. The first of the problems revealed requires a conceptual switch from law to authority. The second commands the establishment of democratically controlled adjudication for sovereign debt restructuring. The third calls for a new conceptualization of the public. While discourse theory normally assumes that the public is characterized by a common lifeworld, this chapter contends that, as shown by the current state of sovereign debt restructuring, a concept of the public adequate for global financial regulation should rely on transnational cleavages as fundamental dividing lines in society that run across, not along, national borders. While this proposal would not reach the level of democracy that allegedly characterizes domestic welfare states, it would be a second-best and realistic solution for a more democratic global financial order.

2 The Role of Law for a Democratic Financial Order in Discourse Theory

The following summarizes Habermas's idea of the relationship between democracy and financial order, originally developed in his reconstruction of the modern welfare state. Habermas conceptualizes the law as a system of rules subject to central enforcement, with separate institutions responsible for making and applying the law, and a distinction between private and public spheres, each governed by its proper law. In his more recent writings on globalization and Europeanization, Habermas generally stuck to the concept of law developed in the context of the welfare state.

2.1 Democracy and Financial Order in the Nation State

To date, Habermas's most in-depth analysis of democracy and the economy is a short monograph from 1973 entitled "Legitimation Problems in Late Capitalism" (LC).[18] It represents an important work in a larger debate on the crisis of the modern

[18] Habermas (1973a). For an English summary, *see* Habermas (1973b).

welfare state during the 1970s. In this debate, the term "late capitalism" characterizes a view that perceived the crisis of the welfare state as the result of inherent contradictions in capitalism. The opposite view feared that union power and clientelist practices would render the democratic welfare state ungovernable.[19]

Arguing in support of the former approach, Habermas distinguished different stages of economic development of modern society. The relevant criterion for this distinction, as well as the main focus of much of Habermas's work, is the question of social integration—of what keeps society together and determines people's collective identity. Habermas held that capitalism's inner contradictions put social integration at risk at each of several ideal-typical stages of development of the modern state. Accordingly, liberal capitalism, characterized by largely unregulated market economies, tends to create cyclical economic crises which threaten social integration through unemployment and ensuing class struggles.[20] In late capitalism, the modern welfare state intervenes in the market in order to avoid or mitigate cyclical economic crises. It creates investment opportunities and provides infrastructure to increasingly monopolistic companies. While this reduces cyclical economic downturns, it increases public debt and inflation. One could therefore say that, according to this view, multiple, permanent financial crises are the late capitalist equivalent of cyclical economic crises characterizing liberal capitalism.[21] They reduce the capacity of states to provide welfare services (generating a rationality crisis), which in turn disappoints citizens and reduces their loyalty (leading to a legitimacy crisis), both contributing to social disintegration. Instead of class struggle, late capitalism encounters crises of the political system. In the end, Habermas observed that late capitalist societies face a choice between breaking the domination of elites and monopolies or switching to more authoritarian forms of government.[22] This late capitalist perspective sharply opposed the "ungovernability" view, which advocated the retreat of government intervention—with considerable success.[23]

From today's perspective, Habermas's LC is outdated in a number of respects. The "great moderation"[24] profoundly shattered LC's assumption that inflation was a permanent feature of welfare states that would undermine their legitimacy among large segments of the population. Instead, inflation and the economic struggles during the late 1960s and 1970s caused modern welfare states to gradually lose the support of capital owners who began pressing for globalization and deregulation.[25] Not unrelated is another fallacy: LC's progress narrative assumed that religion would gradually fade away as a means of social integration during modernity. The rise of religious extremism, a genuinely modern phenomenon,[26] demonstrates that

---

[19] Schäfer (2008). *See, e.g.*, Mandel (1972); Offe (1972).

[20] Habermas (1973a), pp. 42–43.

[21] *Cf.* Schäfer (2008), p. 13.

[22] *See* Habermas (1973a), pp. 66–73, 128–130.

[23] *See* Schäfer (2008), p. 17.

[24] *See generally* Bernanke (2004).

[25] Streeck (2013), pp. 44–45.

[26] *See* Rittberger and Hasenclever (2000), pp. 641–674.

LC was probably right about the interplay between religious and economic forms of social integration, but that it predicted the precise opposite of the development that would actually take place. Nevertheless, in other respects, LC forecasts accurate assessments of the situation in Western welfare states towards the end of the twentieth century. Among them is the idea that communicative rationality may have a decisive function for social integration.[27]

Habermas developed this idea more fully in later works,[28] in respect of political discourse notably in "Between Facts and Norms" (BFN).[29] In this work, almost twenty years after LC and in the midst of the "great moderation," Habermas displayed a much more harmonious view of politics and, in particular, of the relationship between democracy and capitalism. According to this later approach, society in democratic welfare states was held together by communicative action. Habermas considered representative democratic institutions like parliaments, which he mostly ignored in LC, as the keystones of social integration. He recognized them as the places where pragmatic discourse about diverging self-interests converged with socially integrative discourse about ethics and morals. Thus, in democratic institutions, debates in the wider public sphere coalesced into rationally acceptable political decisions, thereby generating loyalty among the people. The administration rendered these decisions effective, while courts ensured respect for fundamental rights. A competitive market economy produced welfare benefits which supported the whole order. Both systems, the administration and the market, required a legal framework. On the one hand, law enabled each system to function effectively by defining enforceable rights, status, and competencies. On the other hand, law tied these systems to the "common good" and to the socially integrative effects of communicative action.[30]

Habermas's idea of society advanced in BFN is not entirely harmonious, however. In fact, Habermas is very much aware of the risk that powerful economic interests might disturb the fragile balance between public and private interests. In this respect, law might become a vehicle for vested interests that threaten social integration. The presumption that law is legitimate might disguise illegitimate power.[31]

2.2 *The Underlying Concept of Law*

BFN's account of the late twentieth century welfare state assigned a key role to law. Three important assumptions, central to understanding the relationship between democracy and economic order, characterize Habermas's concept of law in BFN: (1) law consists of centrally enforceable rules; (2) law-making and law-application

---

[27] *See* Habermas (1973a), p. 140.

[28] Habermas (1981), pp. 369 ff.

[29] Habermas (1992).

[30] *See id.*, pp. 58–59.

[31] *See id.*, p. 59.

require different modes of reasoning and procedures; and (3) one needs to distinguish public law from private law.

2.2.1 Law as Enforceable and Legitimate Rules

A first, important element of Habermas's concept of law invokes Immanuel Kant's doctrine of right.[32] Accordingly, law has a dual character; it consists of rules that are supposed to be both legitimate and effective. Habermas suggests that the legitimacy of law derives from communicative reason expressed in the practice of political discourse. But it is precisely law's origin in political discourse, and hence its contingency, which entails the possibility that people might reasonably disagree with legal rules. This applies *a fortiori* to rules regulating market activity. Some market participants might have strong incentives to violate legal rules that stand in the way of the pursuit of their self-interest. Hence, legal rules require some form of enforcement. Ideally, by being both legitimate and effective, legal rules unite freedom and constraint, allowing their addressees to choose whether to obey the law for intrinsic reasons because they believe it to be legitimate, or for extrinsic reasons because a violation entails negative consequences.[33]

While Habermas discussed the issue of legitimacy extensively, he dedicated relatively little thought to the modalities of law enforcement. His understanding of these modalities seems to follow what one might call a "constraint theory."[34] Accordingly, law enforcement requires centralized or coordinated government institutions with the ability to deploy the full range of police powers and other means that directly compel the addressee of a legal rule. Constraint theories have been highly popular in legal and political theory since early modernity. They may have originated in a modern anthropology that resonated especially well with Protestantism.[35] While medieval scholastics had presumed human nature to be amenable to both good and evil purposes and ends,[36] modernity and the Protestant Reformation firmly established the idea of the *natura corrupta*—the sinful character of human nature since the fall.[37] This was a core theme in Martin Luther's theory of justification.[38] Thomas

[32] *See* Kant (1790), § D.

[33] *See id.*, pp. 46–47.

[34] Goldmann (2015), pp. 339–344.

[35] Note, however, that important work reflecting this anthropology predates the Reformation. *See* Machiavelli (1513 [1891]).

[36] *Cf.* Aquinas (1265–73 [1894]), q. 109, art. II, p. 829.

[37] *See e.g.* Duke of Saxony et al. (1530):

> Also they teach that, after Adam's fall, all men begotten after the common course of nature are born with sin; that is, without the fear of God, without trust in him, and with fleshly appetite; and that this disease, or original fault, is truly sin, condemning and bringing eternal death now also upon all that are not born again by baptism and the Holy Spirit.

[38] *See* Luther (1525 [1924]) (describing man's need for divine redemption after the fall due to his sinful nature). Luther's understanding of state and society is consistent with his theology of justification. *See* Böckenförde (2006), p. 418; Buchrucker (1972), p. 257.

Hobbes' political theory reflected this anthropology when it argued that society requires a Leviathan to keep in check the rational egoists who compose it.[39] After Hobbes, constraint theories of law made their way into legal and political theory and the underlying anthropology became increasingly secularized. Constraint theory reappeared in early capitalist writings in the form of the idea of the *homo economicus*.[40] If self-interest is considered as such a dominant driver of human behavior, it seems obvious that it can only be controlled by directly constraining enforcement mechanisms. The focus on constraint has thus influenced the idea of law of eminent writers in the post-enlightenment era, most prominently that of John Austin,[41] but also that of Marx and Engels.[42] In Habermas's work, constraint theory leads to a conceptual distinction between intrinsic and extrinsic modes of motivation, between legitimacy and enforcement, between discourse and constraint—the latter being limited to classical means of law enforcement.

2.2.2 Relationship between Law-Making and Law-Application

The presumption that, besides being effective, law is also legitimate is quite a demanding one. It applies not only to legislation, which receives its legitimacy from communicative reason brought about by legislative procedures that connect law to the wider public sphere. It also implies that the application of the law to individual cases is legitimate, not merely the expression of arbitrary power, of vested interests and economic preponderance. In other words, some kind of reason needs to connect law-making and law-application, legislation and adjudication.

This is not a trivial issue. Towards the late nineteenth century, the ideas underlying post-enlightenment *Begriffsjurisprudenz*—the view that legal reasoning and legal decisions are objective—increasingly came under stress. The legal realist movement argued that legal reasoning is contingent due to the indeterminacy of language. Power, rather than justice, prevailed in the application of the law.[43] This position was corroborated by the linguistic turn, which argued that the meaning of linguistic propositions like legal rules was determined by their usage in a specific context, not by any intrinsic semantic content.[44] This raised the question whether one could understand the application of the law as guided by reason and not just by power or the random mood of judges, and whether it was possible to consider legal decisions as "right" by any standard.

Habermas provides an affirmative answer to these questions, based on the idea that law-application follows a specific kind of discursive rationality that is different from the rationality of law-making.[45] Unlike Dworkin, Habermas did not assume

[39] *See* Hobbes (1647 [1760]), § 1.

[40] *See* Smith (1776), Ch. 2.

[41] *See* Austin (1832 [2001]).

[42] *See* Marx and Engels (1974), pp. 459, 477.

[43] *See* Holmes (1881).

[44] *See e.g.*, Rorty (1967).

[45] *See* Habermas (1992), pp. 272–291.

that the rationality of law-application depends on the capacity of the judge to find the right answer.[46] Rather, he replaced a subjective standard of rightness with one that is intersubjective. Rightness then becomes a question of intersubjective acceptability. Law-applying discourses follow specific rules which make their results intersubjectively acceptable. Among them are the rules of procedure which determine the issue at stake, allowing some arguments to be presented and excluding others. Legal arguments as such are not determined by rules of procedure, but by the positive law as a reference point. It is the task of the law-applier to rationally reconstruct the law with respect to a specific case.[47] The standard of rightness of legal decisions, the regulative idea of the only right decision, thus becomes a question of procedure and acceptable arguments.

Nevertheless, part of this story is that the judiciary needs to be embedded in a framework of democratic legitimacy.[48] After all, intersubjective rightness is not the same as objective rightness. It involves an element of contingency, which is only acceptable as long as there is a representative parliament that can intervene and change the law in reaction to judicial decision-making. Also, judges need to be democratically selected, whether by election or indirectly by appointment.

2.2.3 The Public-Private Distinction

A further distinction that is crucial to Habermas's understanding of the law is that between public and private law. This distinction, which finds its common law equivalent in specific rules for commercial activities,[49] reflects the emergence of separate public and private spheres in early modern societies as an important requirement of liberal capitalism.[50] Post-enlightenment doctrines of private law hypostatized the idea of the subjective, or private, right as an apolitical institution with a solid foundation in natural law or reason.[51] Nevertheless, the development of the welfare state during late capitalism led to an increasing entanglement of the public and private spheres, characterized by both governmental interventions in the market that restrict liberty, and by the transfer of public services to private actors. This made the liberal capitalist separation of the private and public spheres, and of private and public law, untenable.[52] At the same time, its theoretical justification crumbled away. With the demise of natural law and the law of reason, only positive law remained as a foundation for both private and public law. The establishment of the welfare state laid

[46] *Cf.* Dworkin (1977), p. 14.

[47] *Cf.* Goldmann (2014a), pp. 373–399.

[48] *See* von Bogdandy and Venzke (2015); Möllers (2008), pp. 100–106.

[49] *See* Habermas (1962), p. 90.

[50] *See id.*, pp. 23–32, 158–169 (discussing the entanglement of the public and private spheres since the late nineteenth century).

[51] *See* Habermas (1981b), pp. 525–527; Habermas (1973a), pp. 112–135. This reveals the Kantian element in Savigny. *Cf.* Rückert (1984), pp. 184–186; Thomale (2015).

[52] *See* Habermas (1962), pp. 158–169, 194.

bare the political contingency of the positive law,[53] leading legal theorists to draw different conclusions.[54] On the one hand, Kelsen revealed the ideological character of the distinction between public and private law by pointing out that all law was ultimately state-made.[55] Not surprisingly, his theory shows little concern for individual rights. On the other hand, the ordoliberal school of thought saw subjective rights as functional tools for establishing a capitalist economy. Some of them considered democratic decisions constraining individual rights as risks to the economic order.[56] Both approaches considered public law, respectively private law, as a functional necessity devoid of moral content.[57] They did not offer insights into how one might imagine the relationship between freedom and democracy as a productive one. Capitalism and democracy seemed to defeat each other.

In his earlier work, Habermas followed a similarly pessimistic view in which law served two different purposes in late capitalism. On the one hand, law played the role of a medium between the economy and the welfare state, serving as a functional tool. On the other hand, some legal rules, like constitutional or criminal laws, had the character of an institution within the society as a whole, depending on shared background convictions embedded in the lifeworld.[58] In BFN, in line with his more optimistic view on the relationship between capitalism and democracy, Habermas gave up this position and shifted to what he called the procedural paradigm of the law.[59] Accordingly, freedom and democracy, hence subjective—or private—rights, and objective—or positive—law, mutually precondition each other. Habermas reached this result by observing the communicative practices and procedures of contemporary democracies and by carefully analyzing theories of social contract. The mutual self-interest of citizens to have their private rights guaranteed by an objective legal framework does not provide a sufficient reason for entering into a social contract because one cannot understand private rights as having an intrinsic objective content. Under these conditions, citizens run the risk that the positive law will only recognize the subjective, or private, rights of the stronger, more powerful segments of society. Hence, citizens would only accept a social contract and the legal order it establishes if it guarantees and limits private rights in legitimate ways. This immediately leads to the idea of the equiprimordiality of private and public law, of individual freedom and democracy. By transcending their self-interest in the imaginative moment of a social contract, citizens are able to establish an objective order of positive law which recognizes subjective rights and, simultaneously, provides for procedures that allow limiting their exercise.[60] Private

---

[53] *See id.*, pp. 196–198.

[54] This coincides with the difference between liberal and republican approaches to democracy. *Cf.* Habermas (1992), p. 351.

[55] *See* Kelsen (1967), pp. 281–284.

[56] *See* von Hayek (1960); *see also* Biebricher, chapter "The Concept of Law in Neoliberalism".

[57] This does not apply to the deontological tradition in liberalism. *See* Suttle, chapter "Debt, Sovereign Default, and Two Liberal Theories of Justice".

[58] *See* Habermas (1962), p. 536.

[59] *See* Habermas (1992), p. 502 n. 47.

[60] *See id.*, p. 117.

and public law have equivalent relevance; neither has precedence over the other. In this way, Habermas, following Kant, distinguishes the common good from individual self-interest. The former transcends the latter. A qualitative difference exists between the public and the private interest, hence between public and private law.[61]

This distinction does not amount to some form of systemic fragmentation that would compromise the interaction between politics and the economy.[62] Nevertheless, it entails different types of legitimacy. Public law, including the legal framework for the exercise of private freedom and the acquisition of subjective rights—i. e. market regulation—is geared towards the public interest and requires democratic legitimacy. It needs to be adopted by institutions enabling practical discourse. This creates objectivity in the more modest form of inter-subjective rationality.[63] Private law—i. e. subjective rights acquired through transactions framed by positive law—is geared towards supposedly mutual private self-interest and finds its justification in private autonomy.[64] Accordingly, markets, especially financial markets, are characterized by the interaction between public and private actors. What Pistor considers the "essential hybridity" of the law of finance is in fact a reflection of the equiprimordiality of democracy and freedom.[65]

2.3 Democracy and Financial Order in a Global Context

The preceding analysis reflects Habermas's thinking in a nation-state context. But globalization entails some serious challenges for Habermas's earlier assumptions about the relationship between democracy and financial order. These challenges have become the subject of some of Habermas's more recent writings. In a series of shorter essays, he discusses transformations of the public sphere, challenges for regulatory and enforcement capacities in a multi-level system, as well as the imminent threat of the legitimacy deficit of global decision-making. Nevertheless, his concept of law has remained relatively stable.

In his essay on the constitutionalization of public international law, Habermas finds that legal regulation as a means of social integration is struggling to unfold in the post-national setting.[66] It lacks not only the essential procedural prerequisites of discursive law-making, but also an underlying common lifeworld and corresponding global public that would provide a basis for social integration. Given this context, international organizations should limit their scope of activities to issues

[61] Habermas (1992), pp. 118–123.

[62] For more about the position of systems theory, see Viellechner, chapter "The Limits of Law (and Democracy) in the Euro Crisis: An Approach from Systems Theory".

[63] *See* Habermas (1992), pp. 166–291.

[64] *Cf.* Goldmann (2016), pp. 48–84.

[65] Pistor (2013).

[66] Habermas (2004), pp. 113–193.

which enjoy a high degree of acceptance and legitimacy because they are supported by an underlying moral consensus, namely the prohibition of the use of force and protection from grave human rights violations.[67] By contrast, international organizations should refrain from redistributive activities. At this stage, Habermas left the question open regarding how to regain democratic control of an increasingly globalized economic and financial order whose regulatory needs are currently addressed at best by technocratic responses.

In "The Lure of Technocracy: A Plea for European Solidarity," Habermas takes a very critical stance towards the expansion of technocracy at the expense of democratic authority.[68] This development has been particularly severe in the context of the Eurozone crisis. It has revealed the preference of states for pragmatic, short-term solutions to regain control of the crisis over fundamental, long-term changes to the EU's institutional setting that would enhance democracy. As a consequence, the European idea has remained an elite project with very limited options for citizen involvement. This further endangers social integration in and beyond the nation-state because it uncouples the decision-making processes from representative institutions and removes them to exclusive circles.[69] Combined with the lack of an inclusive European public and an active civil society, these developments result in financial regulation which does not meet the needs or the expectations of the people: "A democratically uprooted technocracy neither possesses the power nor the motive to respect the demands of their constituencies for social justice, social safety, public welfare and public goods against the systemic preferences of a competitive and growth-oriented economy."[70]

Nevertheless, Habermas refuses to accept the "nostalgic option" brought forward, amongst others, by Wolfgang Streeck,[71] i. e. the roll-back to the nation-state.[72] Habermas argues that a policy of economic and financial isolationism is neither prudent, as it would be impossible to isolate a nation and undo globalization, nor necessary, as Streeck underestimates the regulatory capabilities of democracies.[73] Most importantly, in contrast to Streeck, Habermas believes that a democratic public can constitute itself beyond the nation-state, enabling coordinative rule-making by sovereign states to be transformed into common policy-making. There is no reason to think that political, social, and cultural identities are tied to the nation-state or that their evolution beyond national borders leads to a tyranny of the majority or a loss of diversity. The combination of European and national citizenship as representations of the EU's dualistic legitimacy structure is a prime example of how to successfully integrate domestic and global identities into a decision-making process.[74] Solidarity,

---

[67] *See id.*, pp. 172–173.

[68] *See* Habermas (2013a).

[69] *See id.*, pp. 82–92.

[70] *Id.*, p. 92 (author translation).

[71] *See* Streeck (2013).

[72] Habermas (2013b).

[73] *See id.*, pp. 142–145, 149–152.

[74] *See id.*, pp. 152–154; Habermas (2011), pp. 39–69. For the dualistic legitimacy of the Union, *see* von Bogdandy (2000), pp. 284–297.

understood as a mutual interest in the integrity of a common political way of life,[75] derives from a social context that is legally constructed. Hence, in Habermas's view, one possible solution to reunite capitalism and democracy beyond the nation state consists of encouraging solidarity through legal structures and institutions. For the Eurozone crisis, such an approach would require countering technocratic tendencies with more democratic structures and institutions.[76] This would include developing a political union that complements, rather than replaces, the member states and is in line with the duality of European citizenship—represented by the European Parliament—and national citizenship—represented by the Council—and the active promotion of a European public.[77]

Ultimately, Habermas believes that the idea of the welfare state developed more than a decade earlier with respect to the nation-state is in principle a possible model for reconciling democracy and capitalism also on levels beyond the nation state. He does not join with authors who fear the demise of the Keynesian welfare state.[78] Habermas finds that legitimacy is the main problem for a global financial order, just as it was in the late capitalist welfare state—albeit under different auspices: Instead of financial incapacity, deliberate policy choices are preventing the global order from generating the loyalty of the people.[79] Habermas's answer is that the public needs to constitute itself beyond the state, establishing adequate structures for the representation of citizens and nation-states on the international level and effective mechanisms for the regulation of global economic activities. The hope is that representative legal institutions charged with regulating the economy will lead to the emergence of a global public and provide a basis for solidarity. This vision for a global democratic economic and financial order assigns an important role to the law. The concept of law remains unchanged in respect of all three characteristics elaborated above.[80] One may ask whether this is how law actually functions in the context of a global financial order.

3 The Role of Law in Sovereign Debt Restructuring Practice

This section explores the extent to which the discourse theoretical concept of law that was initially developed in the context of the modern welfare state provides a reconstruction of sovereign debt restructurings that is both empirically and normatively satisfactory. To do so, it will apply the concept of law underlying Habermas's

[75] *See* Habermas (2004), p. 104.

[76] *See id.*, pp. 155–156.

[77] *See* Habermas (2004), pp. 93–96; Habermas (2014), pp. 167–192.

[78] *See* Jessop (2002); Streeck (2013).

[79] *See* Schäfer (2008), p. 39.

[80] *See supra* Sect. 2.2.

ideas about democracy and financial order to the contemporary practice of sovereign debt restructuring.

We test the concept of law for its empirical and normative robustness because the global financial order entails both empirical and conceptual challenges and because it follows from Habermas's particular methodological approach, known as rational reconstruction.[81] Rational reconstruction oscillates between the empirical and the normative; it aims to carve out the normative presuppositions underlying contemporary practice. This is also the measure of correctness we apply when testing the theory. The theory might be unsatisfactory, requiring conceptual adjustments to the extent that it does not adequately capture an important element of contemporary practice that is expected under the general normative presuppositions of that practice. By contrast, the structural and institutional framework constituting contemporary practice might need to be adjusted to the extent that it contradicts the general normative presuppositions of that practice. Indeed, in case the application of a theory resulting from rational reconstruction to a particular practice shows a gap between practice and theory, solutions will often include elements of both.

Sovereign debt restructuring is an ideal case study; it represents a particularly difficult case of some of the typical problems pervading the contemporary global financial order.[82] To some extent, sovereign debt crises are the result of unregulated global financial markets which make credit easily available to states. These crises are also a product of regulatory failure on both domestic and international levels. Modern welfare states, whether in developing or developed economies, do not always have adequate mechanisms in place to curb the pileup of debt. Internationally, there is no comprehensive and predictable mechanism to resolve sovereign debt crises. Instead, the resolution of these crises lies in informal, fragmented negotiation processes. Most importantly, in sovereign debt crises, the rationalities of democracy and contemporary financial order clash with particular intensity. Sovereign debt restructuring entails some form of agreement between the debtor state and its creditors about structural adjustment measures and financial relief, each of which have an immense impact on domestic policy.

Before scrutinizing Habermas's concept of law in the context of sovereign debt restructuring, we should emphasize that we consider his analysis of globalization in many respects as correct and helpful for the analysis of sovereign debt restructuring. Sovereign debt restructuring raises questions of solidarity and distribution. As Habermas observes, there is practically no institution available that has the necessary democratic legitimacy for such questions.[83] Instead, sovereign debt restructurings involve technocratic actors and decision-making processes. This is especially true for the role of the International Monetary Fund (IMF) with its high degree of

---

[81] Goldmann (2014a); Habermas (2009); Patberg (2014), pp. 501–521.

[82] For an overview of contemporary sovereign debt restructuring practice, *see* UNCTAD (2015); Das et al. (2012).

[83] *Cf.* Habermas (2004).

technical expertise and comparatively low level of democratic legitimacy, given that the relative shares of the IMF's capital a member possesses determine that member's number of votes. The Paris Club, the informal committee of bilateral debtors, represents another highly technocratic institution lacking in democratic legitimacy.

Any proposal or solution based on Habermas's analysis will, to some extent, rely on the law to regulate the financial order. One should therefore examine whether the concept of law implicit in Habermas's writings about globalization may serve the rational reconstruction of the contemporary practice of sovereign debt restructuring. There are three gaps between Habermas's concept of law and contemporary practice which require conceptual or practical adjustments. These gaps concern the following: (1) the role of soft law and information in sovereign debt restructuring; (2) the law-making role of adjudication in relation to sovereign debt restructuring; (3) and the extremely complex mix of public and private actors, acts, and interests, which make the reconstitution of a global public more difficult than Habermas's writings recognize.

3.1 *Hard and Soft Law in Sovereign Debt Restructuring*

One important aspect of the contemporary practice of sovereign debt restructuring is the role of instruments that are not considered binding international or domestic law. These instruments—including soft law and information—seem to escape a discourse theoretical concept of law. Such instruments play important roles at different stages of a sovereign debt restructuring process.

For example, the IMF carries out Debt Sustainability Assessments (DSA) which frame sovereign debt restructurings in many ways.[84] They provide an estimate as to whether a state is in a financial situation that allows it, with high probability, to roll over or reduce its debt in the foreseeable future without a major correction in the balance of income and expenditure.[85] DSAs are regulated by the internal law of the IMF adopted by the IMF's management as part of its general competence.[86] A DSA consists of two steps. In the first step, the IMF examines whether the debt-to-GDP ratio of a country meets defined benchmarks which correspond with the relative development level of the country in question—the more developed the country, the higher the benchmark. The second step consists of further scrutiny for additional risk factors, which can be higher or lower depending on the outcomes of the first step.

The IMF carries out DSAs for several purposes: as part of its regular bilateral surveillance activities under Article IV of the Articles of Agreement; in order to examine whether a country applying for a loan is eligible; and during the disbursement of a loan. While one might, in general, doubt the significance of the IMF's surveillance

[84] *See* Riegner (2014), p. 6.

[85] *See* Int'l Monetary Fund (2002a), p. 5; Int'l Monetary Fund & Int'l Dev. Ass'n (2004).

[86] *See* Int'l Monetary Fund (2013a, b).

activities, their role in sovereign debt crises renders them highly influential. At the same time, DSAs cannot be reduced to purely technocratic, econometric exercises, as they involve some level of political judgment. First, the predictive power of debt-to-GDP ratios is highly controversial.[87] Second, DSAs involve projections about expected growth and other macroeconomic figures, which are difficult to predict. In particular, DSAs have, at times, underestimated the negative effects of restrictive fiscal policies for growth[88] and social development. Third, DSAs are only as good as the risks included in the assessment, thus they depend on the IMF's assessment of a situation.

Once the IMF has decided that a country is eligible for IMF support, it sets out its plans for policy reform. This involves another array of non-binding instruments, which include Letters of Intent and Memoranda of Understanding. Formally, these documents are non-binding instruments addressed to, or consented with, the IMF.[89] Nevertheless, they are highly effective. The concerned country needs to implement the reform program set out in these instruments in line with specific performance targets.[90] If it fails to do so, it faces sanctions, like the withholding of subsequent installments. This would seriously impede the entire restructuring process.

The terms of a restructuring are also agreed upon in soft instruments. One example of such an instrument is the Agreed Minutes which conclude Paris Club negotiations regarding the restructuring of bilateral debt. Like the entire architecture of the Paris Club, these instruments are formally non-binding. The Agreed Minutes stipulate the details of the deal between the borrower and its lenders, including whether there will be debt relief and the conditions of any debt restructuring. The principle of comparability requires the debtor country to offer any other creditor comparable terms.[91] The members of the Paris Club have the economic power to enforce the terms of the Agreed Minutes. The same applies for the intermediate and outcome documents of bail-out negotiations in the Eurozone. The statement of the Eurozone concerning Greece from February 2015 is one example.[92]

As these examples demonstrated, soft legal instruments play a decisive role in every stage of the restructuring process. In line with what Chris Brummer has observed for financial market regulation, soft legal instruments owe their effectiveness to the power of institutions, reputation, and markets.[93] As a result, soft law

---

[87] *Cf.* Piketty (2014), p. 471 (discussing the controversy surrounding the Reinhardt paper and the 90 % threshold it advocated).

[88] Blanchard and Leigh (2013).

[89] Int'l Monetary Fund (2002b), para. 9.

[90] *Id.*, para. 11.

[91] Paris Club (n.d.); *see* Josselin (2009), p. 531; *see also* Das et al. (2012), p. 16 (emphasizing the discretion the application of the comparability principle gives to the Paris Club).

[92] Council of the European Union (2015).

[93] Brummer (2010), p. 637.

and information may have effects akin to those of hard, binding law, even in the absence of central, official enforcement mechanisms. By contrast, some rules that formally belong to the realm of hard international law in the sense of Article 38 of the Statute of the International Court of Justice may be very ineffective in sovereign debt restructuring. In particular, this concerns economic and social rights. For example, structural adjustment programs often seem to be responsible for a decline in the level of human rights protection.[94] The citizens affected by such measures have few legal safeguards against such measures, because institutions like the IMF do not consider themselves to be bound by human rights. Only recently, domestic constitutional courts have taken effective steps to enforce constitutional guarantees against adjustment programs.[95]

3.2 *Law-Making and Law-Application in Sovereign Debt Restructuring*

In sovereign debt restructurings, domestic and international courts have played an especially important role because the issuance of sovereign debt became classified as *acta iure gestionis* to which no sovereign immunities apply.[96] Decisions of domestic and international courts sometimes have effects for many other cases, countries, and creditors. Such decision-making is not embedded, as it should be according to the discourse theoretical view of adjudication, in a legislative framework representing, by-and-large, those affected by the decisions. Currently, courts engage in a sort of *ersatz* rule-making because there is no comprehensive international legal framework for sovereign debt restructuring for them to rely on.[97]

The avalanche of cases against Argentina before US courts presents a formidable example of domestic judgments that have effects for third states and individuals not within the same jurisdiction. In these cases, New York courts famously interpreted the *pari passu* clause, a boilerplate provision in sovereign bond terms, in an unusual way. Many industry members had thought that this clause secured the formal rank of the bonds,[98] but the state courts held that the clause implied a right of bondholders to equal payment conditions, even if they chose not to participate in a debt restructuring and exchange their bonds for new bonds with a reduction in principal, maturity extensions, and lower yields—so-called uncooperative creditors. On top of this, the courts issued injunctions obliging banks processing Argentina's payments to its cooperative creditors to divert funds and make pro rata payments to non-cooperative

---

[94] Abouharb and Cingranelli (2008); Goldmann (2014b).

[95] *See* Fasone (2014).

[96] *See* Republic of Arg. v. Weltover, 504 U.S. 607 (1992).

[97] *See* Schumacher et al. (2014).

[98] Buchheit and Pam (2004).

creditors.[99] The adverse effects of this decision for Argentina are obvious, but the decision also affects creditors other than the plaintiffs, whether they are US citizens or not. This precedent might severely compromise future restructurings of sovereign debt. The decisions put a premium on free-riding and provide a huge incentive for bondholders not to participate in bond exchanges. They put uncooperative creditors in a position that is more favorable than that of cooperative creditors because the former get the entirety of their arrears paid if Argentina continues regular debt service to its cooperative creditors.[100] These are remarkable conclusions for a view based on creditor equality.[101]

These cases are not isolated instances; there are already copycats.[102] The ruling has influenced sovereign bond restructuring without the possibility of legislative intervention by an institution representing, at least approximately, those affected by it. The EU has allowed courts to render decisions affecting the policies of other member states, not just private citizens, as would normally be the case in trans-border private law disputes. The European Court of Justice (ECJ) decided that German courts can serve Greece a statement of claim challenging its 2012 haircut.[103] If push comes to shove, German courts may have to decide whether the legislative measures enabling the 2012 haircut were in conformity with the Greek constitution—a decision which, in a German context, would be reserved to the German Federal Constitutional Court.[104] This prospect has motivated other courts to engage in seemingly desperate attempts to shoot down the case.[105]

Some claims involve the application of international law, leading to yet another form of adjudication without the possibility of effective legislative correction. International

---

[99] NML Capital, Ltd. v. Republic of Arg., No. 08 Civ. 6978, 2012 U.S. Dist. LEXIS 167272, at *7–8 (S.D.N.Y. 23 Feb. 2012, revised 21 Nov. 2012) (order granting an injunction):

> Whenever the Republic pays any amount due under … the [Exchange Bonds] … the Republic shall concurrently or in advance make a 'Ratable Payment' to Plaintiffs … Such 'Ratable Payment' shall be an amount equal to the 'Payment Percentage' multiplied by the total amount currently due to [Plaintiffs]. Such 'Payment Percentage' shall be the fraction calculated by dividing the amount actually paid or which the Republic intends to pay under the terms of the Exchange Bonds by the total amount then due under the terms of such Exchange Bonds.

[100] *Id.*

[101] Weidemaier and Gelpern (2014).

[102] *See* Export-Import Bank of China v. Grenada, No. 13 Civ. 1450, 2013 U.S. Dist. LEXIS 117740 (S.D.N.Y. 19 Aug. 2013). *But cf.* Wong (2015) (pointing out the more cautious approach in cases against Granada).

[103] Joined Cases C-226/13, C-245/13, C-247/13 and C-578/13, Fahnenbrock et al. v. Hellenic Republic, ECLI:EU:C:2015:383 (11 Jun. 2015).

[104] Grundgesetz [GG] [Basic Law] Art. 100(1).

[105] *Cf.* the judgment of Landgericht [LG] [regional court] Konstanz, 19 Nov. 2013, Case No. II O 132/13 B, arguing that Greece enjoys sovereign immunity. However, this contradicts its finding that the debt instrument belongs to *acta iure gestionis*.

investment tribunals have considered sovereign bonds as investments within their jurisdiction *ratione materiae*.[106] This gives privately appointed panels of three judges the possibility to call into question decisions affecting not only the plaintiff, but the entire success of a sovereign debt restructuring process. Attempts to invoke necessity or good faith as a defense under customary international law have mostly failed, whether before international or domestic courts.[107] In 2015, an investment tribunal seemed to get cold feet when it declined jurisdiction, stating that "sovereign debt is an instrument of government monetary and economic policy and its impact at the local and international levels makes it an important tool for the handling of social and economic policies of a State. It cannot, thus, be equated to private indebtedness or corporate debt."[108] As laudable as the insight into the limits of legitimate judicial decision-making may be, it increases the confusion. It does not create a substantive defense applicable across the board, nor is there a legislature that could guide further courts faced with highly contradictory precedents. Progress in terms of predictability seems to depend on judicial activism, a rare and unpredictable resource.

But there are positive examples. The ECJ has shown judicial self-restraint when assessing the legality of the rescue measures of the European institutions, including the ECB.[109] Even when examining whether the consent of the Commission to the Memorandum of Understanding with Cyprus was compatible with the right to property of the depositors on whom it inflicted financial losses, the ECJ engaged only in a perfunctory review of the proportionality of the measure.[110] Although Habermas accurately points out the legitimacy deficit of the rescue measures,[111] unaccountable judicial law-making would make a bad situation worse. Granted, one may disagree with the stance taken by the ECJ in these cases. Yet, one can hardly claim these decisions were unlawful. Law is malleable—both at the center and at the periphery.[112] Malleability may depend on the institutional context in which a court operates; whether a court must review the decisions of institutions with more democratic legitimacy than the court may influence the court's interpretation.

[106] *See* Abaclat v. Argentine Republic, ICSID Case No. ARB/07/5, Decision on Jurisdiction and Admissibility (14 Aug. 2011).

[107] *See* Bundesverfassungsgericht [BVerfG] [Federal Constitutional Court], Case No. 2 BvM 1/03, 2 BvM 2/03, 2 BvM 3/03, 2 BvM 4/03, 2 BvM 5/03, 2 BvM 1/06, 2 BvM 2/06, 118 Entscheidungen des Bundesverfassungsgerichts [BVerfGE] 124 (8 May 2007); Bundesgerichtshof [BGH] [Federal Court of Justice], Case No. XI ZR 193/14, Neue Juristische Wochenschrift [NJW] 2328 (24 Feb. 2015).

[108] *See* Poštová banka, A.S. and Istrokapital SE v. Hellenic Republic, ICSID Case No. ARB/13/8, Award, para. 324 (9 Apr. 2015).

[109] *See* Case C-370/12, Pringle v. Ireland, ECLI:EU:C:2012:756 (27 Nov. 2012); Case C-62/14, Gauweiler v. Deutscher Bundestag, ECLI:EU:C:2015:400 (16 June 2015).

[110] *See* Case C-8/15 P, Ledra Advertising Ltd v. European Commission, ECLI:EU:C:2016:701 (20 Sept. 2016).

[111] *See supra* Sect. 2.3.

[112] *But see* Pistor (2013).

Of course, there is also the reverse problem of executive decisions without judicial control. Most acts of international organizations, including those by the IMF and the Paris Club, are not subject to judicial review. There is no court that can determine whether the Greek bail-out did or did not meet the IMF's lending requirements as those requirements had been traditionally understood.[113] In cases like this one, one important characteristic of the financial order makes it even more important to have independent judicial review, ideally embedded in a constitutional setting: It is entirely constituted by the law.[114] This comprises products, transactions, and money, its only commodity. Legal certainty is therefore of the essence if we expect markets to work smoothly. Legal uncertainty may not only generate transaction costs, but pull the plug entirely.

3.3 Public and Private Law in Sovereign Debt Restructuring

For Habermas, a democratically legitimate financial order depends on a legally structured public sphere.[115] Sovereign debt restructuring features a conglomerate of private and public actors, instruments, and rules. This ties in with Katharina Pistor's account of the "essential hybridity" of the law of finance.[116] Essential hybridity highlights the fact that private financial transactions have an immediate impact upon the public interest because they increase or decrease the quantity of money in the market and, with it, the indebtedness of public or private actors.[117] This makes it difficult to determine which public spheres should be deemed relevant and to what extent decisions can be legitimately made in the context of private transactions.

The confusion of the public and the private is most acute in sovereign debt disputes governed by domestic private law, as described in the preceding section. The fragmented nature of contractual relations between creditors and their debtors generates coordination problems.[118] To solve these problems, the IMF advocates a contractual approach.[119] Contractual collective clauses might increase certainty and reduce fragmentation in sovereign debt restructuring, but they avoid the issue of the relevant public. Indeed, contractual mechanisms alone, almost by definition, do not constitute a public, or provide for solutions that represent the public interest. Contracts certainly play a role in public law contexts, such as cooperative administrative

---

[113] *Cf.* Int'l Monetary Fund (2014b).

[114] *Cf.* Pistor (2013).

[115] *See* Sect. 2.3.

[116] *See* Pistor (2013).

[117] *Id.*

[118] *Cf.* UNCTAD (2015).

[119] Int'l Monetary Fund (2014a).

arrangements,[120] but such arrangements are always embedded in a public law framework, which gears them towards the public interest. Without that underlying framework, private law serves the self-interest of strategic market actors, not the public interest. Although this might advance commutative and restorative justice, it is inapt to bring about distributive justice. This requires solidarity, for which an actual—or at least an identifiable—public is necessary.

This is easier said than done. In the context of a globalized financial system, democratic institutions and financial activities part ways, especially in respect to the complex arrangements charged with the restructuring of sovereign debt. They involve and affect various constituencies, ranging from taxpayers in debtor and creditor states, private creditors, and international organizations in the field, to third states and private actors that might be indirectly affected by the restructuring.[121] The Greek referendum of July 2015 juxtaposed various constituencies on the domestic and supranational levels, each claiming to have at least an equal say in the decision-making process. Habermas's emphasis on two strands of legitimacy in the EU, one deriving from Union citizenship, the other from citizenship in the EU Member States,[122] faces severe limits in this context. As for the IMF, it certainly does not find itself represented in such a structure. The same goes for creditors from third states and creditors of other Eurozone members indirectly affected by the solution due to path dependencies. Even for the Eurozone, an international framework built around and constituting an international public seems necessary.

But to constitute such an international public is highly difficult. There is no institution, even with minor modifications, designed for that task. The IMF is highly unequal given that voting power is determined by financial capacity, not population or some other representative factor. This perpetuates the financial rationality, which a public must be able to call into question. The Paris Club may have transformed itself from an agency for the enforcement of bilateral debts into an organization sincerely concerned about debt sustainability,[123] but it has not transformed itself into an inclusive, representative institution. The General Assembly of the United Nations may come closest to an institution that could be transformed along the lines of Habermas's suggestion for the European Parliament,[124] but one cannot expect a body of that size to have the necessary resolve for efficient executive decision-making.

Habermas's suggestion that international organizations should simply refrain from decisions is not an option either. In case of an acute debt crisis, any restructuring would likely be better than no restructuring at all, even if it is of doubtful legitimacy. Discourse theory thus leads to a conundrum; it attempts to transfer the late capitalist welfare state model to a global environment, but this environment

[120] *See e.g.*, Schill (2013), p. 27; Napolitano (2003).

[121] Streeck (2013), p. 118, distinguishes between national citizenship and market citizenship as the relevant constituencies. Although we share the underlying concern for democratic self-determination, sovereign debt restructuring involves far more groups than these two.

[122] *See infra* Sect. 2.3.

[123] von Bogdandy and Goldmann (2012).

[124] Habermas (2013b), p. 87.

seems unfit to meet the requirements of the late capitalist welfare state model for a series of practical and theoretical reasons. Discarding the late capitalist welfare state model in favor of a more liberal model does not seem to be an option either, as it would reduce the democratic character of the financial order.[125] The only realistic hope is that of a middle ground between a fully institutionalized, EU-style public institutional setting and the demise of the welfare state model. The structure of transnational discourse may point in that direction.

4 Lessons for Sovereign Debt Restructuring

As has been said above, rational reconstruction approaches issues from both an empirical and a normative angle.[126] Any solution to the problems of Habermas's concept of law identified above may therefore have an empirical and a normative component. In some respects, institutions and procedures might have to change. In other respects, our understanding of the law and of democracy might require adaptation.

We suggest three modifications, which have partly institutional-procedural and partly conceptual implications. They take up the challenges previously identified. All of these proposals are reconstructive in that they engage with current developments, proposing realistic modifications while refraining from any grand institutional redesign. We do not propose, for example, the establishment of a fully-fledged binding international mechanism for sovereign debt restructuring, which—as desirable as it might be—is unlikely to happen in the near future. Our proposals are of an incremental nature. They comprise a shift in focus from binding law towards a broader concept of authority, measures for embedding adjudication in quasi-legislative frameworks, and finally, proposals for the creation of a public on the international level that would neither require grand institutional design nor amount to a demise of the welfare state.

4.1 Towards International Public Authority

In Habermas's view, law is uniquely suited for combining legitimacy and effectiveness. The preceding analysis highlighted the role of soft law and non-legal instruments such as DSAs in effective sovereign debt restructuring. A discourse theoretical approach should not exclude these instruments from its consideration by only focusing on hard, binding international law. Rather, it should recognize that effective soft and non-legal instruments are an important and useful part of global regulatory efforts to the extent that they are legitimate.

---

[125] *Cf.* Habermas (1992), pp. 182–187.

[126] *See* Patberg (2014).

This observation relies on the insight that the "constraint theory" misses much of what motivates human behavior. It draws too strict a line between intrinsic and extrinsic forms of motivation and overlooks that there might be intermediate forms. Foucault's analysis of the development of the modern welfare state shows how governments have used more subtle means—incentives, information, and indoctrination—to motivate people.[127] Modern studies in motivational psychology have provided insights into why such mechanisms are effective. Between purely intrinsic motivational forces—like, for example, entirely personal convictions—and purely external motivational forces—the threat of force, for example, there is a scale of intermediate types of motivation where external factors motivate people because they influence the way people think about their identity, strategies, and the world.[128] Although the motivations of states, companies, and international institutions arguably do not operate in exactly the same way as the individual motivations,[129] it seems that similar forces are at work in the realm of soft law and non-legal instruments.

This is the reason why the proposal focuses on international public authority instead of international law as the relevant concept for identifying effective governance instruments that require legitimacy.[130] For this purpose, one should understand "authority" as "the legal capacity to determine others and to reduce their freedom, i. e. to unilaterally shape their legal or factual situation."[131] A mechanism that can be rightly considered to shape a factual situation does not need to reach the level of physical sanctions. Rather, it is sufficient that the act gives rise to some form of power which the addressee can only avoid at some cost, be it reputational, discursive, ideational, financial, or other. If such authority is public—if it claims to represent the common interest of a certain group—it needs to be democratically legitimate.[132] Thus, identifying an act as one of public authority does not extend any kind of unconditional blessing over it. Instead, it obliges the author to ensure that the act is democratically legitimate.

The ramifications of the concept of authority as we define it here have been set out in full detail elsewhere.[133] Suffice it to say that it does not imply that any instrument of international institutions counts as public authority. Rather, it needs to pass a certain threshold. We define this threshold incrementally, applying a reconstructive approach, which discovers typical acts in the practice of international institutions that usually influence the legal or factual situation of their addressees. These

---

[127] Foucault (1991).

[128] Goldmann, *supra* note 34, pp. 344–358; *see* Goldmann (2016).

[129] For a nuanced defense, *see* van Aaken (2014), p. 435.

[130] von Bogdandy et al. (2008).

[131] *Id.*, pp. 1381–1382.

[132] The international character of public authority derives from its having a basis in international law. *See id.* p. 1383.

[133] The ramifications of the concept of authority as we define it here have been set out in full detail elsewhere. For more on these ramifications, *see* von Bogdandy et al. (2008); Goldmann (2015), p. 359.

acts deserve recognition as "standard instruments," and their legal framework needs to ensure their legitimacy and effectiveness.

As the preceding analysis reveals, sovereign debt restructuring features at least three typical acts that can serve as standard instruments: DSAs, Agreed Minutes or other non-binding instruments resulting from negotiations, and Memoranda of Understanding. Considering these instruments as acts of international public authority recognizes their function for the regulation of sovereign debt restructuring and obliges their authors to ensure their democratic legitimacy.

4.2 Towards Democratically Embedded Adjudication

The problem of un-embedded adjudication requires mostly institutional and procedural responses. Adjudication is indispensable for legitimate sovereign debt restructuring because the latter affects private, individual rights. Adjudication needs to be democratically legitimate and embedded in equally democratic law-making processes.

For many reasons, an international treaty framework would provide a satisfactory solution to the problem of un-embedded adjudication. Such a framework might set up an international insolvency court and stipulate reasonably predictable substantive and procedural rules for the entire restructuring process, including judicial review. Yet such a solution seems highly unlikely, at least in the near future. It is therefore necessary to look for alternatives to this type of framework. We propose a two-pronged strategy: The first prong relies on a certain measure of judicial activism, while the second prong consists of an incremental strategy aimed at establishing a quasi-legislative, soft legal framework.

At present, courts have the power to simply decide not to enforce sovereign debt instruments where enforcement would endanger either the financial situation of the country concerned or the effectiveness of international efforts to achieve debt sustainability. By choosing not to enforce these instruments, courts would avoid interfering with international negotiating frameworks that have a greater chance of involving all affected parties. Specifically, courts should stay such proceedings as long as the debtor country is cooperating in good faith with the creditors to achieve a consensual restructuring. In fact, it is possible to argue that the enforcement of sovereign debt instruments is legally barred in such a situation. As set out elsewhere, this might follow from good faith or sovereign debt sustainability as general principles of law.[134] Good faith, as a widely accepted general principle, governs contractual sovereign debt instruments. If the debtor state, as part of its good faith duties, initiates restructuring negotiations in good faith, rejecting this offer might amount to a violation of good faith. The German Federal Court of Justice recently

[134] *Cf.* von Bogdandy and Goldmann (2012); UNCTAD (2015).

disagreed with this position.[135] Yet it mixed the good faith defense with the necessity defense despite the fact that both defenses have quite different requirements and legal effects.[136] Additionally, one might also argue that sovereign debt sustainability has become a general principle of (international) law.[137] The history of sovereign debt restructuring since the end of the Second World War shows a development from a quasi-colonial setting focused on the enforcement of bilateral debt, to mechanisms aimed principally at social and economic development—even though these mechanisms might often fail in practice. This development has been epitomized by the Heavily Indebted Poor Countries Initiative.[138] Nevertheless, this prong of the proposed strategy is a risky one. Progressive judicial reasoning cannot always be relied on, especially in the case of important countervailing economic interests. Perhaps a more democratic supranational and international judiciary would be more inclined to take such steps,[139] but, for the time being, another safeguard seems more practical.

The second prong of the proposed strategy involves embedding judicial decision-making in a quasi-legislative framework. As part of this prong, soft legal instruments—which we have found to be less ineffective than is sometimes assumed—would corroborate and encourage judicial recognition of good faith and sustainability as general principles of law. The United Nations Conference on Trade and Development has taken this approach in recent years by means of its "Principles on Promoting Responsible Sovereign Lending and Borrowing" in 2012[140] and, more recently, its "Principles for a Sovereign Debt Restructuring."[141] The UN General Assembly adopted a revised version of the latter in September 2015 by an overwhelming majority.[142] Courts might receive further guidance by the principles of the Human Rights Council elaborating the human rights implications of sovereign debt restructuring.[143]

4.3 *Towards a Cleavage-Sensitive Concept of the Public*

The most profound institutional and conceptual problem regarding sovereign debt restructuring concerns the question of how to constitute an international public. As discussed earlier, Habermas's proposal to build a supranational public on the

[135] *See* Buchheit (2004).

[136] Int'l Law Comm'n (2001), Art. 25.

[137] Bohoslavsky and Goldmann (2016).

[138] *See* Guder (2009).

[139] With respect to the ECJ, *see* Vauchez (2014), p. 90.

[140] UNCTAD (2012).

[141] *See* UNCTAD (2015).

[142] *Cf.* U.N. G.A. (2015).

[143] *E.g.* Human Rights Council (2012).

basis of national and supranational citizenship[144] comes under stress in the complex setting of sovereign debt restructuring.[145] We suggest that a middle course situated between Habermas's model and the demise of the democratic welfare state model and its replacement by technocratic regulation is a realistic option.

The structure of global discourse reveals how that option could look: (1) Cleavages in public discourse running across national borders and dividing people in different societies more or less along the same lines create discourses that have a potential for legitimizing the exercise of public authority in sovereign debt restructuring. (2) With regard to sovereign debt restructuring, current world public opinion is divided not only along national or regional borders, but also across national borders. In each state or region, people disagree about the right balance between free markets and governmental regulation, as well as about whether regulation should be on the domestic or international level. These two intersecting cleavages characterize a transnational discourse that has the potential to contribute to the legitimacy of sovereign debt restructuring. (3) This prompts two proposals how one could use that potential. One option is implementing institutional improvements that integrate the different sides of a specific cleavage into sovereign debt restructuring. Another option is to attach special significance to decisions taken in one particular constituency based on a discourse centered on a particular cleavage.

4.3.1 Cleavages in Public Discourse

Democratic nation states gain legitimacy from their ability to bridge deep cleavages in society. Originally formulated by political scientists Seymour Martin Lipset and Stein Rokkan in 1967, the concept of cleavages stems from empirical research revealing the striking stability and efficiency of democracies in Western Europe.[146] According to Lipset and Rokkan, historically developed party systems are the main causes of widespread participation and acceptance of decision-making bodies. Lipset and Rokkan identified the cleavages of Labor versus Capital, State versus Church, and Center versus Periphery as the most crucial divisions structuring political discourse in Western Europe in the preceding decades and century. The decisive question is whether a society manages to institutionalize these discursive divisions in a way that ensures participation on either side of the cleavage in the exercise of public authority. If successful, this institutionalization may stabilize society and contribute successfully to social integration. For instance, during the struggle between Labor and Capital in the nineteenth century, owners and employers, on the one hand, and tenants, laborers, and workers, on the other, were ultimately able to aggregate their interests and form political parties. Hence, the conflict was

---

[144] *See infra* Sect. 2.3.

[145] *See infra* Sect. 3.3.

[146] Lipset and Rokkan (1967).

transformed into a political discourse, the newly founded political parties acted as advocacy coalitions, and the conflict between the two groups did not escalate.[147]

The underlying concept is simple: Political affiliations emerge in crucial, entrenched divisions in society. Cleavages are different from disagreements on other political questions in that they epitomize fundamental conflicts revolving around fundamental values such as the distribution of public goods. These fundamental conflicts determine the political affiliations of people on either side of the cleavage. Hence, cleavages structure discourse in two ways: They separate people on different sides of a cleavage, but allow alliances to form across political, geographic, religious, or ethnic lines among those on either side of the cleavage. If a political system succeeds in institutionalizing either side of a cleavage, the system will enjoy a high degree of stability and legitimacy. This is the story of the post-war party system in Western European states.[148]

Certainly, the post-war party system has lost a good part of its capacity to absorb societal conflict lines. Habermas has observed as early as in 1987 that societal conflicts:

> no longer flare up in domains of material reproduction; they are no longer channeled through parties and associations; and they can no longer be allayed through compensations. Rather, these new conflicts arise in domains of cultural reproduction, social integration and socialization; they are carried out in sub-institutional—or at least extra-parliamentary—forms of protest; and the underlying deficit reflects reification of communicatively structured domains of action that will not respond to the media of money or power.[149]

In hindsight, one might argue that Habermas's quote observed the first societal consequences of globalization that has transformed the structure of cleavages in society. Indeed, globalization might be one of those processes of profound change which Lipset and Rokkan considered essential for the emergence of cleavages.[150] The issue which determines the cleavage needs to be in the center of the public debate.[151] Globalization has led to major social transformations that increasingly politicize the public sphere on a worldwide scale.[152] This has been the object of recent empirical research by Michael Zürn and Pieter de Wilde.[153] The concept of cleavages therefore may have the potential to describe transformations of the public sphere in the wake of globalization.

For this reason, the concept of cleavages lends itself to a discourse theoretical approach. Both the cleavage concept and discourse theory consider the public sphere as the main resource of legitimacy. The idea of cleavages can be used to identify

---

[147] *See generally* Zuckerman (1975); Heitmeyer (1997) (regarding the development of capitalism and social integration); Vester (1997).

[148] Lipset, *supra* note 144, pp. 2–5.

[149] Habermas (1987), p. 394.

[150] Lipset and Rokkan (1967), p. 14; Deegan-Krause (2013).

[151] *See* de Wilde (2011).

[152] *See* Kriesi et al. (2012); Furia (2005). Also, *see* surveys available at www.WorldPublicOpinion.org.

[153] de Wilde and Zürn (2012).

specific transnational discourses relevant to the financial order. Transnational discourses structured along specific cleavages are tantamount to public spheres in which participating groups or individuals align themselves on either side. If the global level—where the two sides of a cleavage meet—succeeds in channeling this disagreement into institutions and procedures that allow for fair and transparent discourse, there may be a realistic chance for transnational social integration. Taking into account discourses characterized by cross-border cleavages may enhance the legitimacy of sovereign debt restructuring.

4.3.2 Two Transnational Cleavages: Market Versus Government and Domestic Versus International

In order to make use of cleavages for sovereign debt restructuring, one first needs to identify the relevant cleavages that characterize discourse in the field. Some claim that "[p]opular agitation around the international politics of public debt tends to express itself in terms of nations versus nations, rather than people versus financial markets."[154] Indeed, Russia's refusal to grant Ukraine a sovereign debt restructuring in 2015 is a case in point for a cleavage that runs along national borders. Similarly, in the history of sovereign debt in the twentieth century, the dominant cleavage was located between the Global North and the Global South, which may also be perceived as a cleavage between the center and the periphery of international finance.[155]

There is evidence, however, that cleavages regarding sovereign debt issues do not necessarily run along national boarders any longer—at least in the European Union.[156] Research on social movements has shown that there are two transnational, intersecting cleavages, which shape the debate about sovereign debt restructuring. The first cleavage resembles—and goes beyond—the traditional labor versus capital cleavage. This cleavage is characterized by two different and competing attitudes concerning the organization of the economy: market liberalism or neoliberalism versus governmental regulation or interventionism.[157] The former attitude refers to a less welfarist approach, which emphasizes the importance of free markets. Proponents of market liberalism prefer requiring debtor states to pay back their debt in order to let market discipline work and to prevent the moral hazard that might derive from overly accommodating debt restructurings.[158] The latter attitude, interventionism, strives for a stronger role of the state in market regulation and the provision of welfare services. It therefore advocates more generous sovereign debt

[154] Schäfer and Streeck (2013), p. 21.

[155] Regarding the center-periphery dynamics in international economic law, *see* Kennedy (2013).

[156] *See* de Witte and Dawson (2016); *see also* Bartolini (2005), pp. 248–281.

[157] For the neoliberal view, *see* von Hayek (1944). For the interventionist view, *see* Keynes (1926); Polanyi (1944). The two views come in many different shades. *See* Hall and Soskice (2001).

[158] The leaked plan of the German Ministry of Finance in November 2015 provides an example of this. *See* Bastasin (2015); Issing (2015).

restructurings, stressing that economic hardship in debtor states and a lack of solidarity undermines the legitimacy of political systems.[159]

There is ample empirical evidence for the existence of the cleavage along neoliberalist and interventionist lines and its relevance for depicting attitudes on sovereign debt restructuring. Donatella della Porta identified the emergence of a global cleavage in both the North and the South in current anti-austerity protest movements.[160] Economic globalization and the consequences of financial markets are in the center of this cleavage between the winners and the losers of globalization. The roots of the cleavage go back several decades; advancement of neoliberalism since the 1970s, the Latin American debt crisis, and the conditionality attached to structural adjustment programs by the IMF have all triggered recurrent protests. Emerging in the periphery, resistance against IMF and World Bank instruments has soon expanded globally. As a consequence, as della Porta rightly observes, the Global North has witnessed an immense wave of anti-globalization protests during the last fifteen years. These protests intensified in the wake of the financial crisis and the ensuing sovereign debt crisis. The Occupy Movement in the capitals of international finance and anti-austerity protests in Spain, Portugal, Italy, and Greece have shown a significant amount of collective identity, organizational capacity, and discursive action. Their claims include demands for a more democratic and just economic or financial system.[161] In the run-up to the Greek bailout referendum of July 2015, many countries witnessed anti-austerity protests and public expressions of solidarity with Greece.[162] The cleavage thus appears to be truly transnational in character. However, it should be borne in mind that this cleavage is not (yet) as deeply entrenched in society as traditional cleavages confined to the nation state, as it is not (yet) supported by powerful and persistent transnational institutions.

Michael Zürn and Pieter de Wilde have identified a second transnational cleavage that structures the debate about sovereign debt restructuring. They argue that a cleavage has emerged between cosmopolitan and communitarian attitudes, whereby the cosmopolitan attitude favors international solutions for global problems, while the communitarian attitude prefers domestic responses.[163] Zürn and de Wilde were able to demonstrate that this cleavage exists beyond the Western world. It relates to contentious issues such as trade, regional integration, migration, and human rights.[164] One can map this new cleavage in the increasing politicization of international institutions,[165] although it falls short of the high degree of institutionalization typical of traditional cleavages on the level of the nation state.

Both cleavages intersect. Cosmopolitan and communitarian views exist on either of the sides of the previously described cleavage between market liberalism and

[159] *See, e.g.*, Guzman et al. (2016); Varoufakis (2015).

[160] della Porta (2015).

[161] *Id.*, pp. 89–97; Fominaya and Cox (2013).

[162] E.g. solidarity protests surrounding the Greek referendum took place in several European capitals, including in Lisbon, Barcelona, Rome, Paris, Berlin and Brussels.

[163] de Wilde (2011).

[164] *See* de Wilde et al. (2014a,b).

[165] *See generally* Zürn and Ecker-Ehrhardt (2011); de Wilde and Zürn (2011); Zürn (2014).

governmental interventionism. In fact, as the literature on the varieties of capitalism[166] and on welfare state models has shown, a variety of views exist regarding the role of the state in regulating markets and providing welfare.[167] This might have a conditional effect on the manifestation of the cleavage with respect to sovereign debt restructurings, as austerity policies will have different effects according to the prevailing model of economic and welfare regulation, affecting the population to varying degrees.[168] Likewise, whether solutions are sought on the national or international level is often a matter of degree rather than an exclusionary position. For example, among those favoring European solutions in the Eurozone debt crisis, some would favor the introduction of Eurobonds,[169] while others think that liability for sovereign debt should remain domestic.[170]

This leads to the following distribution:

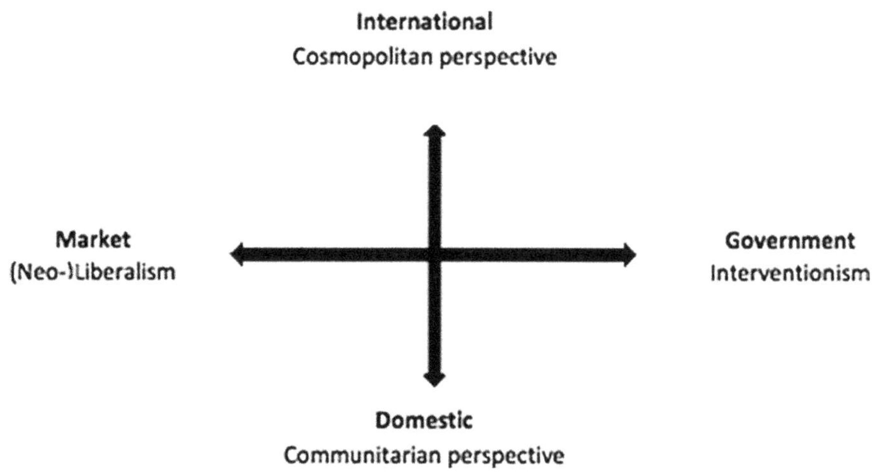

This scheme represents the abstract form of the views emerging from the two mentioned cleavages. The concrete distribution of views might vary from case to case. With respect to the European sovereign debt crisis, Habermas distinguishes six different positions. These positions reflect and further differentiate the two above-mentioned cleavages. According to Habermas, defenders of national sovereignty include

[166] Hall and Soskice (2001).

[167] According to Gøsta Esping-Andersen, the development of institutions predominantly preoccupied with the production and distribution of social well-being led to the rise of the welfare state, with variations of welfare state institutions and policies in capitalist democracies. Esping-Andersen distinguishes the liberal, conservative, and social democratic model of welfare state regulation. *See* Esping-Andersen (1990); Schmidt et al. (2007).

[168] Pierson (2000).

[169] *See* Schulz (2012).

[170] *See* Schäuble (2011).

both "ordoliberal proponents of a lean nation-state" and "republican or right-wing populist proponents of a strong nation-state," while advocates of progressive European integration comprise "economic liberals of various types" and interventionists wishing to regulate the financial market.[171] Proponents of interventionist policies can be further distinguished according to the familiar left-right divisions on the political spectrum, which separates the "Eurodemocrats" from the technocrats.[172] Yet, this distribution is specifically tailored to the Eurozone in 2013 and therefore constitutes only one possibility of how the two transnational, intersecting cleavages in debt restructuring might manifest in practice.

4.3.3 Cleavage Sensitivity in Sovereign Debt Restructuring

The decisive question is how sovereign debt restructuring can take the two cleavages identified above into account and productively channel the legitimating potential of these transnational debates. Again, the reconstructive methodology is most appropriate for advancing incremental developments of existing practice in line with the principles expressed in that practice. The guiding idea behind our proposals is similar to that of the duality of member state and EU—or cosmopolitan—citizenship endorsed by Habermas. Based on this duality, sovereign debt restructuring should represent citizens in two ways: as citizens of a state and in accordance with their affiliation with the different sides of the two cleavages.

Integrating this dual concept of representation into sovereign debt restructuring is very difficult because affiliation with the different sides of the two mentioned cleavages is not formalized like EU citizenship.[173] In fact, these new transnational cleavages lack the institutional embeddedness of the traditional nation-state cleavages, which historically manifested within party structures. Transnational civil society and international social movements do not have the same organizational capacity as political parties. Although the groups initiating and sustaining these cleavages have less organizational capacity, taking into account the identified manifestations of these cleavages is crucial in sovereign debt restructuring to account for the legitimacy problems identified above. Furthermore, as discussed in the previous subsection, in the past two decades, the increasing transnational manifestations of the two cleavages are extremely relevant for sovereign debt restructurings. One option to reflect the cleavages in sovereign debt restructuring negotiations would be to allow the participation of representative civil society groups; another option would be to reconsider the significance of domestic democratic decision-making processes for international sovereign debt restructurings.

With regard to the first option, the idea to involve non-state actors in the institutional framework—and in the decision-making mechanism of an international

[171] Habermas (2013b), pp. 83–84 (translated version).

[172] *Id.*

[173] For an inspired proposal for institutional changes in the European Union, *see* de Witte and Dawson (2016), pp. 214–217.

organization—is not entirely new. The global cleavage between Labor and Capital has been integrated into the structure of the International Labour Organization for a long time, and representatives of workers and employers enjoy a high degree of participation in the organization.[174] The representatives participate in the main bodies along with domestic government representatives and enjoy voting powers. Similarly, certain international economic organizations such as the Organization for Cooperation and Development (OECD) and the Andean Community of Nations and the Southern Common Market (MERCOSUR) provide for the participation of both workers and business representatives.[175] In these organizations, representatives have mostly consultative functions.[176] The level of institutionalization of the various positions emerging from the two intersecting transnational cleavages is far lower. It is difficult to find groups or organizations that could legitimately claim to represent a position. It would therefore appear inappropriate to give direct decision-making power in sovereign debt restructuring negotiations to the representatives of the various positions reflecting these particular cleavages. This would not exclude institutional arrangements for participation that has a consultative function. Such participation should be extended to industry representatives, civil society organizations, unions, and other entities.

The second option, not exclusive to the first, concerns the status attributed by international restructuring operations to democratic decisions taken on the domestic level. The Greek and Icelandic referenda, which took place in the context of a transnational discourse characterized by the two cleavages, provide good examples. One cannot discard such decisions as mere expressions of national interest given that the underlying cleavages are transnational and exist in one way or another in many countries. This is evidenced by the solidarity movement in favor of the Greek government, as well as by an equally vocal countermovement. Yet, a referendum in Greece or Iceland cannot claim to express the will of other states, other states' citizens, or of their private and public creditors. Like Greece and Iceland, other creditors and other states have their legitimate self-interest, for which bargaining-style restructuring negotiations are appropriate. One should therefore attribute some significance, albeit not a dominating one, to domestic democratic decisions like the Greek or Icelandic referenda in debt restructuring negotiations by making them cleavage-sensitive. One way of doing so would be to attribute veto powers to such decisions. Should the debtor country veto the result of negotiations in a democratic procedure framed by a transnational discourse along the two cleavages, creditors would then not be allowed to walk away from the negotiating table—or to threaten the debtor with the prospect of leaving the monetary union. Instead, they would have to continue negotiations and find a different solution. The same applies

---

[174] For a proposal as to how the design of an international financial architecture could draw on the institutional setting of the ILO, *see* Tsotroudi (2014).

[175] *See* other organizations, for example, *Consejo Presidencial Andino, Consejo Consultivo Empresaral*, and *Consejo Consultivo Laboral.*

[176] In the case of MERCOSUR, workers' and employers' representatives can also vote on instruments and policies to be adopted by the organization in the area of social and labor affairs.

to democratic decisions taken in creditor states, provided that discourse is framed along the two cleavages.

This does not give carte blanche to debtor or creditor states. Their citizens need to be aware that such veto powers only work as long as decisions are actually structured by the two transnational cleavages and do not revolve solely around domestic interests. Competent domestic and international courts could decide whether that is the case. They should also become more cleavage-sensitive and respect domestic democratic decisions.[177] One way of doing so would be to impose a stay on enforcement measures as long as there is a duty to negotiate due to a legitimate veto.

5 Towards a Democratic Financial Order

This text has taken a discourse theoretical perspective on the role of law in the relationship between democracy and financial order. We have argued that Habermas's idea of transposing the welfare state model into the global and European arenas implies a concept of law that is doubtful in several respects. This has led us to develop proposals that take into account soft law and information as forms of authority, embed adjudication in quasi-legislative structures, and make sovereign debt restructuring more sensitive to transnational cleavages between preferences for market liberalism or governmental regulation, on the one hand, and domestic or international solutions on the other.

The practical application of our proposal might require more investigation, as would the question of whether it could be useful for other segments of the financial order to ensure that they are squared with democracy. In any case, we hope this chapter has shown that—at least in theory—there are viable alternatives that exist between the unlikely prospect of a fully democratic, welfarist world federation and a return to liberal capitalism and national solutions.

Acknowledgements: We are highly indebted to Franz Ebert for discussions and advice. We would like to thank Armin von Bogdandy, Kolja Möller, Michael Zürn, Floris de Witte and Francesco Costamagna as well as the participants in the workshop "Democracy and Financial Order – Legal Perspectives" at Goethe University Frankfurt in September 2015 for their helpful comments. We are grateful to Tante Hildegard for hosting us during a retreat. This research was enabled by the DFG funded cluster of excellence "Formation of Normative Orders" at Goethe University Frankfurt.

[177] For the ECJ, *see* Komárek (2014).

References

Abouharb MR, Cingranelli D (2008) Human rights and structural adjustment. Cambridge University Press, Cambridge

Aquinas T (1265–73 [1894]) Summa theologica, vol 2. Forzani, Rome

Austin J (1832 [2001]) The Province of Jurisprudence Determined. Cambridge University Press, New York

Avgouleas E (2012) Governance of global financial markets: the law, the economics, the politics. Cambridge University Press, Cambridge

Bartolini S (2005) Restructuring Europe: centre formation, system building, and political structuring between the nation state and the European Union. Oxford University Press, Oxford

Bastasin C (2015) Mr. Schäuble's ultimate weapon: the restructuring of European public debt, Brookings, 15 Dec 2015. http://www.brookings.edu/research/opinions/2015/12/15-schauble-public-debt-weapon-bastasin. Accessed 16 March 2018

Bernanke BS (2004) Chairman, Bd. of Governors of the Fed. Reserve Sys., remarks at the meeting of the Eastern Economic Association: the great moderation, 20 Feb 2004, Washington, DC

Blanchard O, Leigh D (2013) Growth forecast errors and fiscal multipliers [XX] (Int'l Monetary Fund, Working Paper No. 1). IMF, Washington, DC

Böckenförde E-W (2006) Geschichte der Rechts- und Staatsphilosophie, 2nd edn. Mohr Siebeck, Tübingen

Bohoslavsky JP, Goldmann M (2016) An incremental approach to sovereign debt restructuring: sovereign debt sustainability as a principle of public international law. Yale J Int'l L 41:13

Boutros Ghali B (2009) Die Welt braucht ein Parlament. Die Zeit 24. http://www.zeit.de/online/2009/24/uno-reform. Accessed 16 March 2018

Brummer C (2010) Why soft law dominates international finance—and not trade. J Int'l Econ L 13:623

Buchheit LC, Pam JS (2004) The Pari Passu Clause in sovereign debt instruments. Emory LJ 53:869

Buchrucker AE (1972) Luthers Anthropologie nach der großen Genesisvorlesung von 1535/45. Neue Zeitschrift für systematische Theologie 14:250

Council of the European Union (2015) Statement 71/15 of Council of the European Union of Feb. 20, 2015, Eurogroup Statement on Greece (Eurogroup)

Das US, Papaioannou MG, Trebesch C (2012) Sovereign debt restructurings 1950–2010: literature survey, data, and stylized facts (Int'l Monetary Fund Working Paper No. WP/12/203). IMF, Washington, DC

de Tocqueville A (1838) Democracy in America, vol 2. Saunders and Otley, London

de Wilde P (2011) No polity for old politics? A framework for analyzing politicization of European Integration. J Eur Integr 33:559

de Wilde P, Zürn M (2011) Can the politicization of European integration be reversed? J Common Mkt Stud 50:6

de Wilde P, Zürn M (2012) Debating globalization: cosmopolitan and communitarian argumentation. http://paperroom.ipsa.org/papers/paper_12480.pdf. Accessed 18 March 2018

de Wilde P, Junk W, Palmtag T (2014a) Representing globalization conflict in international organizations: cleavage formation beyond the state presented at ECPR general conference, 3 Sept 2014. http://ecpr.eu/Filestore/PaperProposal/bab379c6-8b11-4980-9765-83c1bf34dd46.pdf. Accessed 18 March 2018

de Wilde P, Koopmans R, Zürn M (2014b) Conflicts or cleavage? Contesting globalization in Western Europe and beyond presented at ECPR general conference, 3 Sept 2014. http://ecpr.eu/Filestore/PaperProposal/ce7978ec-3492-4c4f-ba81-459b6ad76667.pdf. Accessed 16 March 2018

de Witte P, Dawson M (2016) From balance to conflict: a new constitution for the EU. Eur Law J, 22:211

Deegan-Krause K (2013) Full and partial cleavages. In: Berglund S, Ekman J, Deegan-Krause K, Knuten T (eds) The handbook of political change in eastern Europe, p 35. Edward Elgar, Cheltenham

della Porta D (2015) Social movements in times of austerity: bringing capitalism back into protest analysis. Polity Press, Cambridge
Duke of Saxony J et al (1530) Confessio Augustana, Art. 2 (C.P. Krauth trans, 1874). http://www.ccel.org/ccel/schaff/creeds3.iii.ii.html. Accessed 16 March 2018
Dworkin R (1977) Taking rights seriously. Bloomsbury Publishing, London
Esping-Andersen G (1990) The three worlds of welfare capitalism. Princeton University Press, Princeton, NJ
Fasone C (2014) Constitutional courts facing the Euro crisis. Italy, Portugal and Spain in a comparative perspective (Eur Univ Inst, Working Paper No. 25). European University Institute, Badia Fiesolana
Fominaya CF, Cox L (2013) Understanding European movements: new social movements, global justice struggles, anti-austerity protest. Routledge, London
Foucault M (1991) Governmentality. In: Burchell G, Gordon C, Miller P (eds) The Foucault effect. University of Chicago Press, Chicago, IL
Friedman M (1962) Capitalism and freedom. University of Chicago Press, Chicago, IL
Furia PA (2005) Global citizenship, anyone? Cosmopolitanism, privilege and public opinion. Global Soc'y 19:331
Goldmann M (2014a) Dogmatik als rationale Rekonstruktion: Versuch einer Metatheorie am Beispiel völkerrechtlicher Prinzipien. Der Staat 53:373–399
Goldmann M (2014b) Human rights and sovereign debt workouts. In: Bohoslavsky JP, Cernic JL (eds) Making sovereign financing and human rights work. Hart Publishing, Oxford
Goldmann M (2015) Internationale öffentliche Gewalt. Springer, Heidelberg
Goldmann M (2016) A matter of perspective: global governance and the distinction between public and private authority (and not law). Glob Const 5:48
Guder LF (2009) The administration of debt relief by the international financial institutions. Springer, Heidelberg
Guzman M, Ocampo JA, Stiglitz JE (2016) Creating a framework for sovereign debt restructuring that works. In: Guzman M et al (eds) Too little, too late: the quest to resolve sovereign debt crises, p 3. Columbia University Press, New York, NY
Habermas J (1962) Strukturwandel der Öffentlichkeit. Luchterhand, Neuwied
Habermas J (1973a) Legitimationsprobleme im Spätkapitalismus. Suhrkamp, Frankfurt a. M.
Habermas J (1973b) What does a crisis mean today? Legitimation problems in late capitalism. Soc Res 40:643
Habermas J (1981a) Theorie des kommunikativen Handelns, vol 1. Suhrkamp, Frankfurt a. M.
Habermas J (1981b) Theorie des kommunikativen Handelns, vol 2. Suhrkamp, Frankfurt a. M.
Habermas J (1987) Theory of communicative action volume two: lifeworld and system: a critique of functionalist reason. Polity Press, Cambridge
Habermas J (1992) Faktizität und Geltung. Suhrkamp, Frankfurt a. M.
Habermas J (2004) Hat die Konstitutionalisierung des Völkerrechts noch eine Chance? In: Der gespaltene Westen: Kleine politische Schriften X, pp 113–193. Suhrkamp, Frankfurt a. M.
Habermas J (2009) Rekonstruktive vs. verstehende Sozialwissenschaften. In: Philosophische Texte, vol 1, p 338. Suhrkamp, Frankfurt a. M.
Habermas J (2011) Die Krise der Europäischen Union im Lichte einer Konstitutionalisierung des Völkerrechts: Ein Essay zur Verfassung Europas. In: Zur Verfassung Europas: Ein Essay, pp 39–69. Suhrkamp, Frankfurt a. M.
Habermas J (2013a) Im Sog der Technokratie: Ein Plädoyer für europäische Solidarität. In: Im Sog der Technokratie: Kleine politische Schriften XII, pp 82–111. Suhrkamp, Frankfurt a. M.
Habermas J (2013b) Demokratie oder Kapitalismus? Vom Elend der nationalstaatlichen Fragmentierung einer kapitalistisch integrierten Weltgesellschaft. In: Im Sog der Technokratie, Kleine politische Schriften XII, pp 138–157. Suhrkamp, Frankfurt a. M.
Habermas J (2014) Zur Prinzipienkonkurrenz von Bürgergleichheit und Staatengleichheit im supranationalen Gemeinwesen: Eine Notiz aus Anlass der Frage nach der Legitimität der Ungleichen Repräsentation der Bürger im Europäischen Parlament. Der Staat 53:167–192

Hall PA, Soskice D (2001) Varieties of capitalism: the institutional foundations of comparative advantage. Oxford University Press, Oxford
Haque MS (2002) Globalization, new political economy, and governance: a third world viewpoint. Admin Theory Praxis 24:103–124
Heitmeyer W (1997) Was hält die Gesellschaft zusammen? Suhrkamp, Frankfurt a. M.
Hobbes T (1647 [1760]) Elementa Philosophica De Cive. Apud Franciscum Grasset, Lausanne
Holmes OW (1881) The common law. Little, Brown, and Co., Boston
Human Rights Council (2012) The effects of foreign debt and other related international financial obligations of states on the full enjoyment of all human rights, particularly economic, social and cultural rights, U.N. Doc. A/HRC/RES/20/1018, July 2012
Int'l Law Comm'n (2001) Responsibility of states for internationally wrongful acts, U.N. Doc. A/56/49, at Art. 25
Int'l Monetary Fund (2002a) Assessing sustainability. https://www.imf.org/external/np/pdr/sus/2002/eng/052802.pdf. Accessed 16 March 2018
Int'l Monetary Fund (2002b) Guidelines on conditionality, Sept 2002. http://www.imf.org/External/np/pdr/cond/2002/eng/guid/092302.pdf. Accessed 16 March 2018
Int'l Monetary Fund (2013a) Staff guidance note for public debt sustainability analysis in market-access countries. IMF, Washington, DC
Int'l Monetary Fund (2013b) The joint World Bank–IMF debt sustainability framework for low-income countries factsheet. IMF, Washington, DC
Int'l Monetary Fund (2014a) Strengthening the contractual framework to address collective action problems in sovereign debt restructuring, Oct 2014. IMF, Washington, DC
Int'l monetary Fund (2014b) The fund's lending framework and sovereign debt – preliminary considerations, June 2014. IMF, Washington, DC
Int'l Monetary Fund & Int'l Dev. Ass'n (2004) Debt sustainability in low-income countries – proposal for an operational framework and policy implications. https://www.imf.org/external/np/pdr/sustain/2004/020304.pdf. Accessed 16 March 2018
Issing O (2015) Some remarks on debt, default, and debt relief (LSE Financial Markets Group Paper Series).
Jessop B (2002) The future of the capitalist state. Polity Press, Cambridge
Josselin D (2009) Regime interplay in public-private governance: taking stock of the relationship between the paris club and private creditors between 1982 and 2005. Global Governance 15:521
Kant I (1790) Introduction to the science of right: general definitions, and divisions. Informotions, Inc., Virginia
Kelsen H (1967) Pure theory of law. Max Knight trans., 2nd edn, pp 281–284. The Lawbook Exchange, Clark, NJ
Kennedy D (2013) Law and political economy of the world. Leiden J Int'l L 26:7
Keynes Maynard J (1926) The end of laissez-faire. Hogarth Press, London
Kirchhof P (2010) §169 Erwerbsstreben und Maß des Rechts. In: Kirchhof P, Isensee J (eds) Handbuch des Staatsrechts, vol 8. C. F. Müller, Heidelberg
Komárek J (2014) National constitutional courts in the european constitutional democracy. Int'l J Const L 12:525
Kriesi H et al (2012) Political conflict in western Europe. Cambridge University Press, Cambridge
Lang ATF (2013) The legal construction of economic rationalities? JL Soc'y 40:155
Lipset SM, Rokkan S (1967) Cleavage structures, party systems and voter alignments. An introduction. In: Lipset SM, Rokkan S (eds) Party systems and voter alignments: cross-national perspectives, p 1. Free Press, New York, NY
Luther M (1525 [1924]) Vom unfreien Willen. Kaiser, München
Machiavelli N (1513 [1891]) Il Principe. Clarendon Press, Oxford
Mandel E (1972) Der Spätkapitalismus: Versuch einer marxistischen Erklärung. Suhrkamp, Frankfurt a. M.
Marx K, Engels F (1974) Manifest der Kommunistischen Partei. In: Marx Engels Werke, vol 4, p 459. Dietz, Berlin

Möllers C (2008) Die drei Gewalten: Legitimation der Gewaltengliederung in Verfassungsstaat, Europäischer Integration und Internationalisierung. Velbrück, Weilerswist
Napolitano G (2003) Pubblico e privato nel diritto amministrativo. Giuffrè Editore, Milano
Offe C (1972) Strukturprobleme des kapitalistischen Staats: Aufsätze zur politischen Soziologie. Campus, Frankfurt a. M.
Paris Club, Que signifie la comparabilité de traitement? http://www.clubdeparis.org/en/communications/page/what-does-comparability-of-treatment-mean. Accessed 16 March 2018
Patberg M (2014) Supranational constitutional politics and the method of rational reconstruction. Phil & Soc Criticism 40:501
Pierson P (2000) Three worlds of welfare state research. Comp Pol Stud 33:798
Piketty T (2014) Capital in the twenty-first century. Belknap Press of Harvard University Press, Cambridge, MA
Pistor K (2013) A legal theory of finance. J Comp Econ 41:315
Polanyi K (1944) The great transformation: the political and economic origins of our time. Beacon Press, Boston, MA
Reinhart CM, Rogoff KS (2010) Growth in a time of debt (Nat'l Bureau of Econ Res, Working Paper No. 15639). National Bureau of Economic Research, Cambridge, MA
Riegner M, Legal F (2014) Frameworks and general principles for indicators in sovereign debt restructuring. Paper for the UNCTAD Working Group on a Debt Workout Mechanism
Rittberger V, Hasenclever A (2000) Does religion make a difference? Theoretical approaches to the impact of faith on political conflict. Millennium: J Int'l Stud 29:641
Rodrik D (2011) The globalization paradox: democracy and the future of the world economy. Norton, New York, NY
Rorty R (1967) The linguistic turn. University of Chicago Press, Chicago, IL
Rückert J (1984) Idealismus, Jurisprudenz und Politik bei Friedrich Carl von Savigny. Kremer, Ebelsbach
Sassen S (2012) Global finance and its institutional spaces. In: Knorr Cetina K, Preda A (eds) The Oxford handbook of the sociology of finance. Oxford University Press, Oxford
Schäfer A (2008) Krisentheorien der Demokratie: Unregierbarkeit, Spätkapitalismus und Postdemokratie, MPIfG Discussion Paper
Schäfer A, Streeck W (2013) Politics in the age of austerity. Polity Press, Cambridge
Schäuble W (2011) Interview, Keine Rettung um jeden Preis. Der Spiegel 33. http://www.spiegel.de/spiegel/print/d-79973965.html. Accessed 16 March 2018
Schill S (2013) Transnational Legal Approaches to Administrative Law: Conceptualizing Public Contracts in Globalization (Jean Monnet Working Paper No. 05)
Schmidt MG et al (2007) Der Wohlfahrtsstaat. Eine Einführung in den historischen und internationalen Vergleich. VS Verlag für Sozialwissenschaften, Wiesbaden
Schulz M (2012) Interview, Daumenschrauben angezogen. Der Spiegel 36. http://www.spiegel.de/spiegel/print/d-87997155.html. Accessed 16 March 2018
Schumacher J, Enderlein H, Trebesch C (2014) Sovereign defaults in courts. http://papers.ssrn.com/sol3/papers.cfm?abstract_id=2189997. Accessed 16 March 2018
Smith A (1776) An inquiry into the nature and causes of the wealth of nations. Raleigh, N.C.: Alex Catalogue.
Streeck W (2013) Gekaufte Zeit: Die vertagte Krise des demokratischen Kapitalismus. Suhrkamp, Berlin
Thomale C (2015) Rechtsfähigkeit und juristische Person als Abstraktionsleistungen: Savignys Werk und Kants Beitrag. In: Gröschner R, Kirste S, Lembcke OW (eds) Person und Rechtsperson: Zur Philosophie der Personalität in den interpersonalen Verhältnissen des Rechts. pp 173–185. Mohr Siebeck, Tübingen
Tsotroudi K (2014) International labour standards as a model for the future: the case of financial regulation. In: Politakis G (eds) Les normes internationales du travail: un patrimoine pour l'avenir. Mélanges en l'honneur de Nicolas Valticos. p 615. Bureau International du Travail, Genève

UNCTAD (2012) Principles on promoting responsible sovereign lending and borrowing. http://unctad.org/en/PublicationsLibrary/gdsddf2012misc1_en.pdf. Accessed 16 March 2018
UNCTAD (2015) Sovereign debt workouts: going forward: roadmap and guide, (18 Apr 2015), http://unctad.org/en/PublicationsLibrary/gdsddf2015misc1_en.pdf. Accessed 16 March 2018
U.N. G.A. (2015) Basic Principles on Sovereign Debt Restructuring, Draft Resolution, U.N. Doc. A/69/L.84 (29 July 2015)
van Aaken A (2014) Behavioral international law and economics. Harv. Int'l LJ 55:421
Varoufakis Y (2015) A new approach to eurozone sovereign debt, Project Syndicate (17 Aug 2015). https://www.project-syndicate.org/commentary/eurozone-sovereign-debt-solution-by-yanis-varoufakis-2015-08?barrier=true. Accessed 16 March 2018
Vauchez A (2014) Démocratiser l'Europe. Seuil, Paris
Vester M (1997) Kapitalistische Modernisierung und gesellschaftliche (Des-)Integration. In: Heitmeyer W (eds) Was hält die Gesellschaft zusammen? Suhrkamp, Frankfurt a. M.
Viellechner L (2016) The limits of law (and Democracy) in the euro crisis: An approach from systems theory. Ger Law J 17(5):747–762.
von Bogdandy A (2000) Das Leitbild der Dualistischen Legitimation für die Europäische Verfassungsentwicklung. Kritische Vierteljahresschrift für Gesetzgebung und Rechtsprechung, 3:284
von Bogdandy A, Dann P, Goldmann M (2008) Developing the publicness of public international law: towards a legal framework for global governance activities. German LJ 9:1375
von Bogdandy A, Goldmann M (2012) Sovereign debt restructurings as exercises of public authority: towards a decentralized sovereign insolvency law. In: Esposito C, Bohoslavsky JP, Li Y (eds) Responsible sovereign lending and borrowing: the search for common principles, p 39. Oxford University Press, Oxford
von Bogdandy A, Venzke I (2015) In whose name? A public law theory of international adjudication [XX]. Oxford University Press, Oxford
von Hayek FA (1944) The road to serfdom. University of Chicago Press, Chicago, IL
von Hayek FA (1960) The constitution of libert . University of Chicago Press, Chicago, IL
von Weizsäcker CC (2014) Die normative Ko-Evolution von Marktwirtschaft und Demokratie, MPIfG Discussion Paper
von Weizsäcker J et al (2013) Mobil, Gerecht, Einig. Die Zeit 43. http://www.zeit.de/2013/43/glienicker-gruppe-europaeische-union. Accessed 16 March 2018
Weber M (1972 [1922]) Wirtschaft und Gesellschaft, 5th edn. Mohr, Tübingen
Weidemaier MC, Gelpern A (2014) Injunctions in sovereign debt litigation. Yale J Reg 31:189
Wong N (2015) NML Capital, Ltd. v. republic of Argentina and the changing roles of the pari passu and collective action clauses in sovereign debt agreements. Colum J Transnat'l L 53:396
Zuckerman AS (1975) Political cleavage: a conceptual and theoretical analysis. British J Pol Sci 5:231
Zürn M (2014) The politicization of world politics and its effects: eight propositions. Eur Pol Sci Rev 6:47
Zürn M, Ecker-Ehrhardt M (2011) Die Politisierung der Weltpolitik: Umkämpfte internationale Institutionen. Suhrkamp, Berlin

Matthias Goldmann is a Junior Professor for International Public Law and Financial Law at Goethe University Frankfurt and Senior Research Affiliate at the Max Planck Institute for Comparative Public Law and International Law, Heidelberg.

Silvia Steininger is a Research Fellow at the Max Planck Institute for Comparative Public Law and International Law, Heidelberg.

The Limits of Law (and Democracy) in the Euro Crisis: An Approach from Systems Theory

Lars Viellechner

Abstract The chapter attempts to explore the fate of law and democracy in the euro crisis from the sociological perspective of systems theory. It consecutively ascertains the performance, the relevance, and the function of the law with regard to the current practice of restructuring sovereign debt in the euro area. While novel forms of regulation such as the European Stability Mechanism attest a remarkable assertiveness of the law, they cannot effectively command economic recovery and must cede to economic imperatives for their part. Under such circumstances, the law can no longer adequately fulfill its function to counterfactually secure normative expectations. Nevertheless, the regulatory experiments in the euro crisis may not be regarded as undemocratic. Rather, the heterarchical processes of mutual observation, recognition, and contestation among the various constituencies involved, including representatives of governments, institutions of the European Union, central banks, national parliaments and peoples via referenda, as well as European and national courts, provide some substitute for the lack of elections and parliamentary decision-making at the European level.

Revised version of the original published article "The Limits of Law (and Democracy) in the Euro Crisis: An Approach from Systems Theory" by Lars Viellechner, German Law Journal 17(5):747–762

L. Viellechner (✉)
University of Bremen, Bremen, Germany
e-mail: lars.viellechner@uni-bremen.de

M. Goldmann, S. Steininger (Eds.), *Democracy and Financial Order: Legal Perspectives*, Beiträge zum ausländischen öffentlichen Recht und Völkerrecht, https://doi.org/10.1007/978-3-662-55568-2_3

1 Introduction

The various supranational and international instruments that aim to ensure the stability of the euro and restructure the sovereign debt of some of the member states of the European Union (EU) in the face of the current financial crisis are not only highly complex in their construction and interaction so that even experts have difficulty in comprehending them.[1] Their legality is also much contested. Meanwhile, the Court of Justice of the European Union (CJEU)[2] and some national constitutional courts[3] have decided on the compatibility of some important rescue measures, notably the establishment of the European Stability Mechanism (ESM) and the Outright Monetary Transactions (OMT) program of the European Central Bank (ECB), with European and national constitutional law respectively, largely approving of them. Nonetheless, each subsequent step towards restructuring sovereign debt within the euro area raises new issues of legality. Thus, it was recently discussed if a debt "haircut" could be made part of additional financial assistance facilities to support Greece.[4] Apart from that, some legal scholars have tried to develop a set of abstract legal principles against which to measure the legitimacy of sovereign debt restructuring in the future.[5]

As a sociological approach, systems theory cannot contribute to the normative debate on the legality and legitimacy of financial market regulation in general and sovereign debt restructuring in particular. It cannot even engage in any kind of "rational reconstruction"[6] that would carve out the normative presuppositions underlying the contemporary practice of financial regulation and, hence, oscillate between the empirical and the normative. It can only describe and analyze the role that the law—and democratic political lawmaking—might assume in view of financial crisis. Such an endeavor is not futile. It may reveal systemic deficiencies in the current practice of financial regulation and thus help policy-makers and lawyers acknowledge which avenues to follow in order to reach their aims.

Nevertheless, the analysis remains difficult because the version of systems theory submitted by Niklas Luhmann,[7] which serves as a tool of analysis here, has never expressly dealt with financial crisis. Neither has Luhmann comprehensively explored

[1] For an overview of the legal instruments, *see* de Gregorio Merino (2012), p. 1613.

[2] *See* Case C-62/14, Gauweiler and Others v. Deutscher Bundestag, ECLI:EU:C:2015:400 (16 June 2015); Case C-370/12, Pringle v. Government of Ireland, ECLI:EU:C:2012:756 (27 Nov. 2012).

[3] For the German perspective, *see* Bundesverfassungsgericht [BVerfG] [Federal Constitutional Court], 142 Entscheidungen des Bundesverfassungsgerichts [BVerfGE] 123 (21 June 2016); 135 Entscheidungen des Bundesverfassungsgerichts [BVerfGE] 317 (18 March 2014); 134 Entscheidungen des Bundesverfassungsgerichts [BVerfGE] 366 (14 Jan. 2014); 132 Entscheidungen des Bundesverfassungsgerichts [BVerfGE] 195 (12 Sept. 2012); 131 Entscheidungen des Bundesverfassungsgerichts [BVerfGE] 152 (19 June 2012); 130 Entscheidungen des Bundesverfassungsgerichts [BVerfGE] 318 (28 Feb. 2012); 129 Entscheidungen des Bundesverfassungsgerichts [BVerfGE] 124 (7 Sept. 2011).

[4] *See* von Bogdandy et al (2015), p. 6; Steinbach (2016), p. 223.

[5] *See* von Bogdandy and Goldmann (2013), p. 39.

[6] Goldmann and Steininger, chapter "A Discourse Theoretical Approach to Sovereign Debt Restructuring: Towards a Democratic Financial Order".

[7] *See generally* Luhmann (1995 [1984]).

international or European law, although he left some short, yet clear-sighted presumptions on the fate of law in the further evolution of world society, which he had already started formulating at the beginning of the 1970s.[8] Only recently have some of Luhmann's followers started to discuss the role of law in the current financial crisis, but their studies focus on the possibilities of political-legal intervention on the private side of financial markets while altogether ignoring the topic of sovereign debt restructuring, which supposedly requires a different assessment.[9]

Hence, the present attempt at analyzing the role of law—and democratic political lawmaking—in coping with the euro crisis from the perspective of systems theory may only draw on some of Luhmann's more general insights concerning the relationship of law, politics, and the economy. In so doing, it cannot claim to deliver an authoritative interpretation of Luhmann's work. It can only offer what appears to be a plausible reading of this version of systems theory.

The survey will consecutively ascertain the performance (2.), the relevance (3.), and the function of the law (4.) with regard to the current practice of restructuring sovereign debt in the euro area. All three terms are employed in everyday language, but they have specific meanings in systems theory. The sociological analysis will also yield some observations on the legitimacy of the regulatory practice in the euro crisis, even though it does not allow for a normative appraisal (5.).

2 Performance

The first observation relates to the performance that the law may achieve with regard to shaping the financial market in general and restructuring sovereign debt in particular. Such a capacity for achievement crucially depends on the relationship between the various social systems, especially politics, law, and the economy. In this respect, it is necessary to explain some of the basic assumptions of systems theory as a social theory. According to Luhmann's most fundamental claim, modern society consists of various social systems, such as religion, politics, law, the economy, the sciences, and the arts that operate self-referentially according to their own rationality. While each system fulfills a function that is indispensable to society as a whole, it cannot directly influence, but only irritate the others. Consequently, external information or stimulation may only be processed according to the inner logic of each system.[10] For Luhmann, therefore, any attempt at social steering by means of politics and law was doomed to fail. In particular, he regarded the "welfare state,"[11] which tried to assume a universal responsibility for prosperity in all spheres of social life, as a useless "effort to inflate the cows in order to get more milk."[12]

---

[8] *See* Luhmann (1971), p. 1; Luhmann (1985 [1972]), pp. 255–264; Luhmann (2004 [1993]), pp. 479–490.

[9] *See* the contributions in Kjaer et al (2011).

[10] *See* Luhmann (1995 [1984]), pp. 12–58.

[11] Briggs (1961), p. 221; Luhmann (1990 [1981]).

[12] Luhmann (1998), p. 369 (my translation).

Still, Luhmann conceded that social systems might presuppose certain features of their environments and rely on them structurally. For example, he assumed that the political and legal systems were linked through a "structural coupling"[13] in the form of the constitution, which allows for them to have a certain impact on each other.[14] He also admitted that politics and law, in their peculiar conjunction through the constitution, "imply the action capacity of the system more than any other structures" and therefore serve as "the primary developmental factor or risk carrier of societal development."[15] In this regard, he came close to Jürgen Habermas, who, when further elaborating on his discourse theory of law and democracy "connect[ed] with an objectifying sociological approach that regards the political system neither as the peak nor the center, nor even as the structuring model of society, but as just one action system among others." Thus, he admitted that politics may, through the medium of law, only provide "a kind of surety" for solving problems of society as a whole.[16]

Gunther Teubner and Helmut Willke took a similar diagnosis as a point of departure for imagining a "reflexive law"[17] that, albeit unable to govern other social systems, may at least stimulate processes of self-reflection within them in order to allow for their mutual consideration and hence social integration in the absence of a central steering agency. Yet, Luhmann was not convinced. For the orthodox strand of systems theory, it is "inconceivable that law could control and regulate the autopoiesis of all social systems,"[18] even in the extenuated sense of a regulation of self-regulation. In this view, none of the social systems may assume a superordinate position, not even as a catalyst or moderator to facilitate coordination among them. It is therefore impossible that political-legal intervention could in any way channel the economic system and effectively cure the deficiencies of a failing financial market.

There may only be hope for a successful "self-constitutionalization"[19] of the economic system. As Teubner has recently demonstrated with regard to the example of plain money reform in the current financial crisis, such a transformation could not only be induced by external pressure, but also by the near-death experience of "hitting the bottom."[20] Supposedly, the relevant parts of society, in this case the financial market, will be able to develop an extraordinary strength that allows them to pull themselves out of the swamp by their own bootstraps when facing an imminent existential threat. A self-regulation of this kind, however, is highly demanding and extremely fragile. It requires the economic system to develop a capacity for

[13] Luhmann (1992a), p. 1419.

[14] *See* Luhmann (1990), p. 176.

[15] Luhmann (1985 [1972]), pp. 259–260.

[16] Habermas (1998 [1996]), p. 251.

[17] Teubner (1983), p. 266; Willke (1992), p. 366.

[18] Luhmann (1992b), p. 397.

[19] Teubner (2004), p. 15. For more detail, *see* Teubner (2012).

[20] Teubner (2011), p. 3.

self-reflection ultimately provoking a willingness to engage in self-restraint, which can neither be induced nor ensured from outside.

The situation appears to be different when it comes to restructuring the sovereign debt of nation-states through supranational and international law, as currently practiced in the EU. In this case, regulation does not encounter insurmountable systemic boundaries because both regulatory means and targets lie within the reach of the political and legal systems. Nation-states as political entities may readily engage with other nation-states by employing the political-legal instruments of international treaties. They may also be able and willing to comply with the secondary legislation of the supranational organizations to which they are members. At the same time, they have the means of administrative law at their disposal to implement the political reforms of public spending that supranational and international law might call for. Indeed, the member states of the EU whose currency is the euro have proved a remarkable capacity and willingness to solve problems by establishing, and complying with, the law of newly erected international financial institutions such as the ESM.[21]

Nonetheless, the effectiveness of political-legal attempts at restructuring sovereign debt may be impaired by two factors. First, whether the reforms of public spending that are politically agreed upon and legally implemented will eventually succeed depends on a favorable development of the economy at large. Politics and law, however, cannot command economic recovery. At this point, the systemic boundaries reoccur. If at all, the legal restructuring of sovereign debt may take the form of what is called "purposive programs," as opposed to "conditional programs."[22] While conditional programs clearly define the conditions and effects of a certain rule, purposive programs solely name a distinctive goal to be reached in a particular case and some aspects to be considered in the process of decision-making, while the path to realizing the goal also hinges on various external circumstances. The conditionality attached to the financial assistance facilities according to Article 13(3) of the ESM Treaty provides an illustrative example of such purposive programs—the term "conditionality" should not cause confusion here.[23] For example, the memorandum of understanding that implements the third assistance program to support Greece under the ESM builds on four abstract goals: (1) restoring fiscal sustainability; (2) safeguarding financial stability; (3) growth, competitiveness, and investment; and (4) a modern state and public administration. It also enlists certain sectors of reform and some specific measures to be adopted by the Greek government in this respect, including reorganization in the areas of taxation, pensions, health care, and justice, among others.[24] Nevertheless, there is no guarantee that the political goals stipulated in the program will in fact be reached. Even if faithfully realized, the political reforms may have adverse effects on the economic system, while changing economic or other social circumstances may thwart their realization in the first place.

[21] *See* Craig (2014), p. 19; Fabbrini (2016).

[22] Luhmann (1966) p. 36.

[23] *See* ESM (2012), art. 13(3).

[24] *See* Eur. Comm'n (2015).

Moreover, as purposive programs grant a generous amount of leeway in their application, judicial control is hampered so that the law loses much of its force.

Second, it is possible that the parties to an international treaty that restructures sovereign debt will not keep their promises. As a matter of fact, international law has long suffered from a lack of authority because the nation-states are simultaneously its authors and addressees. Many commentators have even denied its legal character on these grounds.[25] To be sure, it is nowadays well established that "almost all nations observe almost all principles of international law and almost all of their obligations almost all of the time."[26] Under conditions of economic hardship, however, the debtor states may have no alternative but to disregard their legal obligations. Thus, several member states of the EU have exceeded the deficit thresholds of the Stability and Growth Pact (SGP) in the past.[27]

Apart from that, some observers recognize a significant difference in compliance with the law between member states of the EU from the north and from the south.[28] It is not clear whether this allegation can stand up to objections but, if it is accepted, such divergence can be explained by persisting differences in legal cultures and mentalities that even systems theory acknowledges. Although Luhmann generally assumed a differentiation of social systems on a global scale, he admitted that the political and legal systems of world society are still characterized by a "segmental, secondary differentiation"[29] into nation-states, which entails that, regarding the law, "enormous differences in the different regions of the globe cannot be overlooked."[30] Consequently, as neither upswings in the economy nor changes in mentality may be imposed by command and control, there remains serious doubt as to whether the political-legal attempts at restructuring sovereign debt in the euro area will eventually succeed.

3 Relevance

The second observation concerns the relevance that law may retain in facing the euro crisis. Exposing the argument requires clarifying the basic function of law with regard to society, that is, the question of which problem of society is solved by the differentiation of a specialized legal system. According to Luhmann, each social system only fulfills one particular function for which there is no equivalent, whereas a social system may render various performances with regard to society for which other social systems may well offer alternatives.[31] For example, dispute resolution

---

[25] *See, e.g.*, Austin (1832), p. 208. For an overview of the various approaches, *see* Walz (1930).

[26] Henkin (1979), p. 47.

[27] *See* Eur. Comm'n (2018).

[28] *See* Ladeur (2014), pp. 148–151.

[29] Luhmann (2004 [1993]), p. 487.

[30] *Id.*, p. 481. For an illustration regarding the case of Brazil, *see* Neves (1992).

[31] *See* Luhmann (2004 [1993]), pp. 142–172.

is only a performance, not a function, of the legal system because arbitrators and mediators may also provide it instead of courts. In this understanding, the one and only function of the law is the counterfactual "stabilization of normative expectations."[32] While normative expectations are upheld even if someone acts against them, cognitive expectations are adapted to reality in cases of disappointment. The latter are hence characterized by a preparedness to learn.[33]

Against this background, Luhmann suspected that social structures marked by a cognitive style of orientation would gradually supersede those showing a normative orientation in the evolution of world society.[34] As he explained, there has long been a preference for normative mechanisms of orientation because of their stabilizing function. For this reason, he claimed, such social systems as religion, politics, and law had assumed a predominant role in the past. By contrast, Luhmann found that those social systems that open up and support worldwide social relations, such as the economy, science, and technology, clearly show a cognitive style of orientation. A "shift of evolutionary primacy from normative to cognitive mechanisms"[35] of orientation therefore appeared obvious to him. He even insinuated

> that—in relation to further developmental possibilities—the provision of normative, political-legal mechanisms, which were passed down from high cultures, was a flawed specialisation of human development from which further evolution could not ensue; that we have, with them, established ourselves at a level of the system from which the evolution of social systems toward higher complexity cannot be continued.[36]

At first glance, however, the developments during the current euro crisis do not appear to attest to Luhmann's conjecture on the withering of law in the evolution of world society. At least with regard to European financial governance, a "de-juridification,"[37] or a move to "informal governance,"[38] is barely perceivable. Certainly, the attempts at ensuring the financial stability of the euro area have fundamentally altered the institutional and constitutional structure of the EU.[39] Not only have the European Council and the euro group become the center of political

---

[32] *Id.*, p. 148.

[33] *See* Luhmann (1985 [1972]), pp. 31–40. For an obnoxious example of the distinction between normative and cognitive expectations, *see id.*, p. 33:

> Suppose, for example, one is waiting for a new secretary. This situation contains both cognitive and normative components of expectation. To be sure, the fact that she could be young, pretty and blonde may be cognitively expected; but in these respects it is necessary to adapt to disappointments, i. e. not to insist on blonde hair, ask for it to be dyed, etc. However, it is normatively expected that she should achieve something.

[34] *See* Luhmann (1971), pp. 10–17; Luhmann (1985 [1972]), pp. 261–264.

[35] Luhmann (1985 [1972]), p. 262.

[36] *Id.*, p. 261.

[37] Joerges (2014), p. 251.

[38] Kleine (2013).

[39] *See* Tuori and Tuori (2014); Hinarejos (2015a).

decision-making, while the latter is indeed an informal body whose meetings are highly nontransparent.[40] This "new intergovernmentalism"[41] has also created a new layer of international law that supplements EU law.[42] Most notably, an international treaty between the member states of the EU whose currency is the euro established the ESM.[43] At the same time, some of the newly erected international institutions borrow certain organs of the EU in order to reach their aims, thereby generating a new kind of hybrid law that combines elements of both international and EU law.[44] In particular, the ESM assigns several tasks to the European Commission, the ECB, and the CJEU, in addition to providing for a close cooperation with the International Monetary Fund (IMF).[45] In this way, the respective institutions also attain a preponderant role in European financial governance.[46] Yet none of these transformations results in a decline of law. On the contrary, the recourse to the cumbersome legal constructions here described attests that the member states of the EU whose currency is the euro undertake all efforts to frame their attempt at ensuring the financial stability of the euro area in terms of law.

Even in the rare instances in which European financial governance, for lack of alternatives, resorts to instruments of soft law, a strong normativity prevails. For example, Article 13(3) of the ESM Treaty stipulates that memoranda of understanding shall detail the conditionality of the financial assistance facilities that are granted to ESM member states.[47] Although these agreements specify the general terms of the ESM Treaty on a particular occasion, they are not, in themselves, legally binding.[48] Nevertheless, they are perceived as strictly obligatory because the ESM may refuse to release subsequent payments in the case of non-compliance.

A pronounced reliance on the law also resurfaces with regard to judicial control of the euro crisis. Indeed, it appears that courts have never before been called upon as extensively to monitor and shape a financial crisis.[49] Plaintiffs have turned to any competent jurisdiction in any possible way. Not only have they challenged the public law framework of sovereign debt restructuring in the euro area before both European and national constitutional courts,[50] but they have also sued debtor states in civil proceedings.[51]

Nevertheless, the smashing force and sustained impact of the euro crisis demonstrate how far a globalized economy may gain predominance over all other social

---

[40] *See* Puetter (2006, 2014).

[41] Bickerton et al (2015), p. 703; *see also* Fabbrini (2013), p. 1003.

[42] *See* Dimopoulos (2014), p. 41; Lorz and Sauer (2012), p. 573.

[43] *See* ESM (2012).

[44] *See* Peers (2013), p. 37; Fischer-Lescano and Oberndorfer (2013), p. 9.

[45] *See* ESM (2012), arts. 13, 37–38.

[46] *See* Bauer and Becker (2014), p. 213; Beukers (2013), p. 1579.

[47] *See* ESM (2012), art. 13(3).

[48] *See* Schwarz (2014), p. 389; Meng-Papantoni (2015), p. 3.

[49] *See* Bardutzky and Fahey (2014), p. 341; Hinarejos (2015b), p. 112.

[50] *See* cases cited *supra* notes 2–3.

[51] *See, e.g.*, Case C-226/13, Fahnenbrock and Others v. Hellenic Republic, ECLI:EU:C:2015:383 (11 June 2015).

systems including the law. Although the economy does not supersede the law, legal regulation and control of the euro crisis become highly dependent on extra-legal knowledge. Certainly, the functioning of the explicit rules and principles of law has always built upon an underlying infrastructure of social norms and informal conventions that store the implicit knowledge and practical experience dispersed in society.[52] Moreover, the modern welfare state, which does not only limit itself to averting imminent dangers for its citizens but more expansively assumes the task of risk precaution,[53] has to increasingly rely on scientific findings and technical expertise when taking political decisions. Only in this way can it avoid measures that will miss their targets. It therefore has to cooperate with various non-state actors that gain privileged positions as they participate in the process of law formation.[54]

When it comes to regulating the financial market and restructuring sovereign debt, however, extra-legal knowledge almost entirely determines political decisions that result in legal norms. This development is unavoidable because the assessment and evaluation of what action should be taken in order to achieve financial stability crucially depends on both economic expertise and practical experience in the respective areas of reform. Consequently, Article 13(1) of the ESM Treaty assigns the tasks of assessing the existence of a risk to the financial stability of the euro area, the sustainability of public debt, and the actual or potential financial needs of a member state to the experts of the European Commission, the ECB, and the IMF.[55] Furthermore, Article 13(7) of the ESM Treaty entrusts the same institutions with monitoring compliance with the conditionality attached to the financial assistance facilities granted to ESM member states.[56] Even the courts heavily rely on economic knowledge when reviewing the legal constructions that aim at restructuring sovereign debt in the euro area. Thus, the German Federal Constitutional Court (FCC) heard representatives of the ECB and the German Bundesbank as expert third parties pursuant to Section 27a of the FCC Act in its proceedings on the constitutional complaint against the establishment of the ESM.[57]

The extensive recourse to the law during the current euro crisis may be animated by a firmly held belief in its previous capacity for achievement. At the same time, new tools of legal regulation and judicial control attest a remarkable assertiveness of the law in this context. Nevertheless, the law will inevitably lose relevance to the extent that it cedes to economic imperatives.

---

[52] *See* Ladeur (2006), p. 87; Vesting (2015), pp. 113–115.

[53] *See* Beck (1992 [1986]); Ewald (1986).

[54] *See* Schmitter (1974), p. 85; Ritter (1979), p. 389.

[55] *See* ESM (2012), art. 13(1).

[56] *Id.*, art. 13(7).

[57] *See* Bundesverfassungsgericht [BVerfG] [Federal Constitutional Court], Case No. 2 BvR 1390/12 et al., 135 Entscheidungen des Bundesverfassungsgerichts [BVerfGE] 317, 371 (18 March 2014).

4 Function

As the euro crisis impairs both the performance and the relevance of the law, the question arises of whether the law itself will have to change in order to hold its position in contemporary society. Indeed, Luhmann supposed that a total decline of the law in the evolution of world society was highly improbable because a one-sided reliance of society on cognitive mechanisms of processing disappointments would foreclose any confident orientation and bring with it unbearably high risks.[58] Yet he contemplated that the law would perhaps have to take into account the fact that the emerging world society gives primacy to a cognitive style of orientation. Such a transformation would then imply "the inclusion of cognitive mechanisms in the essentially normative structure of law."[59]

In the most extreme case, the genuine function of the law—the counterfactual stabilization of normative expectations—would be affected by such a transformation. As Luhmann proposed:

> Law would take the form of normed models of behaviour which have been drafted as solutions to recognised problems, are legislated upon, tried and changed according to the rules of experience. Normativity would then only have the function of securing the constancy of expectation as long and in as far as it appears meaningful. Moral and ideological reasoning would then be replaced by a functional critique.[60]

As a matter of fact, this description accurately captures the features of the supranational and international instruments that aim to restructure sovereign debt in the euro area. The legal measures adopted to safeguard the financial stability of the euro area are constantly revised, amended, or complemented as soon as it turns out that changed economic or other social circumstances compromise their goals. For example, after a second financial assistance program had expired, Greece immediately requested further stability support so that the third program was launched under the ESM in 2015.[61]

To be sure, the alterability of the law necessarily follows from its positivization. As Luhmann stated: "Positivity involves precisely the built-in capacity for learning in law despite its contradiction to the basic normative attitude."[62] Moreover, the advent of democracy has considerably enhanced the capacities for altering the law. For Luhmann, it seemed not even "too far-fetched to say that democracy is a consequence of the positivization of law and the ensuing possibilities of changing the law at any time."[63]

Yet, with regard to the supranational and international instruments that aim to restructure sovereign debt in the euro area, the inclusion of cognitive mechanisms

---

[58] *See* Luhmann (1985 [1972]), p. 262.

[59] *Id.*

[60] *Id.*, p. 264.

[61] *See* ESM (2015).

[62] Luhmann (1985 [1972]), p. 262.

[63] Luhmann (2004 [1993]), p. 404.

in the normative structure of the law reaches a new dimension that was unknown before. On the one hand, economic imperatives determine the law. On the other hand, fast-changing social circumstances require constant adaptations of the law. Meanwhile, the courts grant a large degree of leeway in regulating the euro crisis to political experiments, if only not to compromise the project of European integration as a whole. For example, the German FCC finally approved the OMT program of the ECB,[64] even though it had initially expressed strong constitutional objections and submitted its first request for a preliminary ruling to the ECJ.[65] Taken together, these developments cause concern that the law might soon forfeit its normative character entirely in the face of the euro crisis. Under such circumstances, it can no longer adequately fulfill its function to counterfactually secure expectations.

Unfortunately, legal scholarship does not offer much guidance here either. It is largely at loss with assigning a proper role to the law in respect of financial crisis. So far, it has neither carved out any particular contribution that the law could make in taming financial crisis, nor does it more generally reflect on how to regain the autonomy of the law against the pull of economics. On the contrary, many scholars who are interested in law and finance do not pursue genuinely juridical interests. Some of them manifestly explore economic issues with economic methods.[66] Others limit themselves to describing and analyzing the various instruments of financial market regulation.[67] Even some more ambitious legal theories of finance turn out to be predominantly empirical observations on the role of law in the financial system.[68] While much has been gained from this scholarship, legal theory is now confronted with the pressing task of developing a specifically legal epistemology that provides some guidance about how the law is to deal with extra-legal, especially economic, knowledge.[69]

5 Legitimacy

The view from systems theory may finally cast a glance on the normative issues of sovereign debt structuring in the euro area, notably the question of legitimacy. As a sociological position, it may not submit a normative proposal in its own right. It may, however, offer a tentative outlook on the fate of democracy in the current stage of European integration.

Many commentators regard the current attempt at restructuring sovereign debt in the euro area as undemocratic and, hence, illegitimate. In their view, the

[64] *See* Bundesverfassungsgericht [BVerfG] [Federal Constitutional Court], Case No. 2 BvR 2728/13 et al., 142 Entscheidungen des Bundesverfassungsgerichts [BVerfGE] 123 (21 June 2016).

[65] *See* Bundesverfassungsgericht [BVerfG] [Federal Constitutional Court], Case No. 2 BvR 2728/13 et al., 134 Entscheidungen des Bundesverfassungsgerichts [BVerfGE] 366 (14 Jan. 2014).

[66] *See, e.g.*, Avgouleas (2012).

[67] *See, e.g.*, Moloney (2014).

[68] *See* Pistor (2013), p. 315.

[69] *See* Augsberg (2015), p. 457; *see also* Towfigh and Petersen (2015).

various supranational and international instruments aimed at ensuring the stability of the euro are elitist constructions, created by executives and implemented by experts, while evading participation and control by both European and national parliaments.[70]

In contrast, the sociological appraisal may—irrespective of its findings on efficiency—juxtapose a more favorable reading of the continuing political negotiations about how to cope with the euro crisis that ultimately result in the formation of supranational and international law. Indeed, it does not appear erroneous to think that the processes of mutual observation, recognition, and contestation among the various constituencies involved, including representatives of governments, institutions of the EU, central banks, national parliaments and peoples via referenda, as well as European and national courts, bring about a new kind of transnational democracy.[71] It may also be possible to detect a variant of the separation of powers here.[72] In such a setting, democratic rule is not grounded on hierarchical chains of legitimacy and representation. Instead, the heterarchical processes of mutual observation, recognition, and contestation among the various constituencies involved serve as a substitute for the lack of elections and parliamentary decision-making.[73] As some proponents of systems theory assert:

> A non-hierarchical variant of democracy would focus less on common decision through sovereign organized unity of will than on producing a distributed self-observation and observation of others made possible by a "network of networks" and the associated productive association possibilities and constraints, which are so openly dimensioned that far-reaching inclusion of citizens is guaranteed.[74]

It should be noted, however, that this vision of democracy does not include an apology of the status quo of European integration. In no way does it take side with keeping the euro area as it currently stands. On the contrary, continuing contestation on either plane may ultimately provoke or require a "Grexit," for example.

Yet an equivalent of democracy that deserves its name presupposes that choices can freely be made and that alternative avenues are available. Whether these conditions are currently met in the EU may be doubted on good grounds. For some constituencies, a voluntary decision is frustrated by the constraints of economic hardship. For others, it is corrupted by the path dependency of the prior political decision to introduce the euro as a single currency.

---

[70] *See, e.g.*, Scharpf (2011), p. 163; Scicluna (2014), p. 545; Joerges (2015), p. 167.

[71] *See also* Goldmann and Steininger, chapter "A Discourse Theoretical Approach to Sovereign Debt Restructuring: Towards a Democratic Financial Order".

[72] In a different context, *see* Peters (2007), p. 273.

[73] For a related concept of democracy within the nation-state, *see* Rosanvallon (2008 [2006]). For some applications to international law, *see* Krisch (2010), pp. 264–276; Ley (2015), p. 717.

[74] Ladeur (2004), p. 113.

References

Augsberg I (2015) Some realism about new legal realism: what's new, what's legal, what's real? Leiden J Int L 28:457

Austin J (1832) The province of jurisprudence determined. Murray, London

Avgouleas E (2012) Governance of global financial markets: the law, the economics, the politics. Cambridge University Press, Cambridge (UK)

Bardutzky S, Fahey E (2014) Who got to adjudicate the EU's financial crisis and why? Judicial review of the legal instruments of the Eurozone. In: Adams M et al (eds) The constitutionalization of European budgetary constraints. Hart, Oxford, p 341

Bauer MW, Becker S (2014) The unexpected winner of the crisis: the European Commission's strengthened role in economic governance. J Eur Integration 36:213

Beck U (1992 [1986]) Risk society: towards a new modernity (trans: Ritter M). Sage, London

Beukers T (2013) The new ECB and its relationship with the Eurozone Member States: between central bank independence and central bank intervention. Common Mkt L Rev 50:1579

Bickerton CJ et al (2015) The new intergovernmentalism: European integration in the post-Maastricht era. J Common Mkt Stud 53:703

Briggs A (1961) The welfare state in historical perspective. Eur J Soc 2:221

von Bogdandy A, Goldmann M (2013) Sovereign debt restructurings as exercises of international public authority: towards a decentralized sovereign insolvency law. In: Espósito C et al (eds) Sovereign financing and international law: the UNCTAD principles on responsible sovereign lending and borrowing. Oxford University Press, Oxford, p 39

von Bogdandy A et al (2015) Verlustrisiko: Griechenlands Schuldenlast kann und muss im Euroraum erleichtert werden. Frankfurter Allgemeine Zeitung, 23 July 2015, p 6. http://www.faz.net/aktuell/politik/staat-und-recht/griechenland-krise-schuldenschnitt-auch-ohne-grexit-moeglich-13715803.html. Accessed 8 January 2018

Craig P (2014) Economic governance and the Euro crisis: constitutional architecture and constitutional implications. In: Adams M et al (eds) The constitutionalization of European budgetary constraints. Hart, Oxford, p 19

Dimopoulos A (2014) The use of international law as a tool for enhancing governance in the Eurozone and its impact on EU constitutional integrity. In: Adams M et al (eds) The constitutionalization of European budgetary constraints. Hart, Oxford, p 41

ESM (2012) Treaty Establishing the European Stability Mechanism, 2 February 2012. https://www.esm.europa.eu/sites/default/files/20150203_-_esm_treaty_-_en.pdf. Accessed 8 January 2018

ESM (2015) Financial Assistance Facility Agreement Between European Stability Mechanism and the Hellenic Republic and the Bank of Greece and Hellenic Financial Stability Fund, 19 August 2015. https://www.esm.europa.eu/sites/default/files/2015-08-19gr-esm-ffapublicationversion.pdf. Accessed 8 January 2018

Eur Comm'n (2015) Memorandum of Understanding Between the European Commission Acting on Behalf of the European Stability Mechanism and the Hellenic Republic and the Bank of Greece, 19 August 2015. https://ec.europa.eu/info/sites/info/files/01_mou_20150811_en1.pdf. Accessed 8 January 2018

Eur Comm'n (2018) Overview of Ongoing and Closed Excessive Deficit Procedures, 8 January 2018. https://ec.europa.eu/info/business-economy-euro/economic-and-fiscal-policy-coordination/eu-economic-governance-monitoring-prevention-correction/stability-and-growth-pact/corrective-arm-excessive-deficit-procedure/excessive-deficit-procedures-overview_en. Accessed 8 January 2018

Ewald F (1986) L'État providence. Grasset, Paris

Fabbrini F (2016) Economic governance in Europe: comparative paradoxes, constitutional challenges. Oxford University Press, Oxford

Fabbrini S (2013) Intergovernmentalism and its limits: assessing the European Union's answer to the Euro crisis. Comp Pol Stud 46:1003

Fischer-Lescano A, Oberndorfer L (2013) Fiskalvertrag und Unionsrecht: Unionsrechtliche Grenzen völkervertraglicher Fiskalregulierung und Organleihe. Neue Juristische Wochenschrift 66:9

de Gregorio Merino A (2012) Legal developments in the economic and monetary union during the debt crisis: the mechanisms of financial assistance. Common Mkt L Rev 49:1613

Habermas J (1998 [1996]) Three normative models of democracy. In: The inclusion of the other: studies in political theory (trans: Cronin C). Massachusetts Institute of Technology Press, Cambridge (MA), p 239

Henkin L (1979) How nations behave: law and foreign policy, 2nd edn. Columbia University Press, New York

Hinarejos A (2015a) The Euro area crisis in constitutional perspective. Oxford University Press, Oxford

Hinarejos A (2015b) The role of courts in the wake of the Eurozone crisis. In: Dawson M et al (eds) Beyond the crisis: the governance of Europe's economic, political, and legal transformation. Oxford University Press, Oxford, p 112

Joerges C (2014) Law and politics in Europe's crisis: on the history of the impact of an unfortunate configuration. Constellations 21:249

Joerges C (2015) Europe's legitimacy in the crisis. In: Dawson M et al (eds) Beyond the crisis: the governance of Europe's economic, political, and legal transformation. Oxford University Press, Oxford, p 167

Kjaer PF et al (ed) (2011) The financial crisis in constitutional perspective: the dark side of functional differentiation. Hart, Oxford

Kleine M (2013) Informal governance in the European Union: how governments make international organizations work. Cornell University Press, Ithaca

Krisch N (2010) Beyond constitutionalism: the pluralist structure of postnational law. Oxford University Press, Oxford

Ladeur K-H (2004) Globalization and the conversion of democracy to polycentric networks: can democracy survive the end of the nation-state? In: Ladeur K-H (ed) Public governance in the age of globalization. Ashgate, Aldershot, p 89

Ladeur K-H (2006) The postmodern condition of law and societal "management of rules": facts and norms revisited. Zeitschrift für Rechtssoziologie 27:87

Ladeur K-H (2014) Diesseits der Rechtsgemeinschaft: Die "instituierende Gewalt" der sozialen Regeln und die Grenzen der europäischen Integration. In: Kadelbach S, Günther K (eds) Europa: Krise, Umbruch und neue Ordnung. Nomos, Baden-Baden, p 139

Ley I (2015) Opposition in international law: alternativity and revisibility as elements of a legitimacy concept for public international law. Leiden J Int L 28:717

Lorz RA, Sauer H (2012) Ersatzunionsrecht und Grundgesetz: Verfassungsrechtliche Zustimmungsgrundlagen für den Fiskalpakt, den ESM-Vertrag und die Änderung des AEUV. Die Öffentliche Verwaltung 65:573

Luhmann N (1966) Recht und Automation in der öffentlichen Verwaltung: Eine verwaltungswissenschaftliche Untersuchung. Duncker & Humblot, Berlin

Luhmann N (1971) Die Weltgesellschaft. Archiv für Rechts- und Sozialphilosophie 57:1

Luhmann N (1985 [1972]) A sociological theory of law (trans: King E, Albrow M). Routledge & Kegan Paul, London

Luhmann N (1990 [1981]) Political theory in the welfare state (trans: Bednarz J). De Gruyter, Berlin

Luhmann N (1990) Verfassung als evolutionäre Errungenschaft. Rechtshistorisches Journal 9:176

Luhmann N (1992a) Operational closure and structural coupling: the differentiation of the legal system. Cardozo L Rev 13:1419

Luhmann N (1992b) Some problems with "reflexive law". In: Teubner G, Febbrajo A (eds) State, law, and economy as autopoietic systems: regulation and autonomy in a new perspective. Giuffrè, Milan, p 389

Luhmann N (1995 [1984]) Social systems (trans: Bednarz J). Stanford University Press, Stanford

Luhmann N (1998) Der Staat des politischen Systems: Geschichte und Stellung in der Weltgesellschaft. In: Beck U (ed) Perspektiven der Weltgesellschaft. Suhrkamp, Frankfurt am Main, p 345

Luhmann N (2004 [1993]) Law as a social system (trans: Ziegert KA). Oxford University Press, Oxford

Meng-Papantoni M (2015) Legal aspects of the memoranda of understanding in the Greek debt crisis. Zeitschrift für Europarechtliche Studien 18:3

Moloney N (2014) EU securities and financial markets regulation, 3rd edn. Oxford University Press, Oxford

Neves M (1992) Verfassung und Positivität des Rechts in der peripheren Moderne: Eine theoretische Betrachtung und eine Interpretation des Falls Brasilien. Duncker & Humblot, Berlin

Peers S (2013) towards a new form of EU law?: the use of EU institutions outside the EU legal framework. Eur Const L Rev 9:37

Peters A (2007) The globalization of state constitutions. In: Nijman J, Nollkaemper A (eds) New perspectives on the divide between national and international law. Oxford University Press, Oxford, p 251

Pistor K (2013) A legal theory of finance. J Comp Econ 41:315

Puetter U (2006) The Eurogroup: how a secretive circle of finance ministers shape European Economic Governance. Manchester University Press, Manchester

Puetter U (2014) The European Council and the Council: new intergovernmentalism and institutional change. Oxford University Press, Oxford

Ritter E-H (1979) Der kooperative Staat: Bemerkungen zum Verhältnis von Staat und Wirtschaft. Archiv des öffentlichen Rechts 104:389

Rosanvallon P (2008 [2006]) Counter-democracy: politics in an age of distrust (trans: Goldhammer A). Cambridge University Press, Cambridge (UK)

Scharpf FW (2011) Monetary union, fiscal crisis and the pre-emption of democracy. Zeitschrift für Staats- und Europawissenschaften 9:163

Schmitter PC (1974) Still the century of corporatism? Rev Pol 36:85

Schwarz M (2014) A memorandum of misunderstanding—the doomed road of the European stability mechanism and a possible way out: enhanced cooperation. Common Mkt L Rev 51:389

Scicluna N (2014) Politicization without democratization: how the Eurozone crisis is transforming EU law and politics. Int J Const L 12:545

Steinbach A (2016) The "haircut" of public creditors under EU law. Eur Const L Rev 12:223

Teubner G (1983) Substantive and reflexive elements in modern law. Law Soc Rev 17:239

Teubner G (2004) Societal constitutionalism: alternatives to state-centered constitutional theory? In: Joerges C et al (ed) Transnational governance and constitutionalism. Hart, Oxford, p 3

Teubner G (2011) A constitutional moment? The logics of "hitting the bottom". In: Kjaer PF et al (ed) The financial crisis in constitutional perspective: the dark side of functional differentiation. Hart, Oxford, p 3

Teubner G (2012) Constitutional fragments: societal constitutionalism and globalization (trans: Norbury G). Oxford University Press, Oxford

Towfigh EV, Petersen N (eds) (2015) Economic methods for lawyers. Edward Elgar, Cheltenham

Tuori K, Tuori K (2014) The Eurozone crisis: a constitutional analysis. Cambridge University Press, Cambridge (UK)

Vesting T (2015) Rechtstheorie, 2nd edn. Beck, Munich

Walz GA (1930) Wesen des Völkerrechts und Kritik der Völkerrechtsleugner. Kohlhammer, Stuttgart

Willke H (1992) Societal guidance through law? In: Teubner G, Febbrajo A (eds) State, law, and economy as autopoietic systems: regulation and autonomy in a new perspective. Giuffrè, Milan, p 353

Lars Viellechner is Associate Professor of Constitutional Law, Constitutional Theory, Legal Philosophy, and Transnational Law at the University of Bremen.

Rational Choice and Its Limits

Emanuel V. Towfigh

Abstract This chapter asks the fundamental question of whether the concept of a market-oriented (economic) order can be reconciled with the idea of democracy from the perspective of rational choice approaches to the law. Europe has been facing great economic challenges for the past years—sovereign debt; fiscal and monetary policy; financial market regulation; trade and investment agreements. Some observers argue that prioritizing an economic rationale in the policy response to these challenges comes at the expense of democracy by undermining its most vital preconditions (such as equality and solidarity), while their antagonists state that in fact democratic decision-making is undermining financial stability and long-term welfare of societies[1]. This contribution will establish that both positions contribute important insights and yet display too narrow a field of vision. Combining the arguments puts the cart before the horse: Democratic decision-making undermines, among other things, financial stability—and thus long-term welfare of societies—because it follows a logic that is primarily economic.

Revised version of the original published article "Rational Choice and Its Limits" by Emanuel V. Towfigh, German Law Journal 17(5):763–778
Parts of this manuscript are based on the book "Das Parteien-Paradox: Ein Beitrag zur Bestimmung des Verhältnisses von Demokratie und Parteien" by Emanuel V. Towfigh, Mohr Siebek 2015.
I gratefully acknowledge fruitful comments by the editors, Matthias Goldmann and Silvia Steininger; earlier drafts of this manuscript have profited from feedback by Katharina Towfigh, as well as from my commentator, Agniezka Janczuk-Gorywoda, and other participants at the workshop Democracy and Financial Order at the University of Frankfurt.
As always, any and all remaining misconceptions in this text are attributable to my own limited understanding only.

[1] In some sense, this can be understood as a variant of the question whether a market economy is helpful (if not a precondition) for a democratic order; for a recent example of such an argument *see* von Weizsäcker (2014a), p. 13.

E. V. Towfigh (✉)
EBS Law School, Wiesbaden, Germany
e-mail: emanuel@towfigh.net

M. Goldmann, S. Steininger (Eds.), *Democracy and Financial Order: Legal Perspectives*, Beiträge zum ausländischen öffentlichen Recht und Völkerrecht,
https://doi.org/10.1007/978-3-662-55568-2_4

1 The Economic Paradigm[2]

When I say "economic logic" or "economic paradigm," I am not using this vocabulary in the language of everyday life. Rather, I am using this terminology as a shortcut or code for Rational Choice Theory's behavioral model of the *homo oeconomicus*. The core ideas of this model are that resources are scarce, people will behave as in order to maximize their individual utility—or, to use a criticized word, employing some sort of cost-benefit analysis—to foster their self-interest, and that incentives and restrictions are thus major levers for influencing behavior. If two or more people interact in such a way that one's utility is dependent on both one's own and another person's action, then we talk about strategic interaction, and can analyze these situations with the tools of game theory. Markets can be understood to be a particular game theoretic setting, using competition to identify a price. Public Choice Theory, and more generally the study of political economy, extends the idea of actors behaving rationally—in the terms of Rational Choice Theory—to the political realm. This does not mean that Public Choice Theory assumes that politics is only about money; rather, it uses general insights on human behavior as a framework to study human behavior in a specific field, namely politics. Finally, Social Choice Theory reflects on aggregating individual preferences in such a way that the ultimate collective decision maximizes social welfare; its insights are important when construing the common weal or when analyzing democratic decision-making procedures.

In the first part of the following two Sections, this chapter shows that a somewhat shrouded economic idea is at the heart of the prevailing doctrinal perspective on democracy, and that this allows for a remarkably powerful description and explanation of the political order. Many of the shortcomings of the political order, however, have severe implications on, among other things, financial stability, and thus on welfare.

At the heart of this chapter lies an attempt to explain the limits of a rational choice driven perspective by drawing on behavioral insights: First, by looking at the risks of a descriptive behavioral theory, and second, by showing—in contrast—the expectations that rational choice theory can shape anyway. Finally, this contribution will show the usefulness of this model to explain how competitive behavior influences morals and markets.

2 An Economic Theory of Democracy[3]

2.1 *The Law of Democracy*[4]

The economic perspective on democracy is not new; it can be traced back to authors such as Schumpeter and Downs. Many observers will reject the claim that this view of democracy is dominant, however, and most lawyers will categorically deny that

[2] *See* Towfigh and Petersen (2015), pp. 18–31.

[3] *See generally* Downs (1957).

[4] *See generally* Issacharoff et al. (2012).

the prevailing legal doctrine is a manifestation of a rational choice approach to democracy. But if we have an unemotional look at the ideas underlying constitutional theory and democratic institutions, we can descriptively state that modern democratic thought is saturated with economic concepts: To construct a collective will, the political discourse aims at reflecting the interests of citizens, bundling them into platforms and programs. Competition is used as a mechanism to select among these the citizens best suited to fulfill the common weal. And decision-makers are chosen and controlled such that aggregation of the citizens' interests—necessary for the construction of both collective will and common weal—are secured, and the resulting policies are implemented. This constitutes the *Leitmotiv* of political orders on both shores of the Atlantic, namely in Germany and in the United States.[5] If we boil the idea down to its essence, we can describe our political order as a system of interest aggregation through competition. There are several elements that can easily be connected to the economic model of democracy; rational choice—and, in the political context, public choice—studies precisely the ways to maximize one's utility and to further one's self-interest; competition—often dubbed "market"—is a central mechanism in economic thought, one of the few substantial concepts that the field is genuinely concerned with apart from method; and "aggregation", which is the core interest of social choice theorists.

2.2 *Politics as Markets*[6]

Even though the connection of political practice and theory of democracy to economics seems pretty straightforward today, it took a while for it to be recognized in legal scholarship. In their seminal 1998 Stanford Law Review paper *Politics as Markets,* Samuel Issacharoff and Richard Pildes made this connection. Issacharoff once wittily remarked in a conversation that the idea went from being harshly criticized, to being commonplace in virtually no time, depriving its authors of any praise. The triumph of the description of democratic institutions in economic terms is probably due to its strikingly plausible explanation of the political everyday reality.

If the political discourse is the basis for furthering one's self-interest, then collective action is a major problem. Therefore, platforms are built; they reduce information costs and coordinate voters with like-minded interests. Political parties are the entrepreneurs on this market, offering ready-made bundles, mobilizing for elections, organizing majorities on the one side of the aisle and effectuating political control on the other side. Acting in competition through elections creates incentives for the professionalization of personnel, making politics a profession. Here too, political parties help candidates by serving as a commitment and signaling

[5] Towfigh (2015), p. 55.

[6] *See generally* Issacharoff and Pildes (1998), pp. 643 f.

devices, so politicians can make credible offers, and they are a screening instrument in choosing political personnel to further their platform. Voters choose among the menus they are presented with by the platforms, and have been likened to consumers of policies.[7]

2.3 Market Failures and Failures of Markets[8]

But *Politics as Markets* was not so much a paper in praise of this system, but rather served as a contrast agent to render the shortcomings of the U.S. political system—which has since gone defunct—both visible and understandable. Indeed, the economic paradigm allows a better understanding of why democratic decision-making was apt to disappoint time and again. If everyone behaves rationally in terms of rational choice theory, then political entrepreneurs have incentives to disregard the interests of non-voters, for example the interests of future generations—a political myopia—of voters in other constituencies. This has especially become a problem in international contexts, specifically in the European Union. As there are no European parties, there are barely any incentives to see the big European picture, giving rise to scattered regionalism.

Ian Goldin and Tiffany Vogel argue that in the time preceding the financial crisis (2007–2009), the connection and intertwining between global forms of governance and their local counterparts were largely ignored. As a consequence, a "crisis limited to the local level transformed into a crisis of international magnitude, which is called 'systemic'."[9]

One of the basic messages Robert A. Axelrod gave in his seminal work about the agent-based models of the complexity of cooperation—which ties in to Goldin's and Vogel's observations smoothly—is that no level of political and regulatory control is "sufficient as an island of governance control".[10] Therefore, from his viewpoint, it is imperative that the global financial system is governed together at all levels, sizes, and sectors, and not independently from another in a vacuum.[11] In consequence, as projects taken by only a few countries are extremely likely to be inherently inefficient, as well as ineffective, many systemic risks—for example, the financial crisis, modern pandemics, bioterrorism risks, risks emerging from the internet, climate change—[12] will require international collaboration and coordination.[13] In the light

[7] *See* Ortiz (2000), p. 754 ("[W]e might well view voters in modern mass democracy more as political consumers than as political principals.").

[8] *See generally* Levinson (1999), p. 1745.

[9] Goldin and Vogel (2010), p. 11.

[10] *Id.*

[11] *See generally* Axelrod (1997).

[12] Goldin and Vogel (2010), p. 11.

[13] *See generally* Axelrod (1997), p. 11.

of an ever-increasing number of state and non-state actors, collective action problems will inevitably increase and contribute to systemic fragility, as they will bring with them a momentous multiplication of interests.[14]

Likewise, a focus on the cost-benefit calculus entices politicians to exploit the voters' rational ignorance in favor of special interest group issues—such as by giving in to lobbyism. In other words, politicians are motivated to design policies where few benefit hugely at the expense of many who are just below the threshold of having the resources to assemble the information necessary to unmask such policy. Germans may remember what has since been dubbed the *Mövenpick* law, a break on hotel room VAT, that was only uncovered by the press after its entry into force as a clandestine provision in the "Law to Accelerate Growth". It is estimated that this led to a tax loss of 960 million Euros in the 2013 fiscal year alone.[15] Such bargains, reinforced through logrolling, illustrate how an economic understanding of democracy and its procedures may endanger a society's long-term (economic) welfare.

From another perspective, these phenomena have also been described as "intellectual hazard", namely the tendency of behavioral biases to interfere with accurate thought and analysis within complex organizations.[16] One commonly distinguishes different types of intellectual hazard, *inter alia* the so-called "incentive bias", which leads to effects like the infamous "cognitive dissonance".[17] Geoffrey P. Miller and Gerald Rosenfeld illustrate this phenomenon through the imagination of a person working in a complex institution who may stay under pressure or may be motivated to see things in a particular way. The actor's problem is of such a nature that the information available to him suggests a type of interpretation which is contradictory to his own interests. This inconsistency creates cognitive dissonance—in consequence, he feels uncomfortable to see things in a way that might have the potential to threaten his interests. He will work to overcome his uncomfortable state by superseding concerns about possible contradictory or unfavorable competing effects.[18]

If we now think about the political scene and consider politicians to be in the position of such actors who are constantly confronted with the economic way of thinking as primary logic of today's society, they might somehow unconsciously adopt this logic and apply it as a yardstick for their own operations. Consequently, this incentive bias may cause intellectual hazard, which has a tendency to threaten an accurate analysis. Incentive bias may also become manifest in self-serving behavior, which can be observed in real life in forms like the *Mövenpick* Law: In the case of self-serving behavior, the actor knows that there is causal connection between the

[14] Goldin and Vogel (2010), p. 12.

[15] Beschluss [Resolution], Bundesrat Drucksachen [BR] 485/12 (Ger.).

[16] Miller and Rosenfeld (2009), p. 808.

[17] *See* Pompian (2012), p. 83.

[18] Miller and Rosenfeld (2009), p. 816.

facts, but consciously decides to ignore them, distorting the analysis and suppressing information with the intention to promote the actor's self-interests.[19] Miller and Rosenfeld claim that this kind of intellectual hazard might be a major compounding factor in financial crises in general and especially in the crisis of 2008.[20]

B. Guy Peters, Jon Pierre, and Tiina Randma-Liiv identify the "loss of memory and willingness" as that the "most glaring" factor for losing governance control during the period leading up to the crisis.[21] This created a blind spot so that governments were not capable of seeing the real menace of economic failures coming from markets with insufficient supervision. They conclude that governance is destined to fail if the ideas being used to manage a society and an economy tend to dim, disguise, and falsify information rather than to supply accurate interpretation.[22] These observations strongly support the theory of cognitive dissonance and incentive bias, as well as the viewpoint presented in this piece, that democratic decision-making may undermine financial stability precisely because its primary logic is economic.

Therefore, in the aftermath of the financial crisis, Miller and Rosenfeld plead for technocratic governance reform:

> Ideally, the leadership and staff would be individuals who are not directly affiliated with the institutions that breed intellectual hazard … [as this problem] will not be effectively addressed if the personnel in the agency charged with identifying systemic threats to financial stability are simply recycled regulators [who] … will not bring new ideas to the table. A preferable solution would be to establish … [a] truly independent board, composed largely of people from outside the government, selected according to some principle of merit rather than political connections, and adequately funded and protected against retaliation for expressing unpopular views ….[23]

Another example can be seen in what political economists call the "opportunistic business cycle". There is plausible evidence the administration in power tries to manipulate fundamental macro-economic data—for example, the unemployment or growth rates— through unsustainable short-term measures—especially through fiscal and monetary policies—to beef up their political legacy and to enhance the prospects of re-election.[24] As economic measures are typically extremely debatable, it is barely possible to make a certain case as to whether such a measure was an opportunistic flash in the pan or a sustainable policy innovation.

Moreover, rent-seeking political entrepreneurs have incentives to collude and to build cartels on political markets, just as corporations do on commercial markets. Through political parties, they circumvent some of the features regulating the political market. For example, these political entrepreneurs effectively shortcut the separation of powers by combining political patronage and coordination of personnel

---

[19] *Id.* p. 808.

[20] *See generally id.*

[21] Peters et al. (2011), p. 14.

[22] *Id.*

[23] Miller and Rosenfeld (2009), pp. 837–839.

[24] Belke (1996); Nordhaus (1975), pp. 187–189.

across the three branches of government. Finally, patronage leads to political representatives being dependent on their party, giving political parties the leverage to pursue their own class of interests, namely party interests.

The main point stressed by political scientist Mancur Olson in his seminal book "The Logic of Collective Action",[25] is that smaller, agile, and versatile groups are likely to dominate bigger, more cumbersome groups in seeking to influence governance regulation and legislation. Olson predicts that those small and smart kinds of groups could outperform more immobile and inflexible citizen-based groups, which often grow hidden and are rather concealed. In consequence, groups representing shareholders'—or in fact citizens'—interests are likely to see themselves in a situation of great disadvantage in competing with financially powerful industry lobbies. Therefore, it is evident that in the pre-crisis period, mighty financial trade and financial associations were putting pressure on politics concerning regulation and supervision.

Clinging to the idea that democratic politics are best understood as market activities, the remedies suggested have remained in the realm of the economic toolbox. If competition on the political market leads to distortions, namely to market failure, it is then argued that we need better regulation of the political market. In analogy to the guardians of competition protecting commercial markets, many call for the courts—the Supreme Court in the U.S., the Federal Constitutional Court in Germany—to take on the role of the umpire of the political process.

Some, however, have raised doubts. Daryl Levinson has put them in a nutshell with his pun—"Market Failures and Failures of Markets"—,[26] asking whether we observe market failure—to be countered with market regulation—or whether the problem is more severe in the sense that actually the market as an instrument fails altogether in politics.

3 Is Public Choice Immoral?[27]

James Buchanan and Geoffrey Brennan, two of the most illustrious proponents of public choice theory, have asked more pointedly whether, along the same lines, public choice may be immoral. While it seems far-fetched to consider a theory which merely claims to describe a reality as immoral, applying an economic rationale, one may come to the conclusion that the behavioral costs of an economic theory of democracy may outweigh its descriptive benefits.

The remainder of this chapter briefly[28] follows up on three questions: (1.) What are the risks connected to behavioral theory, even if it claims to be merely descriptive? (2.) How do expectations shaped by rational choice theory influence behavior?

[25] Olson (1971).

[26] Levinson (1999), p. 1745.

[27] *See generally* Brennan and Buchanan (1988), p. 179.

[28] For a more extensive set of arguments, especially with view to the field of politics, *see* Towfigh (2015), pp. 149–180.

And (3.) how does competitive behavior interfere with fiscal considerations in a democratic setup? The chapter will argue that an institutional regime which, in following the commonplace "politics as markets idea", constitutes democratic process as interest aggregation through competition, in fact lowers decision quality in terms of societal welfare, and therefore, in the context of this conference, undermines, as the conveners have put it, the financial stability of polities. The three arguments will be about the challenges of a descriptive behavioral theory, about rational expectations, and about competitive behavior.

3.1 Risks of a Descriptive Behavioral Theory

First, this section explores the risks of economic theory. The reproach of economic theory exerting influence on human behavior is often rebuffed with the reflexive argument that economics, at least when discussing the law, is mostly descriptive and not normative. Rational choice theory aims at explaining behavior, maybe even at predicting it, but it is not meant to be prescriptive. Even if behavior that is in line with the theory is called rational—a word carrying a positive connotation in everyday language—it does not contain a valuation; its antonym is not irrational but non-rational. In this sense, a descriptive theory may provide an accurate description or an inaccurate one, may have predictive power or not, but it does not say anything about the way the world ought to be. But even descriptive theory is not as innocent as this response may wish to pretend. Geoffrey Brennan and James Buchanan raise the issue pointedly; they explain that colleagues experimenting with rats

> must take into account how their own behavior might influence the behavior of the rats they study. But they need not worry at all about the influence of their research on the behavior of other rats. Other rats do not read or understand economists' conversations about rats; the behavior of those other rats will remain totally unaffected by the reporting of the results of the experiments or by new analyses "explaining" such results to economists.[29]

But economists, other social scientists, and sometimes even lawyers and politicians, do read results of experiments. For them, when evaluating their choices, the question how the world is—and how people behave—may be at least as important as how the world should be; the question how the world is extensively studied by rational choice theorists. To the extent that their insights are appreciated by a wider audience, they become performative in the sense of shaping the understanding and the interpretation of concrete lifeworld situations and by creating expectations of how humans will behave in such situations. As most people in most situations do not align their behavior to invariant—say, moral—behavioral rules but rather condition their own actions on the behavior of others—conditional cooperators—[30]

[29] Brennan and Buchanan (1988), p. 182.

[30] Gächter (2007); Fischbacher et al. (2001), p. 397; Frey and Meier (2004), p. 1720; Keser and van Winden (2000), pp. 23–24; *cf.* Fehr and Fischbacher (2003), p. 788.

the expectation of how others will behave is of eminent importance. A descriptive behavioral theory such as public choice—fuelling expectations of other behaving as *homines oeconomici* and explaining what constitutes a rational reaction to such behavior—will thus develop into a self-fulfilling prophecy. For conditional cooperators, such theory may even become an *ex ante* justification for egoistic behavior; you maximize your own utility because if everyone else behaves that way and you do not, you will perish ("sucker aversion"). This may even hold for well-wishing altruistic actors because vanishing in competition renders achieving altruistic goals impossible altogether, while submitting to some degree of egoism may secure chances of reaching them. Thus, there may be behavioral contagion effects.

3.2 Rational Expectations

But even if nobody reads economic scholarship, a rational choice perspective of democracy may shape expectations. Two behavioral effects are particularly noteworthy, namely framing and crowding out.

3.2.1 Framing: "The Name of the Game"[31]

Varda Liberman and colleagues have conducted experiments in which two subjects repeatedly played a prisoner's dilemma game. In every round, each player could choose to cooperate or to defect—without the options being labeled that way. If both cooperated, they each earned 40 cents; if both defected, they did not earn anything. If one cooperated while the other defected, the cooperator had to pay 20 cents to the experimenter, while the defector earned 80 cents. The payoff matrix looks like this:

Prisoner's Dilemma		Moves *Player 2*	
		Cooperate	Defect
Moves *Player 1*	Cooperate	*Player 1*: +40 cents *Player 2*: +40 cents	*Player 1*: −20 cents *Player 2*: +80 cents
	Defect	*Player 1*: +80 cents *Player 2*: −20 cents	*Player 1*: 0 cents *Player 2*: 0 cents

Game theory explains that rational actors should defect, and thus predicts that they will end on the individually and collectively worst situation. The twist of Liberman's experiment was that the game was presented as "Wall Street Game" to one group of subjects, and as "Community Game" to the other group; there were no other differences. To sum up the results, in the Wall Street Game, approximately one

[31] *See generally* Liberman et al. (2004), p. 1175.

third of subjects cooperated, while two thirds cooperated in the Community Game. Bilateral cooperation was observed in half the cases in the Community Game, while the rational equilibrium—the option where both players defect—was only observed in 19 percent of games. The opposite was true for the Wall Street Game. In this iteration of the game, half the players played the rational equilibrium, coming away empty-handed and bilateral cooperation was only observed in 13 percent of cases. While subjects were presented with the same substantial decision, the presentation of the task—and expectations regarding their fellow players' behavior—made all the difference.

In politics, the situation may even be exacerbated, as real-life situations are more equivocal and thus more difficult to interpret. According to an economically informed interpretation, a superior may not be friendly to her employees because she has come to appreciate them, but rather because she is cold and calculating and expects a greater personal benefit from being friendly. The employees' reactions to her friendliness may well depend on the interpretation of her motives.

3.2.2 Crowding-Out: "A Fine Is a Price"[32]

There are additional results of experiments that point in the same direction, showing that the economization of a decision context may lead to encourage egoistic behavior, and to "crowd out" altruistic behavior. In a controlled twenty week field-experiment, Uri Gneezy and Aldo Rustichini studied the behavior of parents when picking up their children from kindergarten in ten Israeli kindergartens. In the first four weeks, they merely observed how many parents picked up their children ten or more minutes late. At the beginning of the fifth week, six of the ten kindergartens introduced a fine of ten NIS (approximately three U.S. dollars) for each child that was picked up ten minutes or more late. At the beginning of the seventeenth week, the fine was abolished without further explanation. The effect of the introduction of the fine was dramatic. Within a short timespan, the number of children who were picked up late nearly doubled. Interestingly, this effect was not reversed—at least not promptly—when the fine was rescinded.

The authors offer two possible explanations; the second, more widely appreciated one, is the focus here. It is based on the idea of social norms that are somewhat orthogonal to rational choice ideas. According to this explanation, before the introduction of the fine, there is a tacit understanding that the contract provides for the kindergarten to take care of the children until pickup time. After that time, it is a sign of generosity of the personnel to continue oversee the children; to overstrain this generosity would contravene social norms. With the introduction of the fine, the understanding of the situation changes: The payment becomes a price for the delayed pickup, and the overtime supervision becomes a tradable commodity. In

[32] *See generally* Gneezy and Rustichini (2000), p. 1.

such a situation, aligning one's behavior to one's best interest is not condemnable. The social norms are thus summed up as being:

> Parents feel justified in their behavior by a social norm that states, approximately: "When help is offered for no compensation in a moment of need, accept it with restraint. When a service is offered for a price, buy as much as you find convenient." ... Perhaps a third social norm is needed: "Once a commodity, always a commodity".[33]

Similar effects have been shown empirically for the siting of permanent repositories for nuclear waste[34] and for blood donations.[35] And there are studies that show that such effects may also work in the opposite direction, for example (and overly simplified for the purpose of brevity), being reminded of the Ten Commandments may make you more honest.[36]

All in all, these empirical findings show how important the decision context is beyond incentives and restrictions, and how sensitive people react to the specific setting a decision task or problem is embedded in.

3.3 *Competitive Behavior*

Competition is a specific form of following self-interest in a special situation. We should not be surprised to see the described behavioral effects extend to this domain. But as experimental and econometrical studies show, markets and competition create even more far-reaching behavioral effects.

3.3.1 Decisions-Making in Markets: "Morals and Markets"[37]

In an experimental study which has received broad academic and public attention, Armin Falk and Nora Szech were able to show that individual decisions taken in a competitive environment, modeled to resemble markets, were less moral in the sense that the market environment increases the disposition to impose substantial negative consequences of one's own behavior on a noninvolved third party. To study behavior in such situations, the experimenters confronted subjects with a drastic and irreversible decision; the participants of the study had to decide whether they wanted to receive a certain sum of money or instead save a young and healthy

[33] Gneezy and Rustichini (2000), p. 14.

[34] Frey and Oberholzer-Gee (1996), p. 359.

[35] *See* Titmuss (1997); Mellström and Johannesson (2008), pp. 852–857; *see also* Engel (2007), p. 385. *See generally* Ostrom (2000), p. 137.

[36] Mazar et al. (2008), p. 635.

[37] *See* Falk and Szech (2013), p. 707; *see also* Luetge and Rusch (2013), p. 714 (criticizing Falk and Szech's conclusions drawn from the mice experiment); Falk and Szech (2013), p. 714 (responding to Luetge and Rush's criticisms).

mouse's life by forgoing the money which would then be spent on providing end-of-life care to the mouse.[38] In the individual-decision treatment, each subject had the choice to earn €10 or to save a mouse's life. In a bilateral treatment, a buyer and a seller would negotiate how large a share of €20 each would get; if they executed the contract, each received their respective sum and the mouse lost its life. Buyer and seller had a veto position, however, and could reject conclusion of a contract altogether, thus saving the mouse's life. In rational choice terms, the two described situations—unilateral decision and bilateral decision by seller—were equivalent. Finally, there was a multi-lateral decision situation in which nine sellers and seven buyers negotiated prices with each seller having one mouse at her or his disposal.[39]

In the independent, unilateral situation, 45.9 percent of subjects would agree to let a mouse die for €10, but in the bilateral situation 72.2 percent of subjects and in the multilateral situation 75.9 percent of subjects were willing to give away a mouse's life for €10 or less. The experimenters tried to assess how much money they had to pay in the unilateral situation to reach the figures observed in the bilateral and multilateral situation; €47.50 helped reach 72 percent, but they stopped at €50 per mouse before having reach the three-quarters threshold.

The experiment itself does not teach us much about the mechanism that drives this robust, non-rational behavior, but the authors offer three plausible explanations. First, in a plurilateral situation, at least two parties need to agree, so there might be a diffusion of responsibility and a reduced feeling of guilt. Second, the interaction with others reveals information about prevalent social norms. This may shape and change the expectation regarding behavior of other actors; if you observe others breaking ethical standards, then such behavior may seem admissible and thus motivate you to behave the same way. Third, markets may focus your attention on material aspects—such as negotiation and competition—reducing the attention that is directed at the negative consequences of one's own action. Moreover, in the multilateral situation, the logic of substitutability may rule; "if I don't sell the mouse, someone else will", and one will (silently) mumble "and I will go out empty-handed; this way, at least I earn some money".

Of course, this study only gives us hints regarding distortions in market-like competitive environments. It does, however, support an often-voiced intuition. It does tell us something about the difference between decisions made in solitude and isolation, if you will, and decisions taken in market-like group environments. This does not preclude the market to still be a better mechanism than many other environments. Critics of the study have correctly argued that the overall cooperation levels in centrally planned economies are typically substantially lower than in market economies.[40] What we do see is that individual responsibility leads to a lower focus on one's own utility.

---

[38] The subjects did not know the mice were surplus mice from other laboratory experiments and therefore moribund, and that the experiment was not so much about active killing, but rather about extending the lifespan or saving the mice's lives. In the post-experimental de-briefing, the subjects were informed about this fact. *See* Falk and Szech (2013), p. 707.

[39] A number of additional treatments were run to ensure robustness of the observations. *See* Falk and Szech (2013), pp. 709–710.

[40] *See generally* Brosig-Koch et al. (2011), p. 1373; Ockenfels and Weimann (1999), p. 275.

3.3.2 Evolution in Markets: "Does Studying Economics Inhibit Cooperation?"[41]

Finally, markets can have an impact on the evolution of values and tastes.[42] Two effects play an important role here, namely selection and adaptation, and they are difficult to disentangle at times. A number of behavioral experiments[43] have shown that students of economics display less pro-social and more egoistic behavior when compared to students of other disciplines. Basically, these studies revealed that this effect was present when the students took up their studies, and also that it aggravated over time. This supports the conclusion that there is both a selection and an adaptation effect; typically, people who follow their self-interest more strictly tend to choose economics as a field, and studying economics also seems to amplify the focus on one's individual utility. Such effects show, once more, that a descriptive behavioral theory may have substantial effects on real behavior.

4 Conclusion

Now, what do we make of this? Do not misunderstand—there is nothing wrong with indulging in self-interested behavior—at least at times—and there is certainly nothing wrong with competition. But the question is which instruments and models lead to the best results. For the exchange of goods, we seem to have figured out, in theory and empirically, that there is not a much better arrangement than a regulated market. But maybe these insights do not extend to politics. In a globalized world with international challenges, and especially within the framework of the European Union, a nation-state oriented economic model of democracy will inevitably bring about political myopia and hard-headed regionalism.

So let us respond to the fundamental question of this chapter. Democracy, the way we understand and operationalize it today, may indeed put financial stability and long-term societal welfare at risk—not because it follows too little an economic rationale, but rather because it has absorbed too much of it. If the observations expressed in this chapter are correct, then regulating political competition—for example, by supreme or constitutional courts stepping in to assure a level playing field for political competition—cannot be the solution. Regulation may soothe some of the most pressing problems connected to this understanding of democracy, but only in the short term. Ultimately, only a fundamentally rethought approach to democratic theory will be able to resolve the deep-rooted flaws of our current political

---

[41] *See generally* Frank et al. (1993), p. 159.

[42] *See* Bowles (1998), p. 75 ("Markets and other economic institutions do more than allocate goods and services: they also influence the evolution of values, tastes, and personalities."); von Weizsäcker (2014b), pp. 28 f.

[43] *See generally* Carter and Irons (1991), p. 171; Frank et al. (1996), p. 187; Frank et al. (1993), p. 159; Yezer et al. (1996), p. 177. For an overview, *see* Hole (2013), p. 1.

institutions regime. It will require disrupting the nexus of self-interest and collective decision-making. Independent institutions with a highly functional expertise—such as the European Central Bank—may be one of the cornerstones of such institutional architecture. Constitutional theory has a great task to face.

Acknowledgements I gratefully acknowledge valuable contributions by Svenja Huemer and fruitful comments by the editors of this special issue; earlier drafts of this manuscript have profited from feedback by Rebekka Herberg and Katharina Towfigh, as well as from my commentator, Agnieszka Janczuk-Gorywoda, and other participants at the workshop Democracy and Financial Order at the University of Frankfurt.

References

Axelrod RR (1997) The complexity of cooperation: agent-based models of competition and collaboration. Princeton University Press, Princeton, NJ

Belke A (1996) Politische Konjunkturzyklen in Theorie und Empirie: Eine kritische Analyse der Zeitreihendynamik in Partisan-Ansätzen. Mohr Siebeck, Heidelberg

Bowles S (1998) Endogenous preferences: the cultural consequences of markets and other economic institutions. J Econ Lit 36:75

Brennan G, Buchanan JM (1988) Is public choice immoral? The case for the "Nobel" lie.Va L Rev 74:179

Brosig-Koch J et al (2011) Still different after all these years: solidarity behavior in East and West Germany. J Pub Econ 95:1373

Carter JR, Irons MD (1991) Are economists different, and if so, why? J Econ Persp 5:171

Downs A (1957) An economic theory of democracy. Harper & Brothers, New York

Engel C (2007) Verhaltenswissenschaftliche Analyse: eine Gebrauchsanweisung für Juristen. In: Engel C et al (eds) Recht und Verhalten, p 363. Mohr Siebeck, Tübingen

Falk A, Szech N (2013a) Morals and markets. Sci 340:707

Falk A, Szech N (2013b) Response. Sci 341:714

Fehr E, Fischbacher U (2003) The nature of human altruism. Nature 425:785

Fischbacher U et al (2001) Are people conditionally cooperative? Evidence from a public goods experiment. Econ Lett 71:397

Frank RH et al (1993) Does studying economics inhibit cooperation? J Econ Persp 7:159

Frank RH et al (1996) Do economists make bad citizens? J Econ Persp 10:187

Frey BS, Meier S (2004) Social comparisons and pro-social behavior: testing "conditional cooperation" in a field experiment. Am Econ Rev 94:1717

Frey BS, Oberholzer-Gee F (1996) Fair siting procedures: an empirical analysis of their importance and characteristics. J Pol Anal Manag 15:353

Gächter S (2007) Conditional cooperation: behavioral regularities from the lab and the field and their policy implications. In: Frey BS, Stutzer A (eds) Economics and psychology: a promising new cross-disciplinary field, vol 19, p 30–33. CeDEX Discussion Paper No. 2006-003, April 2006. The University of Nottingham, Nottingham

Gneezy U, Rustichini A (2000) A fine is a price. J Legal Stud 29:1

Goldin I, Vogel T (2010) Global governance and systemic risk in the 21st century: lessons from the financial crisis. Global Pol 1:4

Hole AD (2013) How do economists differ from others in distributive situations? Nordic J Pol Econ 38:1

Issacharoff S, Pildes RH (1998) Politics as markets: partisan lockups of the democratic process. Stan L Rev 50:643

Issacharoff S et al (2012) The law of democracy: legal structure of the political process, 4th edn. Foundation Press, Westbury, NY

Keser C, Van Winden F (2000) Conditional cooperation and voluntary contributions to public goods. Scand J Econ 102:23
Levinson DL (1999) Market failures and failures of markets. Va L Rev 85:1745
Liberman V et al (2004) The name of the game: predictive power of reputations versus situational labels in determining prisoner's dilemma game moves. Pers Soc Psychol Bull 30:1175
Luetge C, Rusch H (2013) The systematic place of morals in markets. Science 341:714
Mazar N et al (2008) The dishonesty of honest people: a theory of self-concept maintenance. J Mark Res 45:633
Mellström C, Johannesson M (2008) Crowding out in blood donation: was titmuss right? J Eur Econ Assoc 6:845
Miller GP, Rosenfeld G (2009) Intellectual hazard: how conceptual biases in complex organizations contributed to the crisis of 2008. Harv J L Pub Poly 33:807
Nordhaus WD (1975) The political business cycle. Rev Econ Stud 42:169
Ockenfels A, Weimann J (1999) Types and patterns: an experimental East-West-German comparison of cooperation and solidarity. J Pub Econ 71:275
Olson M (1971) The logic of collective action: public goods and the theory of groups. Harvard University Press, Cambridge, MA
Ortiz DR (2000) Duopoly versus autonomy: how the two-party system harms the major parties. Colum L Rev 100:753
Ostrom E (2000) Collective action and the evolution of social norms. J Econ Persp 14:137
Peters BG, Pierre J, Randma-Liiv T (2011) Global financial crisis, public administration and governance: do new problems require new solutions? Pub Org Rev 11:13
Pompian MM (2012) Behavioral finance and wealth management. Wiley, Hoboken, NJ
Titmuss RM (1997) The gift relationship from human blood to social policy. The New Press, New York
Towfigh EV, (2015) Das Parteien-Paradox: Ein Beitrag zur Bestimmung des Verhältnisses von Demokratie und Parteien. Mohr Siebek, Heidelberg
Towfigh EV, Petersen N (2015) Economic methods for lawyers, pp 18–31. Edward Elgar International Academic Publisher, Cheltenham
Towfigh EV, Rational choice and its limits. German LJ 17(5):763–778
von Weizsäcker CC (2014a) Adaptive preferences and institutional stability. J Institut Theoret Econ 170:27
von Weizsäcker CC (2014b) Die normative Ko-Evolution von Marktwirtschaft und Demokratie. Ordo 65:13
Yezer AM et al (1996) Does studying economics discourage cooperation? Watch what we do, not what we say or how we play. J Econ Persp 10:177

Emanuel V. Towfigh holds a Chair in Public Law, Empirical Legal Research, and Law & Economics at the Law School and is Professor of Law & Economics at the Department of Management and Economics of the Business School at EBS University, Wiesbaden, Germany. He is also a Research Affiliate at the Max Planck Institute for Research on Collective Goods in Bonn, Germany.

Constitutional and Administrative Pluralism in the EU System of Banking Supervision

Matej Avbelj

Abstract This chapter examines the relationship between the developing European Union (EU) system of banking supervision and the theories of constitutional pluralism. It questions the remaining epistemic, explanatory, and normative value of these theories with regard to the EU system of banking supervision. The argument is broken down into three sections. First, the chapter briefly describes the system of banking supervision in the European Union and the pluralist challenges that it spurs. Second, it schematically maps out the leading theories of constitutional pluralism to test, by way of their application to the field of EU banking supervision, their epistemic, explanatory, and normative value. Finally, to the extent that this value has diminished, the chapter offers another pluralist theory, not a constitutional one, which could supplement the identified epistemic, explanatory, and normative gaps. This is a theory of administrative pluralism.

1 Introduction

This chapter examines the relationship between the European Union (EU) system of banking supervision, as it has emerged in the aftermath of the EU financial and economic crises, and the theories of constitutional pluralism. It asks what, if any,

Revised version of the original published article "Constitutional and Administrative Pluralism in the EU System of Banking Supervision" by Matej Avbelj, German Law Journal 17(5):789–798

M. Avbelj (✉)
Graduate School of Government and European Studies, Kranj, Slovenia
e-mail: matej.avbelj@fds.si

M. Goldmann, S. Steininger (Eds.), *Democracy and Financial Order: Legal Perspectives*, Beiträge zum ausländischen öffentlichen Recht und Völkerrecht,
https://doi.org/10.1007/978-3-662-55568-2_5

is the epistemic, explanatory, and normative value of these theories with regard to the system of EU banking supervision. First, the chapter briefly describes the system of banking supervision in the EU and the pluralist challenges that it spurs. Second, it schematically maps out the leading theories of constitutional pluralism to test, by way of their application to the field of EU banking supervision, their epistemic, explanatory, and normative value. Finally, to the extent that this value has diminished, the contribution offers another pluralist theory, not a constitutional one, which could supplement the identified epistemic, explanatory, and normative gaps. This is a theory of administrative pluralism. This leads to the conclusion that constitutional and administrative pluralism should be seen as complementary rather than in opposition. By approaching the EU system of banking supervision through the lenses of constitutional and administrative pluralism together, its growingly complex, increasingly variegated legal, and political landscape can be adequately understood and explained. In addition, this chapter provides an appropriate normative guidance to ensure the EU's viability in practice.

2 The EU System of Banking Supervision

After the outbreak of the financial and, later economic crises, the EU has proposed and implemented a wide range of reforms to its financial sector. Their scope and depth have remained partially unaccounted for—due to various reasons, but mainly due to the complexity of the crisis situation, the short timeframe, and tense, extremely politically loaded atmosphere. Theory has clearly been surpassed by practice, and it is now, already with the benefit of hindsight, trying to catch up and compensate for that epistemic delay. The practice of emerging financial regulation in the EU is thus developing in response to concrete and imminent practical challenges. The emergence is also subject to the necessary constraints of political and transnational compromises in the EU and its member states. Even if the new EU financial regulatory system was envisaged as coherent, it has fallen short of that goal. The product, which has been described as part of the EU's silent revolution,[1] is not absent of internal contradictions, competence overlaps, duplications, and less than efficient solutions. As such, there is doubt the system can deliver the regulatory outcomes it promised.[2] Although not perfect, the European System of Financial Supervision ESFS was created and widely accepted as a good idea; yet, it still awaits implementation.[3] The following Section considers the ESFS's main traits.

[1] Buras (2013), p. 2.

[2] For a detailed report, *see* the IMF (2013).

[3] Ferran (2014); Speyer (2013).

2.1 The European Banking Supervisory Authorities

Since 2008, the EU system of financial supervision *lato sensu* emerged and is constituted of two pillars. The first pillar stands for financial supervision *stricto sensu* (ESFS), which is intended to ensure the functioning of the single market. It is made of four institutions: The European Banking Authority (EBA),[4] the European Securities and Markets Authority (ESMA),[5] the European Insurance and Occupational Pensions Authority (EIOPA),[6] and the European Systemic Risk Board (ESRB).[7] They are coordinated by the Joint Committee. By their legal form, these institutions are EU agencies with their own legal personality. With their national counterparts, their task is to coordinate a decentralized system of financial supervision *stricto sensu*. This is structured around three basic divides: The level of supervision, the sector of supervision, and the type of supervision.

The supervision takes place on the supranational and national level, so that the named supranational agencies are in charge of the more systemic, EU-wide overview, whereas the supervisory institutions on the national level execute day-to-day competences on the ground. The sectors of supervision are banking (EBA), securities (ESMA), and insurance (EIOPA). The supervision can be micro-prudential, which is focused on the financial soundness of individual financial institutions, or macro-prudential, which is concerned with the viability of the financial system as a whole. EBA, ESMA, and EIOPA are in charge of the former, whereas the ESRB is tasked with the latter.

2.2 The European Banking Union

The second pillar involves the banking supervision aimed at safeguarding the viability of the Eurozone. It sets up the European Banking Union (EBU). This is composed of two parts: The Single Supervisory Mechanism (SSM) and the Single Resolution Mechanism (SRM). A third part, typical of banking unions,[8] is the not yet fully created Common Deposit Guarantee Scheme (DGS). The Single Resolution Fund (SRF) currently fulfills its role, albeit in a limited manner. In the future, subject to political compromise, the European Stability Mechanism (ESM) might replace the DGS.[9] As in the case of the ESFS, the EBU is also organized as a decentralized system, operating on the supranational and national level. It exercises two basic functions of supervision and resolution, this time in a single banking sector.

[4] European Banking Authority (2016).

[5] European Securities and Markets Authority (2016).

[6] European Insurance and Occupational Pension Authority (2016).

[7] European Systematic Risk Board (2016).

[8] IMF (2013), p. 9.

[9] For a more detailed discussion, *see* Howarth and Quaglia (2013), p. 103.

2.2.1 The Single Supervisory Mechanism

The SSM rests on a sophisticated division of competences between the European Central Bank (ECB) and the National Competent Authorities (NCA). Their joint endeavor represents a number of principles,[10] which, on the one hand, concern the organizational structure of the supervision and, on the other hand, concern its quality standards. The organizational principles encompass the principles of conferral, integrity and decentralization, homogeneity within the SSM, consistency with the single market, and the principle of proportionality. The latter builds a bridge to the qualitative principles, such as use of best practices, independence and accountability, risk-based approach, adequate level of supervisory activity for all credit institutions, and effective and timely corrective measures.[11] The most basic "constitutional" principle is the principle of conferral, on the basis of which the ECB has only those supervisory powers that have been transferred to it, while the residual supervisory powers remain with the NCA.[12]

In line with the principle of integrity and decentralization, the system of supervision emerged as a single, but decentralized, unity. The close and sincere co-operation between the ECB and NCA ensures and implements the necessary continuity and consistency of supervision across the Union.[13] The principle of homogeneity, standing for a harmonized set of substantive standards for supervision, plays an important role in meeting that objective.[14] These harmonized standards—also known as the single rulebook[15]—directly connect with the principle of consistency with the single market and the main regulatory agency in its financial leg, the European Banking Authority (EBA). In so doing, a bridge between the EBA, explicitly tasked with drafting the single rulebook mentioned above, and the SSM develops by connecting the EBU and the EFSF *stricto sensu* in the larger whole of the ESFS *lato sensu*. But before looking at that relationship in depth, the governance inside the SSM requires more focus.

In the absence of a single supervisory authority, the ECB supervises the so-called significant banks, whereas the less significant banks—in principle—remain under the supervisory authority of NCA.[16] In this relationship,[17] the ECB has a somewhat

[10] European Central Bank (2014), pp. 6–9.

[11] *Id.*

[12] *See also* Moloney (2014), pp. 1609, 1618 who also observed that "*the allocation of supervisory power under the SSM is specific and enumerated.*"

[13] European Central Bank (2014), p. 7.

[14] *Id.*

[15] *Id.*, pp. 7–8.

[16] *Id.*, p. 10. A bank is considered significant if it meets any of the following conditions: (a) The total value of its assets exceeds €30 billion or—unless the total value of its assets is below €5 billion—exceeds 20 % of national GDP; (b) it is one of the three most significant credit institutions established in a Member State; (c) it is a recipient of direct assistance from ESM; and (d) the total values of its assets exceeds €5 billion and the ratio of its cross-border assets and/or liabilities in more than one other participating Member State to its total assets and/or liabilities is above 20 %. Notwithstanding the fulfillment of these criteria, the SSM may declare a bank significant to ensure the consistent application of high-quality supervisory standards.

[17] *See* Council Regulation (EC) No. 1024/2013 of 15 Oct. 2013, art. 6, 2013 O.J. (L 287) 63–89 9 [hereinafter Council Regulation No. 1024/2013].

elevated, but not directly superior, position to the NCA. While EU law prescribes a duty of cooperation in good faith between the ECB and the NCA,[18] the ECB holds ultimate responsibility for the overall effective and consistent functioning of the SSM.[19] To ensure that this objective is met, the NCA must assist the ECB in the execution of its tasks and must follow the ECB's instructions in that respect.[20] This has led some authors to conclude that the overall legal infrastructure of the SSM privileges the ECB over the NCA.[21] The same has been said of the SRM.[22]

2.2.2 The Single Resolution Mechanism

As the second building block of EBU, the SRM establishes a supranational system for restructuring banks in grave financial trouble. This system has both a preventive and a curative leg. The preventive leg builds on the SSM by introducing a requirement for the national authorities and financial actors to draw up recovery and resolution plans on how to deal with situations in which supervision has identified a potential financial stress or failure of a bank.[23] It also includes an authorization for early intervention into a failing bank before its financial situation deteriorates irreparably.[24] Even if that fails, the curative measures set in: The program of resolution, backed up by a reinforced cooperation and coordination between national authorities, particularly in cases involving cross-border banking groups.[25]

Similar to the SSM, the governance of the SRM is decentralized, relying on cooperation between the national resolution authorities (NRA) and the Single Resolution Board (SRB), the EU agency in charge. The division of competences follows the rationale adopted in respect to the SSM, so that the SRB oversees the banks supervised by the ECB, whereas the NRA remains responsible for the less significant banks in need of resolution. The resolution process carries a risk of financial burden-sharing—mutualization of debt—inside the Eurozone, creating from the start a delicate political issue. The issue has resulted in a limited fiscal-backstop as the last resort to support governments,[26] in the form of the SRF,[27] and an overall delayed

---

[18] *Id.*, at art. 6(2).

[19] *Id.*, at art. 6(1).

[20] *Id.*, at art. 6(3).

[21] Moloney (2014).

[22] *Id.*

[23] European Commission Memo (2014)

[24] *Id.*

[25] *Id.*

[26] Schoenmaker (2014), p. 4.

[27] The SRM Regulation provides that the prescribed contributions of national banks to the SRF are levied by the respective Member States and transferred by them to the SRF, following the special Agreement on the Transfer and Mutualization of Contributions to the Single Resolution Fund (Council of Europe 2016).

implementation of SRM.[28] The latter's system of governance, which tries to accommodate the supranational and national interests by requiring swift action when the need emerges, represents a reflex of this delicate political balancing inside the Eurozone. The ECB normally starts the resolution process. The SRB, in consultation with the NRA, prepares the resolution scheme, which must be adopted by the Commission and the Council and then executed by the NRA under SRB supervision.[29]

2.2.3 The European Bank Authority

Finally, the EBA provides the link between the two pillars of the ESFS *lato sensu*. Established in 2011, the EBA adopts the common standards for financial services in the European Union and performs the so-called stress tests of the main EU financial institutions. Following the establishment of EBU, the EBA remains responsible for creating a single rulebook for financial services in the EU, for developing a single supervisory handbook, for supervising consistency in bank supervision across the twenty-eight countries in the single market, and for conducting the EU-wide stress tests.[30] The single rulebook acts as a material bedrock on which the two parts of EBU are built. Nevertheless, this should not create the impression that EBA is supreme over EBU. To the contrary, the establishment of the EBU and the newly acquired supervisory role of the ECB will probably weaken the role of EBA,[31] which has previously been appraised as too narrow with respect to its functions and too broad as a matter of EU institutional and constitutional law.[32] While the latter is largely due to its question-begging legal basis of Art. 114 TFEU, the former involves the fact that EBA is circumscribed in its supervisory, regulatory, and enforcement powers due to the constraints attached to its legal status of an EU agency by the *Meroni* doctrine.[33]

The link between ESFS *stricto sensu* and the EBU hinges on a relationship between the EBA and the ECB, which—to make things even more complicated—depends simultaneously on a relationship between the single market and the Eurozone, between the EU-28 and the EU-19. They stand for two different visions of Europe: One purely economic and the other more political. This complex arrangement appears in two circumstances: First, the specific voting arrangement inside the EBA reflects this complexity[34] because it seeks to find a suitable balance between

[28] The build-up of SRM started in January 2016.

[29] Moloney (2014), p. 1640.

[30] *Id.*

[31] *See* the fears expressed in the British Parliament "that the Single Supervisory Mechanism proposals may seriously undermine the authority of the EBA in its relations with the ECB." (UK Parliament 2016).

[32] *See generally*, Fahey (2011), p. 581.

[33] Case 9/56, Meroni & Co., Industrie Metallurgiche, SpA v. High Auth. of the European Coal and Steel Cmty., 1958 E.C.R. 133.

[34] Howarth and Quaglia (2013), p. 25.

the participating and non-participating Member State.[35] Second, complexity is expressed through the system of mutual supervisory cooperation between the EBA and the ECB, whereby the ECB is bound to act in accordance with EU law, including using the single rulebook prepared by the EBA.[36] As constitutionally independent, the ECB is also subject to an EU agency, which is a creation of EU secondary law.[37] It has been rightly observed that the relationship between the two falls nothing short of a constitutional conundrum in terms of the institutional balance set up under the Treaty.[38]

In short, the system of EU banking supervision, as part of the broader ESFS, exhibits a deeply plural composition. First, it features a plurality of regimes, whereby banking supervision is simultaneously conducted as part of the single market as well as of the Eurozone, the two not necessarily pursuing exactly the same objectives. The plurality of regimes at the same time represents a plurality of constituencies: Banking supervision on the single market takes place in the name of and for twenty-eight member states, whereas inside the Eurozone the constituency counts only nineteen member states. Next, there is a plurality of regulatory levels. Banking supervision is conducted on the supranational and national level through an intricate system of coordination. This coordination involves a plurality of institutions, which both on the supranational and national level are divided between the institutions of constitutional character—primary institutions—and their administrative counterparts—various supranational and national administrative agencies.

This plurality must be connected in order for the system of EFSF—and banking supervision inside it—to function as a viable common whole and exhibit as few internal contradictions and conflicts as possible while being able to contribute to the efficient achievement of the objectives for which it was created. In other words, plurality has to grow into pluralism. To do so, a theory of pluralism must provide a roadmap to that end. The theories of constitutional pluralism are prominent and best-suited candidates to fit that role. Can they also provide an adequate descriptive, explanatory, and normative guidance for the EU system of banking supervision? This a question addressed in the following Section.

---

[35] *See* Statement by the Council on the Proposal for a Regulation of the European Parliament and of the Council Amending Regulation (EU) No 1093/2010 Establishing a European Supervisory Authority (European Banking Authority) as regards the Conferral of Specific Tasks on the European Central Bank Pursuant to Council Regulation (EU) No 1024/2013, Council of Europe (2016). For details, *see* Regulation 1022/2013 of the European Parliament and of the Council of 22 October 2013 Amending Regulation (EU) No 1093/2010 Establishing a European Supervisory Authority—European Banking Authority—regarding the Conferral of Specific Tasks on the European Central Bank pursuant to Council Regulation (EU) 1024/2013, 2013 O.J. (L 287) 20–22 (EU).

[36] *See* Council Regulation No. 1024/2013, *supra* note 17, at para. 32.

[37] *Id.*

[38] Moloney (2014), p. 1665.

3 Theories of Constitutional Pluralism and the EU System of Banking Supervision

In 1995, Neil MacCormick first introduced into the EU legal theoretical landscape the idea of constitutional pluralism, which eventually diversified into multiple theories of constitutional pluralism.[39] In response to the German Constitutional Court's *Maastricht* decision, MacCormick was one of the very few scholars, if not the only one, who argued that this widely and harshly criticized ruling had "a sound basis in legal theory."[40] This theory was pluralist, rather than monist. Pursuant to this theory, "the legal systems of Member States and their common legal system of EC law are distinct but interacting systems of law, and hierarchical relationships of validity within criteria of validity proper to distinct systems do not add up to any sort of all-purpose superiority of one system over another."[41] Yet, it took another piece, a few years later, for the theory to be explicitly called constitutionally pluralist and cast in more concrete terms. MacCormick thus defined, albeit vaguely, constitutional pluralism as a situation of plurality of institutional normative orders, each with a functioning constitution, where each acknowledged the legitimacy of every other within its sphere while refraining from asserting constitutional superiority over another.[42] As applied to the European integration, constitutional pluralism entails a strongly decentralized conception of the EU whose constitutional architecture is much closer to confederation than to federation.[43]

Thus, constitutional pluralism first emerged as an EU-specific theory. Nevertheless, Neil Walker attempted to generalize it by extending its theoretical reach to describe the overall phenomenon of the post-Westphalian constellation.[44] As he has compellingly argued ever since, the state is no longer an exclusive unit of legal and political organization. The link between autonomy and territorial sovereignty has been severed and the exclusivity of the territorially limited claims towards ultimate legal authority have given way to the competition of various functional- but equally plausible—claims towards ultimate legal authority. Alongside the state, new sectorally and functionally oriented polities have emerged and exist on the sub-state, trans-state, supra-state, and other non-state levels.[45] Besides extending the reach of constitutional pluralism, Walker also furnished it with a new objective to rehabilitate the language of constitutionalism, which has faced growing marginalization and irrelevance precisely when its values and social-engineering capacity are needed most.[46]

---

[39] What follows draws closely on Avbelj and Komárek (2012), pp. 2-9.

[40] MacCormick (1995), pp. 259, 265.

[41] *Id.*, p. 265.

[42] MacCormick (1999), p. 104.

[43] MacCormick (2001).

[44] Walker (2002), p. 333.

[45] Most recently, *see generally* Walker (2014).

[46] *See* Avbelj and Komárek (2012), p. 4.

Yet, with the launch of the process of EU documentary constitutionalism destined to result in the Treaty Establishing the Constitution for Europe (TECE), the idea of constitutional pluralism again turned explicitly toward the EU. Driven by the event, as is usual in EU scholarship, constitutional pluralism started drawing attention in wider scholarly circles, pushing itself into the mainstream and simultaneously diversifying itself. A single idea of constitutional pluralism evolved into many theories of constitutional pluralism. In my previous work, I have tried to distinguish at least between six theories of constitutional pluralism.[47]

Joseph Weiler developed the first of these—socio-teleological constitutionalism. His special brand of European constitutionalism has three dimensions: (1) The formal, (2) the normative, and (3) the sociological dimension. According to the formal dimension, the EU already has a constitution, developed in the interaction between the national judicial and political branches, and therefore did not need a special, documented one resembling the statist constitution. Pursuant to the normative dimension—the key pluralist component in this conception—the EU is founded on the principle of constitutional tolerance, which sends a deeply normative message of necessity and desirability of mutual recognition between the self-reflexive individuals and the Member States in their eternal pursuit of a decent life. Finally, in sociological terms, constitutional tolerance is said to be exercised on a daily basis between all the actors of the integration—from the lowest-ranked official to the highest judicial authority.[48]

Epistemic meta-constitutionalism, advanced by Neil Walker, offers constitutionalism redefined pluralistically as a meta-framework above and beyond the constituent entities of European integration. It stresses the need of fostering dialogue, mutual-learning, and cross-fertilization,[49] while acknowledging that each entity is a distinct epistemic site and has limits.[50] Epistemic meta-constitutionalism distances itself, more than Weiler's approach does, from the classical hierarchical constitutional structure; at the same time, it remains in favor of the EU's own "documented" constitution because of the potentially positive effects a constitution-making process could have on integration.[51]

The third version of constitutional pluralism is best fit universal constitutionalism, recently dubbed cosmopolitan constitutionalism.[52] It also recognizes the pluralist structure of European integration. But unlike the epistemic meta-constitutionalism, this version situates the plurality in a universal framework of substantively homogeneous, shared principles and values of political liberalism which lie at the base of the modern constitutionalism. Political liberalism should be relied upon

[47] The ensuing paragraphs draw directly on Avbelj (2008), pp. 1, 11–22.

[48] Weiler (2003), p. 23.

[49] Walker (2000), p. 14.

[50] Walker (2002), p. 338.

[51] Walker (2005), p. 398.

[52] Kumm (2009), p. 258.

as a universal language for measuring and balancing the competing claims of the entities constituting European integration and for finding a best fit solution for the integration as a whole.[53]

The fourth, harmonious discursive constitutionalism,[54] joins the quest of universal constitutionalism, but also differs from it in two respects: First, it differs with regard to the intensity of the plurality and its recognized implications, and second, with regard to the degree of anticipated or assumed universalism. Harmonious discursive constitutionalism is slightly more disposed towards plurality. It refrains from making strong claims about the actual substantive universality of principles and values, and insists only on the procedural dimension of universalizability of arguments through which actors across different entities of the integration can justify their claims to authority.[55] Constitutional pluralism, in this sense, provides for a shared discursive—e.g. procedural framework—rather than for universally shared substantive foundations.

The fifth version, multilevel constitutionalism, was authored by Ingolf Pernice and has been very popular among German scholars.[56] This approach also proceeds from the presumption of considerable substantive unity and homogeneity of values between the constituent entities of the integrated whole, which can function as a composite of two independent constitutional layers—national and supranational. They nonetheless form part of a single European constitution. Multi-level constitutionalism presupposes one European sovereign as well as a single answer in any constitutional conflict that might arise.[57] In so doing, the theory most closely approaches the classical, e.g. non-pluralist constitutional account.

In direct contrast with the five holistic accounts of constitutional pluralism, the sixth version, pragmatic constitutionalism argues that the classical constitutional paradigm should be abandoned along with its sovereignty conundrum in the pursuit of universality, coherence, and integrity. Constitutional language should switch from the whole to the particular, from the constitutionally holistic to the constitutionally atomistic approach. Accordingly, European integration should be completely re-constructed and established as a directly-deliberative polyarchy,[58] characterized by a pragmatic, experimentalist approach to governance with a range of private and public actors entangled in an array of policy networks.[59]

It follows from the most representative theories of constitutional pluralism that they are concerned with the plurality of legal, specifically constitutional, orders. This constitutional preoccupation with supreme legal acts and legal authorities necessarily entails considerations of sovereignty, its locus and role, and the importance

---

[53] Kumm (2005), pp. 262, 292.

[54] Maduro (2003).

[55] *Id.,* p. 525.

[56] Pernice (2002), pp. 511, 514.

[57] *Id.,* pp. 518–519.

[58] Gerstenberg and Sabel (2002), pp. 289, 292.

[59] *See generally*, Marks et al. (1996a, b).

of demos and underlying shared substantive values. Thus, the theories of constitutional pluralism, other than pragmatic constitutionalism, have a predominantly holistic focus. They are occupied with questions of the more or less hierarchical EU framework—e.g. with the challenges of achieving and preserving the EU common whole. In short, the key question that the majority of the theories seems to be addressing is whether European integration has a viable legal nature, which boils down to the relationship between the EU and national constitutional orders. Even more concretely, the theories eventually judicialize this relationship, making the question of supremacy subject either to a final determination by the national or EU judiciary, or, at least, to creative judicial dialogue.[60]

Among the pluralities brought about by the system of EU banking supervision, the plurality of constituencies falls most squarely within the traditional ambit of constitutional pluralism. This plurality takes place inside the EU common whole as it concerns the relationship among the EU, its twenty-eight member states constituting a single market, and the nineteen members of the Eurozone. This differentiated constitutional framework raises challenges of how to accommodate the divergent interests of the partly overlapping national constituencies within the single common whole of the EU. Differing from classical constitutional pluralism, these questions have not been judicialized (yet). Instead, they have been left in the hands of high politics.

There are slight, but important, differences regarding the plurality of regimes. The relationship between the single market and the Eurozone exemplifies the differentiated integration inside the EU legal order, not in the EU common whole.[61] The question raised here is already posited on a lower scale. It does not concern the constitutional framework of the EU as a whole. Instead, it centers on the unity of the EU legal order by finding a balance ensuring that the legal regime of Eurozone does not detract from, or undermine, the wider but shallower legal regime of the single market, or vice versa. Unlike the constituencies' pluralism—an example of classical constitutional pluralism that Daniel Halberstam described as systems pluralism[62]—the regime pluralism is about ensuring coherence between different, semi-autonomous fields of competences inside a unitary and hierarchical EU legal order. In other words, the regimes of the single market and the Eurozone have not made claims to the existence of autonomous legal, let alone constitutional, orders. Their plurality is not constitutional.

The same, albeit reinforced, conclusion applies to the plurality of regulatory levels. Here, the issue is how to exercise and divide a plethora of administrative competences—supervisory, regulatory, and executive—between the national and supranational levels. Obviously, these questions are not directly constitutional in nature. The proper allocation of administrative competences and their efficient execution is a matter of administrative rather than constitutional law. This is not to

[60] *See generally, e.g.*, Martinico and Pollicino (2012).

[61] *See, e.g.*, Avbelj (2013), pp. 191, 191–212.

[62] Halberstam (2012), p. 85.

suggest that constitutional questions are irrelevant or that they cannot arise here. On the contrary, they are always present in the background because any administrative division of powers must be set in a proper constitutional framework. The constitutional pluralism of the EU as a whole dictates and simultaneously conditions the pluralism of regulatory levels. This pluralism normally does not raise constitutional dilemmas. But as practice shows,[63] sometimes the allocation of administrative powers translates into a more fundamental problem related to the principle of conferred competences. In admittedly few, but sensitive areas, it can give rise to the notorious *Kompetenz-Kompetenz* conundrum, which traditionally has been at the heart of constitutional pluralism.

If the plurality of regulatory levels cannot assimilate easily under the classical theories of constitutional pluralism, such assimilation is even more difficult for institutional plurality. In contrast with regulatory plurality, this last example of plurality, spurred by the EU system of banking supervision, is internal to—and does not apply across—the EU and national legal orders. Within the constitutional confines of the EU and national legal orders, this plurality addresses the nitty-gritty administrative details of actual and concrete division of labor between the ordinary, constitutionally-based institutions and organs (or institutions of primary EU law, in case of the EU), and derived, usually administrative, yet independent, agencies as statutory creations. This institutional plurality is clearly set up in a single, monist, either national or EU constitutional order, and cannot be described as constitutional plurality. To a certain extent, it can be captured by what Halberstam called institutional pluralism.[64] Institutional pluralism arises when "multiple actors carry out the same function within a single system,[65] [so as to] execute the same law, in the same territory, regarding the same matters and the same individuals or targets."[66]

It follows from this brief presentation of the leading theories of EU constitutional pluralism and the types of plurality emanating from the EU system of banking supervision, that constitutional pluralism's epistemic, explanatory, and normative value is relatively low with regard to these forms of plurality. Only the plurality of constituencies can be nicely subsumed under the classical constitutional pluralism, whereas the other forms of plurality occur on a sub-constitutional level. It seems that they might be more aptly branded as forms of administrative rather than constitutional pluralism. The next Section sketches out what administrative pluralism might stand for, what its relationship to the constitutional pluralism is, and how either of them or both together could, or could not, contribute to the viability of the EU system of banking supervision.

---

[63] *See* Bundesverfassungsgericht [BVerfG] [Federal Constitutional Court], Case No. 2 BvR 2728/13, 2 BvR 2729/13, 2 BvR 2730/13, 2 BvR 2731/13, 2 BvE 13/13, 134 Entscheidungen des Bundesverfassungsgerichts [BVerfGE] 366 (14 Jan. 2014), paras. 1–24 [hereinafter Judgment of Jan. 14, 2014].

[64] Halberstam (2012).

[65] *Id.*, p. 109.

[66] *Id.*, p. 110.

4 Administrative Pluralism and the EU System of Banking Supervision

Administrative pluralism, unlike its constitutional counterpart, is a far less, if at all, developed theoretical phenomenon. Its origins can be traced back to the idea of global administrative law (GAL) in the early 2000s. GAL was a response to the post-Westphalian global constellation in which a plethora of non-statist actors started to engage in rule-making, creating legally binding or soft-law measures for public and private actors alike. As these non-statist actors and their juris-generative practices most closely resembled national administrative actors and their practices, the term GAL was coined.[67] The construction of GAL had to be embedded in a broader legal paradigm. Several authors tried to assimilate it under global constitutionalism as another example of constitutional pluralism.[68] Others insisted that GAL was a legal paradigm in its own right.[69] Among them, Nico Krisch, in an attempt to divorce GAL from constitutionalism, argued in favor of pluralist GAL.[70] This perspective discourages creating a clearly structured institutional order and accepts mutual challenges, even open confrontations between different regimes and different levels in global regulatory governance; these were not resolved in a hierarchical legal way, but rather in a heterarchical way, usually in a politically-based, pragmatic manner.[71]

Scholars have attempted to transpose a similar theoretical approach to the level of the EU.[72] De Lucia,[73] for example, baptized the execution of EU law, mostly founded on numerous techniques of informational, procedural, and institutional co-operation laid down in secondary law, and occurring vertically and horizontally between the EU and the national administrative units, as administrative pluralism. Hartmann,[74] while using the language of administrative constitutionalism, has been even more explicit and detailed. He notes that "the multilevel nature of European administration has evolved into a multidimensional concept of regulation, legal planning, and trust-building."[75] This administrative cooperative scheme is legally inclusive,[76] based on functional openness and responsivity, aiming at institutionalizing reflexive administrative standards "for transcending territorially limited topologies of national legal preconditions."[77] Developed as a response to growing legal

[67] Kingsbury et al. (2005), pp. 15–61.

[68] *See, e.g.*, Peters (2009), p. 397.

[69] Kingsbury et al. (2005).

[70] Krisch (2006), p. 278.

[71] *Id.*, p. 278.

[72] *See generally*, de Graaf et al. (2012).

[73] de Lucia (2012), pp. 17, 17–45.

[74] *See generally* Hartmann (2013), p. 695.

[75] *Id.*, p. 704.

[76] *Id.*, p. 705.

[77] *Id.*, p. 706.

plurality, functional differentiation, and "normative inconsistencies created by the executive pluralism,"[78] in the EU, administrative constitutionalism is said to be a functional paradigm,[79] capable of "endogenously internalizing the multiplicity of the legal phenomena that are developed on the European and Member States levels, without trying to impose an overarching hierarchy of legality."[80] This model of governance still lacks robust judicial controls and standards, but it could evolve through the judicial dialogue if conducted in pluralist terms.[81]

Administrative pluralism as presented here—including Hartmann's approach despite his different terminology—captures well the pluralities created by the EU system of banking supervision. As already noted, the regulatory and institutional plurality occurs on the sub-constitutional and therefore administrative level. Also noted are the complex, not infrequently overlapping and conflicting interactions between different somewhat independent supervisory, regulatory, and executive national and EU organs, either administrative in nature or in practice. As described above, they face and spur challenges that, due to their occurrence on the sub-constitutional level, go under constitutional pluralism's radar. Administrative pluralism, as attested to by GAL, appears to have the capacity to explain these phenomena, not only as part of EU governance, but as an incidence of a broader, sweeping movement taking place on transnational and sometimes even global level. In pursuit of the problem-solving-capacity, the contemporary models of governance have witnessed a shift from the international and intra-constitutional level to a mezzo-administrative level that is filled with specialized, expert-based, and independent administrative authorities.

Administrative pluralism is also normatively attractive. It prescribes co-operation, dialogical accommodation, compromises, and avoidance of direct confrontation. It has been suggested that, being more political in nature,[82] administrative pluralism offers more opportunity for democratic contestation and consequently legitimization. All of that, as national constitutional challenges and other concerned voices prove,[83] is very much needed for the democratic foundation of the EU system of banking supervision. In normative terms, administrative pluralism, not unlike constitutional pluralism, emphasizes self-reflexivity[84] and mutual-learning in an experimental and not hierarchical manner.

In this way, administrative pluralism is truly pluralism and not just administrative plurality. As argued elsewhere in defense of principled legal pluralism, pluralism is much more than plurality. It is a connected plurality.[85] In light of the normative spirit of pluralism, which stands for a double commitment to the plurality and to the

[78] *Id.*, p. 709.

[79] *Id.*

[80] *Id.*, p. 708.

[81] *Id.*

[82] *Id.*; Krisch (2006).

[83] Judgment of Jan. 14 (2014), *supra* note 63.

[84] Hartmann (2013), p. 706.

[85] On the need to distinguish between pluralism and plurality, *see generally* Walker (2008), p. 336.

common whole, different sites of plurality—constitutional legal orders, regimes, constituencies, regulatory levels or institutions—should not just co-exist; rather, these pluralities should connect in a common, non-unitary, pluralist whole. This is possible in virtue of a developed self-reflexivity, which requires the sites taking part in a pluralist environment to be open to the claims of other sites and be willing and capable of reconsidering their own foundations as a response to their environment. This self-reflexivity is not and cannot remain unlimited, so long as the sites of plurality continue to exist as different epistemic sites.[86]

This means that conflicts between different sites of plurality are not excluded.[87] If conflicts do occur, pluralism requires they be performed in a dialogical, deliberative, and principled way, in light of the normative spirit of pluralism. Such performance, for example, could include defending particular claims on their own chosen basis while demonstrating commitment to a bigger picture of the common whole. This administratively pluralist normative requirement can be seen in the Council Regulation (EU) No. 1024/2013. The regulation prescribes a co-operative, mutually respective relationship between the ECB, the EBA, and others, including national supervisory authorities. It even calls for their semi-institutionalization in the form of concluded memoranda of understanding and ECB's participation in the Board of Supervisors of EBA.[88]

While the intensity of pluralist connections between different types of plurality inside the EU might be stronger than in other functional transnational regimes, this difference remains one of degree rather than kind. Thus, administrative pluralism appears in descriptive, explanatory, and normative terms, to be a generic theory capable of adapting to a plethora of juris-generative sites, marked by sub-constitutional pluralities connected by varying degrees of intensity.

5 Conclusion

If conducted on the basis of the above described pluralism, the viability of the EU system of banking supervision would be enhanced. To achieve that objective this pluralism needs to draw together its constitutional and administrative face. Despite the fact that constitutional pluralism's epistemic, explanatory, and normative value to the EU system of banking supervision is diminished, this does not mean that constitutional pluralism ought to be discarded in favor of administrative pluralism. To the contrary, while administrative pluralism still needs to be theoretically reinforced, its role is to supplement rather than to supplant constitutional pluralism.

[86] For a more in-depth discussion, *see* Avbelj (2012).

[87] *See, e.g.,* Dawson et al. (2015), p. 151, in observing many potential strains in the relationship between the ECB and the EBA, as well as between the participating and non-participating Member States, but simultaneously noting "a series of governance safeguards to both protect the cooperative nature of EBA-ECB relations and to address the concerns of … all Member States." *Id.*

[88] Council Regulation 1024/2013, art. 3, 2013 O.J. (L 287) (EC).

Constitutional and administrative pluralism are closely related but mutually exclusive. Administrative pluralism first describes and then explains a widespread subnational, national, and transnational phenomenon of growth and fragmentation of administrative functions on the sub-constitutional level. It is also a normative theory, which provides guidance for the viable functioning of a hence identified administrative plurality. The latter is not reserved to constitutionally pluralist settings, but also exists in a constitutionally monist environment, such as a—federal—state.

Even in a constitutionally hierarchical setting, the administrative competences are exercised by a number of institutions of public, hybrid, and private stature, which can be situated in more or less semi-autonomous unities charged with administrative tasks *lato sensu*. In a constitutionally monist environment, the constitutional straightjacket on the administrative plurality is tighter, making the achievement of administrative pluralism less difficult. Nevertheless, the increasingly dynamic practices and overall functional differentiation present an unstoppable need for differentiation and, hence, pluralization of administrative functions, even inside a monist state.

A pluralist setting, such as the EU, enhances the pluralization of administrative functions. There, constitutional and administrative pluralism presuppose and complement each other. Constitutional pluralism, as an overlap of different and not entirely harmonious theories, enables, requires, and limits the development of administrative pluralism. An autonomous constitutional site is an autonomous juris-generative site with its own institutions, executing constitutional, judicial, legislative, and administrative competences. A plurality of such autonomous constitutional sites leads to a plurality of administrative sites. With both constitutional and administrative plurality, each doing their job on their respective level of regulation, the need for connecting the two—and hence for constitutional and administrative pluralism—increases. With more plurality involved, the challenge of ensuring pluralism grows.

As a result, while constitutional pluralism, on a first sight at least, remains ill-equipped to describe, explain and normatively guide the new economic and financial infrastructure in the European Union, this does not mean that as a theory it has become defunct or passé. To the contrary, the need for constitutional pluralism has increased, but it needs to be complemented by a lower-level pluralism: administrative pluralism. The two together, following the meta-prescriptions of principled legal pluralism, remain one of the most compelling theoretical accounts for describing, explaining and normatively guiding the ever-changing European Union, now and in the future.

References

Avbelj M (2008) Questioning EU constitutionalisms. German LJ 9:1

Avbelj M (2012) Can European integration be constitutional and pluralist–both at the same time? In: Avbelj M, Komárek J (eds) Constitutional pluralism in the European Union and beyond. Hart Publishing, Oxford

Avbelj M (2013) Differentiated integration—farewell to the EU-27? German LJ 14:191

Avbelj M, Komárek J (eds) (2012) Constitutional pluralism in the European Union and beyond. Hart Publishing, Oxford

Buras P (2013) The EU's silent revolution. In: European Council on foreign relations. http://www.ecfr.eu/page/-/ECFR87_EU_SILENT_REVOLUTION_AW.pdf. Accessed 16 Sept 2016
Council of Europe (2016) Agreement on the transfer and mutualisation for contributions to the Single Resolution Fund. http://register.consilium.europa.eu/doc/srv?l=EN&f=ST%20 8457%202014%20INIT. Accessed 16 Sept 2016
Dawson M, Enderlein H, Joerges C (2015) Beyond the crisis: the governance of Europe's economic, political, and legal transformation. OUP, Oxford
de Graaf KJ, Jans JH, Prechal A, Widdershoven RJGM (eds) (2012) Pluralism in European Administrative Law: Proceedings of the Second REALaw Research Forum. Paris, Zutphen
De Lucia L (2012) Administrative pluralism horizontal co-operation and transnational administrative acts. Rev Eur Admin L 5:17
European Banking Authority (2016) http://www.eba.europa.eu/. Accessed 16 Sept 2016
European Central Bank (2014). Guide to banking supervision. ECB, Frankfurt. https://www.bankingsupervision.europa.eu/ecb/pub/pdf/ssmguidebankingsupervision201411.en.pdf
European Commission Memo (2014) EU Bank Recovery and Resolution Directive (BRRD): frequently asked questions (15 Apr 2014). http://europa.eu/rapid/press-release_MEMO-14-297_en.htm
European Insurance and Occupational Pension Authority (2016) https://eiopa.europa.eu/. Accessed 16 Sept 2016
European Securities and Markets Authority (2016) https://www.esma.europa.eu/. Accessed 16 Sept 2016
European Systematic Risk Board (2016) https://www.esrb.europa.eu/home/html/index.en.html. Accessed 16 Sept 2016
Fahey E (2011) Does the emperor have financial crisis clothes? On the legal basis of the European Banking Authority. Mod L Rev 74:581
Ferran E (2014) European banking union: imperfect, but it can work. European Corporate Governance Institute OUP, Oxford
Gerstenberg O, Sabel CF (2002) Directly-deliberative polyarchy: an institutional ideal for Europe? In: Joerges C, Dehousse, R (eds) Good governance in Europe's integrated market, p 289. OUP, Oxford
Halberstam D (2012) Systems pluralism and institutional pluralism in constitutional law: national, supranational and global governance. In: Avbeli M, Komárek J (eds) Constitutional pluralism in the European Union and beyond, p 85. Hart Publishing, Oxford
Hartmann M (2013) Administrative constitutionalism and the political union. German LJ 14:695
Howarth D, Quaglia L (2013) Banking union as Holy Grail: rebuilding the single market in financial services, stabilizing Europe's banks and 'completing' economic and monetary union. J Common Mkt Stud 51:103
IMF (2013) A Banking Union for the Euro Area, IMF Staff Discussion Note (Feb 2013). https://www.imf.org/external/pubs/ft/sdn/2013/sdn1301.pdf
Kingsbury B, Krisch N, Stewart RB (2005) The emergence of global administrative law. Law Contemp Probs 68:15
Krisch N (2006) The pluralism of global administrative law. Eur J Int'l L 17:278
Kumm M (2005) The jurisprudence of constitutional conflict: constitutional supremacy in Europe before and after the constitutional treaty. Eur LJ 11:262
Kumm M (2009) The cosmopolitan turn in constitutionalism: on the relationship between constitutionalism in and beyond the state. In: Dunoff JL, Trachtman JP (eds) Ruling the world: constitutionalism, international law and global governance, p 258. CUP, Cambridge
MacCormick N (1995) The Maastricht Urteil: sovereignty now. Eur LJ 1:259
MacCormick N (1999) Questioning sovereignty: law, state and nation in the European Commonwealth. OUP, Oxford
MacCormick N (2001) A comment on the governance paper (Jean Monnet Ctr., Working Paper No. 6/01, 2001). Jean Monnet Chair, NYU, New York. http://www.jeanmonnetprogram.org/archive/papers/01/012501.html

Maduro MP (2003) Contrapunctual law: Europe's constitutional pluralism in action. In: Walker N (ed) Sovereignty in transition: essays in European law, p 502. Hart Publishing, Oxford
Marks G, Hooghe L, Blank K (1996a) European integration from the 1980s: state-centric v. multi-level governance. J Common Mkt Stud 34:341
Marks G, Scharpf FW, Schmitter PC, Streeck W (1996b) Governance in the European Union SAGE, London
Martinico G, Pollicino O (2012) The interaction between Europe's legal systems: judicial dialogue and the creation of supranational laws SAGE, London
Moloney N (2014) European banking union: assessing its risks and resilience. J Common Mkt L Rev 51:1609
Pernice I (2002) Multilevel constitutionalism in the European Union. Eur L Rev 27:511
Peters A (2009) The merits of global constitutionalism. Ind J Global Legal Stud 16:397
Schoenmaker D (2014) On the need for a fiscal backstop for the banking system (DSF Policy Paper Series, Paper No. 44, 2014). Duisenberg School of Finance. http://www.dsf.nl/wp-content/uploads/2014/10/DSF-Policy-Paper-No-44-On-the-need-for-a-fiscal-backstop-to-the-banking-system.pdf
Speyer B (2013) EU monitor. In: Böttcher B (ed) EU banking union: right idea, poor execution. Deutsche Bank Research, Frankfurt a. M.
UK Parliament (2016) The impact of banking union on the EBA and the ESRB. http://www.publications.parliament.uk/pa/ld201213/ldselect/ldeucom/88/8806.htm. Accessed 16 Sept 2016
Walker N (2000) Flexibility within a meta-constitutional frame: reflections on the future of legal authority in Europe. In: De Búrca G, Scott J (eds).Constitutional change in the EU: from uniformity to flexibility? p 14. Hart Publishing, Oxford
Walker N (2002) The idea of constitutional uluralism. Mod L Rev 65:317
Walker N (2005) Europe's constitutional engagement. Ratio Juris 18:387
Walker N (2008) Four visions of constitutional pluralism. Eur J Legal Stud 2:336
Walker N (2014) Intimations of global law. CUP, Cambridge
Weiler JHH (2003) In defence of the status quo: Europe's Constitutional Sonderweg. In: Weiler JHH, Wind M (eds) European constitutionalism beyond the state, p 23. CUP, Cambridge

Matej Avbelj is Associate Professor of European Law at the Graduate School of Government and European Studies, Kranj, Slovenia.

Debt, Default, and Two Liberal Theories of Justice

Oisin Suttle

Abstract There is a fundamental disconnect between the public discourse about sovereign and external debt in comparison to private domestic debt. The latter is predominantly viewed through a Humean lens, which sees economic morality in terms of contingent social institutions, justified by the valuable goods they realize; while sovereign and external debt is viewed through a Lockean lens, which sees property, contract, and debt as possessing an intrinsic moral quality, independent of social context or consequences. This chapter examines whether this Lockean perspective on sovereign and external debt is compatible with the dominance of Humean approaches to the domestic economy. It considers and rejects the most plausible argument for reconciling these views, which emphasizes the different qualities of cooperation in the international and domestic economies. It further argues that many standard objections to a Humean approach to sovereign debt suggest, not the Lockean approach, but rather a Hobbesian international moral skepticism. Concluding that the Lockean approach is unmotivated, this chapter instead advances a Humean account of sovereign debt and default. It shows how taking seriously the demand for institutional justification and the idea of persons and peoples as free and equal provides an account of the duties of states—whether creditors, debtors or third parties—in sovereign debt crises. It further examines the implications of each approach for democratic choice about sovereign default.

Revised version of the original published article "Debt, Default, and Two Liberal Theories of Justice" by Oisin Suttle, German Law Journal 17(5):799–834

O. Suttle (✉)
Queen's University Belfast, Belfast, Northern Ireland
e-mail: o.suttle@qub.ac.uk

M. Goldmann, S. Steininger (Eds.), *Democracy and Financial Order: Legal Perspectives*, Beiträge zum ausländischen öffentlichen Recht und Völkerrecht,
https://doi.org/10.1007/978-3-662-55568-2_6

1 Introduction

This chapter is about the ways that we do, and should, think and talk about the moral status of cross-border debt relations, and, in particular, sovereign and quasi-sovereign debts. It is motivated by a puzzle. There is a fundamental disconnect between recent public discourse about the Eurozone sovereign debt crisis, and the ways we commonly analyze economic affairs within domestic polities. Whereas domestically, we typically think about economic affairs in terms of institutions, outcomes, efficiency, and distributive fairness, Eurozone sovereign debts have been discussed through a dominant lens of responsibility, obligation, and the intrinsic moral duties of debtors, tempered only by duties of charity and humanity on the part of creditors.

This disconnect, and the moralizing of cross-border debt, has substantially limited the options for resolving the debt crisis, including in particular by limiting the scope for restructuring. It has shaped the legal responses to the debt crisis, and to sovereign and external debt generally. It has informed debates within and between democratic polities about the choices that fall to them to make, and about who should make those choices, given competing claims and cross-border relations. How we understand the morality of sovereign debt is thus fundamental to any judgment we might make, about either the democratic credentials or the substantive justice of our legal and political responses to this crisis. Insofar as those responses claim to track underlying moral rights and duties, and particularly given the absence of comprehensive democratic processes and institutions through which they can be legitimized, it is doubly important that we clarify our thinking on the underlying moral issues.

I argue the disconnect expresses a deeper tension between two fundamentally different traditions of liberal thinking about economic affairs, which I label Lockean and Humean. The Lockean understands economic relations as having an intrinsically moral quality, while the Humean sees the economy in institutional and instrumental terms. Notwithstanding the domestic dominance of Humean approaches, discussions of sovereign debt seem clearly to express the Lockean perspective.

The first question that I ask is whether and to what extent it makes sense to adopt these different approaches in analyzing domestic and international debt. In particular, I ask whether differences in the nature of cooperation in international financial markets might explain these different approaches. Notwithstanding the initial plausibility of this position, I conclude that it cannot do so. Nor, I argue, can the differences be explained by any of the other challenges typically posed to theories of global economic justice. In so far as these challenges constitute objections to Humean approaches, they are equally fatal to the Lockean perspective, motivating instead a Hobbesian skepticism.

I therefore dispense with the Lockean approach and turn to a second question, namely how we might develop a Humean approach to international financial markets, and specifically to sovereign debt restructuring. There are many Humean approaches domestically, each suggesting a different approach internationally. I focus on one, developing what I see as the best expression in the international debt context of Rawls' *Justice as Fairness*. I show how understanding economic justice as concerned with the justification of social institutions can generate specific principles for the governance of debt relations and the resolution of debt crises, and how those principles in turn support conclusions about the duties of debtors and creditors that are quite different to those suggested by the dominant Lockean approaches. Finally, I consider the implications of these diverse approaches for questions of governance, and in particular how claims to democratic choice might be applied to cross-border debts.

2 Two Liberal Perspectives on Economic Morality

We can identify two distinct liberal traditions of thinking about the morality of economic life. The first, deriving from John Locke, finds its most prominent contemporary expression in the right libertarianism of Robert Nozick. The second runs from Thomas Hobbes through David Hume, Jeremy Bentham, and John Stuart Mill to—in modern Anglo-American thought—John Rawls and his successors.

These traditions are distinguished not by the economic institutions they prescribe, but by the ways they understand those institutions as justified. For Lockean liberals, economic relations have an intrinsically moral character. Real and personal property derive from our inherent self-ownership.[1] Contracts bind as promises, the breach of which violates the natural rights of the individuals to whom we make commitments.[2] The move from natural rights to economic morality does not run through consequences, except perhaps at a low threshold level.[3] Humean liberals, by contrast, understand the economy as institutional, instrumental, and ultimately contingent.[4] Property and contract are institutional expressions of the scheme of cooperation that we label society, and it is together with the rest of that scheme and—at least in modern iterations—in terms of the volume and distribution of valuable goods that it realizes, that they fall to be justified.[5] Humean liberals need not be consequentialists, but they will likely deny there is any intrinsic moral quality

[1] Locke (1988 [1689]), p. 285; Nozick (1974), p. 150.

[2] Locke (1988 [1689]), p. 277. Lockeans can most plausibly invoke Kant for this claim, although Nozick understands the self-ownership argument as similarly expressing a Kantian injunction against instrumentalizing persons. Nozick (1974), p. 30.

[3] Thus, in Locke, our natural right to appropriate depends *inter alia* on a claim about what is necessary for persons to make use of the world. Locke (1988 [1689]), p. 286. Further, the proviso to leave "as much and as good" introduces a potential, if quite limited, consequentialist constraint. *Id.* p. 291; Nozick (1974), p. 178.

[4] We might equally label this second tradition Hobbesian. Given both Hobbes's moral egoism, and his appropriation by international relations realists, however, Hume seems a more suitable namesake.

[5] *See generally* Hume (2000 [1738]), § 3.2; Hobbes (1996 [1651]); Bentham (1843), § 1.8; Rawls (2001). p. 114. Kant's recognition of property as relational, and in consequence deriving from social contract, most clearly places him in this category. Kant (1999).

to economic rules, of the kind imagined by Lockean liberals.[6] Indeed, as Nozick's argument suggests, Humeans must necessarily deny this; for if they concede the natural rights account of property, they will find little conceptual space left in which to realize their utilitarian or egalitarian commitments.

The Lockean reasons directly from political morality to just institutions governing economic activity. The Humean, by contrast, must appeal to the human sciences, most prominently economics, but also sociology, psychology, and political science, to identify optimal institutions, as defined by her underlying social welfare function.[7] These might be the same institutions that the Lockean approach favors—security of property, freedom of contract—but how these are justified is quite different. Indeed, despite their popularity among *soi-disant* libertarians, such prominent free-market liberals as Hayek and Friedman fall clearly on the Humean side of this line: They defend market freedoms not for their intrinsic worth, but for their social consequences.[8]

These traditions represent fundamentally different understandings of the relationship between the individual and society. For Lockeans, individuals and their rights are prior to, and impose limits on, society.[9] For Humeans, rights derive from society and are defined and justified by the function they play within the social scheme.[10]

The tension between these approaches is a recurring feature of political debate in liberal states. J.M. Keynes, writing in 1926, tells the story of their temporary reconciliation at the hands of nineteenth-century *laissez faire* economists.[11] The efficiency of markets generates a happy coincidence between protecting natural rights

---

[6] They do not deny, of course, that economic rules serve important moral functions, making human society possible, but deny only that they have force or content apart from their function in particular societies. *See, e.g.*, Hume (2000 [1738]), at §§ 3.2.2.12, 3.2.3, 3.2.5, 3.2.6.6. Admittedly, some Humean liberals' accounts of liberty lead them towards a middle-ground. *See generally, e.g.*, Dworkin (2000).

[7] This comes out clearly from Rawls's discussion of the basic structure and the need to continuously adjust basic institutions to ensure that they realize social justice over time. Rawls (1996), p. 265.

[8] *See generally* von Hayek (2001); Friedman (2002), pp. 12–20. By contrast, while I focus on right-leaning Lockeans, who identify the intrinsic morality of the economy with property and contract, there are also leftist Lockeans, who ground egalitarian prescriptions in the intrinsic moral quality of particular relations. Consider, most prominently, Marx's concerns with exploitation and alienation. *See* Kymlicka (2002), pp. 180, 190–192.

[9] Recall that Locke understands government as instituted for the protection of property, and hence denies it can have general authority to interfere with property. *See* Locke (1988 [1689]), p. 360; *cf.* Nozick (1974), p. ix.

[10] This holds as much for deontological left-liberals, such as Rawls, as it does for utilitarian liberals, such as Mill. Recall, Rawls's basic liberties are themselves products of social cooperation, rather than a remainder of pre-social natural rights. For Hume, there are natural virtues, which we can understand apart from social cooperation; but the virtues of economic justice, including property and contract, are firmly social and conventional. Hume (2000 [1738]), at §§ 3.2.1.17-19, 3.2.2.9-11, 3.2.6.4. Natural rights play a role in Hobbes's theory, but these are limited to liberty rights in the state of nature. A small residue remain under the commonwealth, but impose no duties on others, whether individuals or the state. Any claim rights, which we can assert against others, are purely institutional.

[11] *See generally*, Keynes (2015 [1926]).

and advancing social welfare. Early utilitarians and libertarians thus found an overlapping consensus in support of secure property, free contracting, and the minimal state.

Two World Wars, the Great Depression, and Keynes's own theoretical innovations undermined that consensus, forcing states to choose between natural rights and social welfare. In Roosevelt's New Deal, the United States chose the latter. In the UK, the same choice was made in stages, from the free trade debates of the 1900s through the industrial unrest of the 1920s to post-war nationalizations and the welfare state. As John Ruggie observes, the post-war Atlantic social model was that of embedded liberalism, in which markets are understood as tools, contingently valuable for the realization of social goals.[12]

The Atlantic consensus around the interventionist state lasted, to varying degrees, into the 1970s, when faltering growth and persistent inflation stimulated renewed interest in the free-market models of neo-classical economics. The Reagan/Thatcher revolution was not, on this account, a simple reassertion of the Lockean morality of property. Rather, it was the return of an overlapping consensus between Humean and Lockean liberals on the virtues of markets in both vindicating natural rights and delivering social goods. Admittedly, the language of market freedom and individual responsibility has achieved a new salience in recent decades. In the domestic context, however, any plausible defense of property and markets must still be, at minimum, supported by a claim about their social efficiency, rather than relying exclusively on the natural rights of individuals.[13]

It is this dominance of Humean reasoning in domestic politics that makes discourse about the Eurozone crisis, and indeed sovereign defaults generally, so puzzling. In contrast with the domestic case, the Lockean morality of debt plays a prominent role here.[14] In Germany in particular, the language of responsibility has been central.[15] However, those more open to flexibility similarly express underlying

---

[12] *See generally,* Ruggie (1982), p. 379.

[13] *See, e.g.*, Cohen (1981), p. 6. Many would argue these stories have again diverged since 2008 and that austerity policies pursued in various countries represent the prioritizing of property and contract at the expense of liberal equality and indeed social stability. This may be true, but for my purposes the more important point is that these domestic policies have continued to rely on both individual and social arguments for their legitimacy. Recall, for example, prominent invocations of the ostensible inverse correlation between sovereign debt and economic growth.

[14] A comprehensive overview of these public debates, and the different moral claims invoked therein, is beyond the scope of this chapter. I have included examples of the kinds of discourse with which I am concerned. As examples, they are open to challenge on their representativeness. It would require another paper entirely to rebut these. I can only hope the points made here will sound familiar to anyone who lived through, and paid attention to, Europe's public debates since 2008, including on the Fiscal Compact, banking union, Eurozone bail-outs and, most dramatically, Greek sovereign default.

[15] *See, e.g.,* Steward and Smith (2015) (quoting German Finance Minister Wolfgang Schäuble's insistence that "we must say that the reasons, the cause for the difficult journey to be undertaken by Greece, that the reason for this is to be found in Greece, and not outside Greece, and definitely not in Germany"). Piketty (2015) (providing contemporary criticism of this aspect of German public discourse).

assumptions of responsibility and obligation.[16] Nor is this attitude limited to politicians, whose statements might be explained by the dynamics of negotiations and elections. Substantial majorities of Europeans have been willing to impose substantial social costs in order to maintain the principle that debts must be repaid.[17] Domestically, we are all Humeans, but external debt is a wholly other matter.[18]

Institutional and sociological explanations might be offered for these divergent judgments. Politicians, responsible to domestic electorates, have little incentive to consider the interests of outsiders, leading creditors to insist on repayment of debts regardless of costs to debtors. Different degrees of mutual visibility and identification lead citizens to favor debt relief for compatriots, while showing less concern for outsiders. My goal is different, however. I want to examine whether there is a principled justification for this divergence. Are there good reasons why we *should* take a Lockean view of cross-border debts, while understanding our domestic economic relations in Humean terms? And if not, then how should we think about these debts?

3 Financial Markets, Default, and Cooperation

My starting point, then, is the prominence of a Lockean morality of debt in the discourse of sovereign and quasi-sovereign restructuring, and how, if at all, this can be reconciled with Humean, and specifically left-liberal, approaches domestically. A successful reconciliation must highlight some difference between the domestic and international contexts, some feature that is present in one but not the other, and explains their different moral structures. Morally significant differences do, of course, exist, many of which are canvassed in the existing global justice literature.[19] The question is whether these differences can explain the Lockean tone of sovereign debt discourse.

The most plausible candidate for this purpose is the nature of cooperation across these two domains. Hobbes, Hume, and Kant each understand rights as a function

[16] *See, e.g.*, Hollande (2015) (quoting French President Francois Hollande's statement that, "Of course Greece must honor its commitments. But they are not contesting that … What Greece is asking for is flexibility—that's understandable").

[17] Ipsos European Pulse (2015) (finding, in the immediate aftermath of the Greek referendum, sixty-one percent of Europeans agreed that austerity was harming the Greek economy, while seventy-three percent believed Greece should still repay all debts); Ipsos Public Affairs (2015), pp. 6, 10. Admittedly, the latter judgment referred to the risk of other countries defaulting, and so is not a pure case of the Lockean perspective. Nonetheless, the overall impression is not of citizens understanding debt as a social institution serving shared purposes.

[18] It is perhaps no coincidence that David Graeber opens his book criticizing the moralizing of debt with an anecdote about sovereign lending. Graeber (2011), pp. 1–4.

[19] There are ongoing debates between cosmopolitan and anti-cosmopolitan liberals about how far their domestic theories commit them to egalitarian or other economic duties beyond the state. Rawls himself, for example, denies economic egalitarianism is appropriate across borders. However, his international view remains Humean in its underlying structure. Rawls (1999), p. 37; *cf.* Pogge (1994), p. 195.

of social institutions.[20] Rawls goes further, characterizing rights and entitlements—including those to economic goods—as products of social *cooperation*.[21] It is only through cooperation that these goods become possible, and the problem of social justice is substantially the problem of how we justify the institutions that distribute the products of that cooperation.[22] The image of society as a fair scheme of social cooperation is central to Rawls's domestic theory, and the idea of production as social and cooperative, rather than individualistic and transactional, is essential to his rejection of libertarian entitlement. If international financial markets are not cooperative in the required sense, this might explain why they are subject to distinct principles of justice.[23]

Why does cooperation matter? It matters because, in Rawls' account, it is the fact that social primary goods are a product of social cooperation that gives rise to problems of distributive justice in the first place.[24] The libertarian challenge to liberal equality understands property as owned by individuals, and hence sees distributive justice as inevitably violating those individuals' rights.[25] Rawls, by contrast, understands social primary goods as coming into existence through cooperation amongst all of those individuals who comprise society, and coming to individuals through, and contingent upon, social institutions.[26] Each of us cooperates in the production of those goods. None of us could have access to them in the absence of the cooperation of others. In consequence, none of us has a pre-social entitlement to them.[27] The problem of distributive justice is the problem of how to distribute such cooperative goods among those who cooperated to produce them. Our claims arise as participants in the scheme of social cooperation, and are justified to other participants under Rawls's model of hypothetical consent.[28] It is only because there is cooperation that distributive questions arise at all.

[20] Hobbes (1996 [1651]), pp. 124–125, 147–154, 200; Kant (1991 [1793]), p. 73; (1999), pp. 136–138; Hume (2000 [1738]), § 3.2.6.

[21] *See, e.g.*, Rawls (1999 [1971]), p. 10.

[22] Rawls (2001), p. 50.

[23] In fact, Rawls understands cooperation in two distinct senses. The first explanatory sense sees cooperation as the source of, and prerequisite for the production of, social primary goods, including the basic liberties and economic goods. The second normative sense understands *social* cooperation as free cooperation on fair terms for the rational advantage of each participant. This chapter focuses, in what follows, on the first explanatory sense. Samuel Freeman has argued against the extension of Rawls's difference principle internationally on the basis that the international system is not cooperative in the second, normative, sense. Freeman (2007), p. 266; *cf.* Sangiovanni (2007), p. 3. As this argument does not support the Lockean approach that I challenge, I do not discuss it here. *Cf.* Abizadeh (2007), pp. 318, 318–358 (criticizing Freeman's work).

[24] Rawls (2001), p. 50.

[25] Nozick (1974), p. 185.

[26] Rawls (1999 [1971]), p. 62.

[27] It is for this reason that, *pace* Nozick, Rawls understand social primary goods as being society's to distribute.

[28] For a discussion of the extent to which Rawls's theory is based on participation, rather than luck egalitarianism, *see* Freeman (2007), p. 111.

Brian Barry challenges the relevance of this story to the international economy, which he suggests is characterized not by cooperation in this sense, but by "mere exchange."[29] Rather than being produced through cooperation amongst peoples, this implies we should understand goods in the international economy in the libertarian mode: They come into existence already owned by one people or another; and any scheme of distributive justice must therefore involve taking from some to give to others.

I have argued elsewhere that Barry's challenge is implausible in the case of international trade.[30] As domestic economies adjust production to focus on areas of comparative advantage, increased production becomes possible that could not have been achieved by individual peoples acting alone. This increased production constitutes a cooperative surplus, and institutions governing international trade determine its distribution. But is the same true of international financial markets, international investment, and cross-border debt? In these latter cases, we might think, what is at stake is the potential expropriation by one people of resources produced exclusively by, and hence the pre-cooperative entitlement of, another.

To explore this suggestion, I next sketch two hypothetical examples, of a physical and a financial asset, showing how different understandings of the facts lead to different normative conclusions.

Consider, first, an oil drillship, manufactured and owned in Industria, that drills for oil in the territorial waters of Extractia. The drillship need never dock in, or otherwise physically interact with, Extractia. It receives supplies from, and sends oil directly to, Industria. It thus starkly illustrates the idea of a valuable productive asset that is brought into a state that plays no role in its creation or maintenance. Assuming *arguendo* that we recognize states' claims to the natural resources within their territories, we might agree that the oil produced, and the revenues flowing therefrom, constitute a cooperative surplus. Neither Industria nor Extractia could have obtained these without the contribution of the other.[31] We might think, in consequence, that questions of distributive justice, in Rawls' sense, arise with respect to that oil and revenue, and that Extractia's and Industria's claims on that oil and revenue fall to be justified in distributive terms. However, we might think, Industria's claim to the ship itself is different: It derives not from cooperation in the extraction of oil, but rather from prior rights under the distinct scheme of social cooperation in Industria.[32] There may still be bases on which Extractia might be justified in expropriating it, but they cannot run through any account of cooperation in the production of social goods.

---

[29] Barry (1982), pp. 232–233.

[30] Suttle (2014), pp. 1059–1060.

[31] Of course, it is possible another ship could have extracted the oil, or that this ship could have extracted other oil elsewhere, but what matters is that these goods and profits were produced through cooperation of both drillship owner and territorial state. That I could have cooperated with someone else does not alter the fact that I actually cooperated with you, giving you a claim on our joint production. An alternative line of thought emphasizing the marginal contribution of particular cooperators and the possibility of replacing them with others leads to Gauthier's contractarianism rather than Rawls' contractualism. *See generally* Gauthier (1986).

[32] Similarly, the territorial state's claim on the oil still in the ground is distinct from its cooperation with the drillship.

I will return to and further problematize this story in a moment. However, before doing so, let's consider how it might translate to a second example involving financial assets and financial markets. Where money is loaned across borders, we might analogize this to the drillship in the above example.[33] The lender presumably holds the money to be loaned before the loan is made and, as such, that money cannot be regarded as a product of cooperation with the borrower. We might regard the interest payable as a cooperative surplus, analogous to the oil revenue in the first example.[34] This might lead us to distinguish between the justification appropriate to an amendment of interest rates or maturity dates and that required to disclaim repayment of principal. Economically, including from the perspective of investors, such distinctions are irrelevant.[35] They have, however, played a prominent role in the Eurozone debt crisis, suggesting that policymakers' underlying moral assumptions reflect something like this view.[36]

This argument, however, ignores an important feature of the debt relationship, namely the relation between default risk and interest rate. Interest rates are not simply a function of the profits that a borrower expects to derive from the borrowed funds, and hence of the production enabled by the cooperation between lender and borrower. Rather, they are a function of, *inter alia*: (1) The lender's cost of capital, which, in an efficient market, is likely to closely track; (2) the returns available from other possible investments; and (3) the lender's and the market's perception of the risk associated with the loan, including, in particular, the default risk posed by the borrower.[37] This suggests a number of implications.

Most obviously, it suggests that default is internal to the scheme of cooperation constituted by lender and borrower. The possibility that the borrower will default is part of the basis on which the returns from that cooperation are apportioned. More importantly, assuming (perhaps naively) that the lender has accurately priced the default risk, the borrower—together with other members of the class of borrowers—has paid for the asset itself through this risk premium.[38] The asset is thus itself a product of the lending relation. Focusing on another component—the lender's cost

---

[33] We might distinguish these cases based on the legal form employed. The drillship owner has a property right, while the lender has a contractual claim. Certainly, for Locke, property and promise have distinct bases. However, these questions of legal form are not relevant to my present concern, namely whether the relevant transaction is cooperative in the required sense.

[34] The symmetry is unsurprising. We might retell the oil exploration story as involving a foreign loan to a domestic company to purchase a foreign manufactured ship, with the loan being serviced through revenues from the oil extracted.

[35] This does not need to imply lenders are unconcerned with repayment, although in practice their main interest may be in a revenue stream rather than a future capital sum. Rather, it is because an appropriate amendment of maturity and interest rate can have exactly the same impact on a lender's financial interest as a default on principal.

[36] *See, e.g.*, Strupczewski (2015) (commenting on the insistence on distinguishing adjusting terms from writing down principal).

[37] *See, e.g.*, Merton (1974), pp. 449–470.

[38] In this view, the part of the interest covering the lender's cost of capital or opportunity cost constitutes payment for the temporary use of the capital borrowed, while the risk premium covers any potential loss of that capital.

of capital—leads to a similar point. For a loan, or any investment, to be economically rational, the borrower must at least offset the lender's cost of capital.[39] In the context of financial markets, lenders are often intermediaries; they borrow in one market and lend in another. Their title to the assets loaned is thus itself a function, not of some property relation that is prior to social cooperation, but rather of the lending relation itself. It is only because the borrower seeks to borrow that the lender has any assets to lend. Cooperation is thus logically, and often temporally, prior to entitlement.

The image of cross-border financial transactions as transfers of assets that are prior to cooperation thus seems irretrievably flawed. This need not mean the analogy between financial and physical assets fails, however. Instead, it suggests we further problematize the drillship case, and the many others for which it here stands. We might first observe that non-financial investors must make the same trade-offs between risks and rewards that we observe in financial transactions. It is for this reason that the cost of capital, and hence returns on investment, are higher in many developing countries. We might also observe that the drillship owner, no less than the financial investor, needs returns to cover both business risk and capital cost. Insofar as this is the case, we again find that the asset itself can be understood as a product of cooperation, rather than existing prior to it.

The upshot, then, is that cross-border investment—whether through transfers of financial or physical assets—is properly regarded as cooperative; and that the goods resulting from that cooperation include not only revenues deriving therefrom, but also the invested assets themselves.[40]

We might inquire whether this story holds equally for government borrowing to fund a current budget deficit, rather than investment.[41] This is less obviously a productive cooperative endeavor. Rather, the lender's resources support the borrower's present consumption. Again, however, we can see the relation as cooperative insofar as it serves, from the perspective of both borrower and lender, to time-shift consumption and, from the perspective of the lender, to convert present surplus production into future revenue. It is only international borrowing, private and public, that makes it possible for countries as a whole to save. Indeed, as Locke himself recognizes, money and its equivalents are in this sense inherently cooperative. It is only through our joint agreement to regard money as a thing of value that we can

[39] *See, e.g.*, Modigliani and Miller (1958), pp. 263–265.

[40] We cannot push this argument too far. It requires a sufficiently stable long-term practice of investment to allow investors to cover risk and capital costs through returns on successful investments. If all or substantially all debtors defaulted, the situation would be more plausibly one of expropriation by debtor peoples of creditors' assets. That said, this would rapidly undermine the practice of cross-border lending itself. The fact that creditors commonly come to terms with defaulting debtors, who in turn regain access to capital markets, suggests this is generally not the case.

[41] This is a difficult distinction to draw in practice. Borrowing to support current expenditure on, for example, public salaries, might still be understood as investment, whether because of public services' long-term economic value, such as health, education, or because financing these through debt may facilitate capital spending elsewhere in the economy. Non-investment deficit borrowing may thus be largely illusory; but to the extent it exists, this paragraph suggests how we should think about it.

derive any value from production that goes beyond our own immediate needs, and thereby avoid Locke's own proviso against waste.[42]

It is important to note that the fact that financial markets and property claims are cooperative does not mean that the investor has no better claim on assets than does the territorial state. There may be many reasons to recognize the continuing validity of their property right. The argument supporting that right, however, is internal to the relevant cooperative scheme, the ends it pursues, and the mutual justification of claims as between the participants therein. It is not a natural rights claim of the kind imagined by libertarians, and perhaps implicitly accepted by anti-cosmopolitan Rawlsians.

4 Three Models of Justice Beyond the State

It appears, then, that international investment and debt concern the distribution of benefits and burdens from cooperation, rather than simply the protection or abrogation of pre-existing rights. Yet, before we can conclude that they are matters for distributive justice, we must acknowledge a prior question, of whether relations across borders are relations of justice at all. Might it be that relations between persons across borders, and between persons in one state and the institutions of another, simply are not relations of a kind to which judgments of justice are appropriate? While I will not argue for an answer to this question here, it is worth highlighting the implications different possible answers would have for the specific puzzle posed in this chapter.

The key point to highlight is that, if relations across borders are not relations of justice, then the upshot is not the Lockean natural rights morality of property. Rather, in that case, no judgments of justice are appropriate thereto. If I do not stand in a relation of justice towards another person or institution, then I can have no claim of justice against them in respect of their actions. This is Hobbes' position, as expounded today by international relations realists.[43] The Lockean morality of property is itself a theory of economic justice, supporting claims about the justice or injustice of particular acts. The debate between Lockeans and Humeans is a debate about the appropriate standard of justice; but those who deny that insiders and outsiders stand in relations of justice deny that *any* standard is appropriate.[44]

---

[42] Locke (1988 [1689]), p. 293. Long-term trade imbalances and corresponding financial flows reflect surprisingly closely Locke's account of money as a cooperative institution.

[43] Hobbes (1996 [1651]), pp. 110–119; Mearsheimer (2014), pp. 30–36. While more institutionalist than realist, similar moral skepticism appears in Goldsmith and Posner (2007).

[44] While Thomas Nagel recognizes this distinction, he nonetheless assumes a Lockean morality will apply in the absence of other duties of socio-economic justice. *See generally* Nagel (2005), p. 113. Rawls is at least clearer that his quasi-libertarian principles represent a substantive account of justice, rather than the absence thereof. For an excellent overview, *see* Caney (2005), pp. 125–129 (highlighting the differences between Rawls's minimalism and genuine skepticism).

Sect. 3 focused on the discontinuity between the domestic Humean and international Lockean approaches, as representing what appeared to be the dominant structure in contemporary discourse. But, the possibility of thoroughgoing international moral skepticism suggests that there are various other ways we might understand the relationship between our domestic and international principles of economic justice.[45] Let me therefore sketch a typology of these, before examining their implications for the discontinuous international Lockean that is my main target at this stage.

First, in moving to the international, we might remain within our preferred Humean approach, whichever that may be, deriving principles by analogous reasoning to that used domestically. If our domestic principles are based ultimately on welfare maximization, then we would expect international principles to be similarly grounded.[46] We would need, presumably, to address such challenges as the population across which welfare required to be maximized, the difficulties of interpersonal comparison beyond the state, the efficiency effects of national responsibility, and so on.[47] Our reasoning would, however, be recognizably analogous to that used domestically. If, instead, we derived our domestic principles through social contract reasoning, we would apply similar procedures internationally. Again, we will face questions, about the identity of the parties to any such contract, and the appropriate way to model their interests,[48] but we will recognize a meta-ethical continuity between domestic and international theory. This is the approach that I adopt in the later parts of this contribution.

Second, we might agree with the Hobbesian approach that the international economy is not a suitable object for evaluation in terms of justice. On this view, it is not simply that our approach—whether utilitarian, contractualist or otherwise—has different implications in the international context. Rather, some fundamental premise that is required to get our method going does not hold internationally. We might think, for example, that a degree of mutual sympathy was a prerequisite to judgments of justice, and that this sympathy was absent beyond the state;[49] or that the coercive power of the state was required to make it rational to act on reasons of justice;[50] or, perhaps, that justice was itself a virtue internal to coercive political institutions that are absent beyond the state.[51] The upshot, in each case, would be to

[45] While Hobbes's arguments are not the only ones motivating such skepticism, for convenience I label all such views Hobbesian.

[46] For the classic statement of this position, *see generally* Singer (1972), p. 299.

[47] Garcia (2003), pp. 89–90 (discussing the first challenge); Miller (2007), p. 56 (discussing the second challenge); *id.* p. 71 (discussing the third challenge).

[48] Rawls (1999), p. 23 (for Rawls's approach to both) and *see generally* Tan (2000) (criticizing that approach).

[49] *See generally* Miller (2009), p. 291 (advancing elements of this view); Walzer (1983) (offering a stronger statement thereof).

[50] *See generally* Nagel (2005); Hobbes (1996 [1651]), pp. 91–92, 96, 100–101; *cf.* James (2012), Ch. 3.

[51] *See generally, e.g.*, Nagel (2005); Blake (2005), p. 257; Risse (2012); Valentini (2012) (suggesting this idea in a more qualified form).

distinguish two contexts: (1) A domestic context, in which actions, institutions, and relations are appropriately subject to judgments of justice; and (2) an international context, in which they are not. This would not mean, however, that states' policies towards outsiders were not subject to any judgments of justice. Rather, their justice would fall to be judged in terms of their implications for insiders, who are in relations of justice amongst themselves.[52]

Third, we might conclude that, while the international economy is indeed subject to judgment in terms of justice, reasoning about justice beyond the state has a different structure to reasoning about justice domestically. Perhaps domestically justice is utilitarian, but internationally it is contractualist. Or, domestically, justice is based on natural rights whereas internationally it is based on hypothetical agreement. Or, domestically, it is understood in Humean terms, but internationally it is Lockean. This last approach is the discontinuous view that I suggested earlier was evident in the discourse of sovereign debt, and against which I argued in Sect. 3.

I should say, before proceeding, that I find the first approach more plausible than the second, but I find both first and second far more plausible than the third. To hold, as the first approach might, that the *content* of justice is different internationally and domestically, seems easier to accept than, as the third requires, that the *grounds* of justice, and the *structure of ethical reasoning*, are different in each context. Certainly, we should place the burden of argument on the proponent of such a discontinuity. Further, it makes little sense to adopt this third approach by default, as some seem to, because we disagree about the conclusions of the first approach. Disagreement seems more plausibly to motivate the skepticism of the second approach than the equally controversial, and domestically disfavored, intrinsic morality of the third.

Beyond this intuitive skepticism, the third approach faces daunting challenges in reconciling the two—by assumption incompatible—sets of principles, where the two interact. How is this the case? Assume, first, that as among members of a society, whether these be citizens, residents, or some other class, the morality of markets is understood in Humean terms. Property and contract are justified as elements of an institutional scheme that is, in turn, justified by the goods it realizes for members—whether understood in utilitarian, egalitarian, prioritarian, or other terms. Unless this society is completely closed, those property and contract rules will necessarily impact on, and may often be applied to, outsiders. How should they be applied and justified in such cases?

The first approach, which reasons in the same way *vis-à-vis* insiders and outsiders, can answer this question in a relatively straightforward way. It might mandate applying the same principles to outsiders and insiders, albeit this might require broadening the outcomes over which those principles are justified. For example, we

[52] Freeman (2007), p. 304 (highlighting the ways principles of domestic distributive justice may determine policies affecting outsiders). Similarly, realists emphasize how duties to insiders restrict statesmen's freedom to pursue cosmopolitan goals. Morgenthau (1966), pp. 235–249; Kennan (1985), pp. 205–218.

might justify property and contract rules as optimizing some function defined over the outcomes for insiders, subject to a side constraint in terms of their impact on the basic rights and self-determination of outsiders. There is no fundamental discontinuity between moral reasoning with regard to insiders and outsiders, so resolving conflicting claims is internal to the relevant theory.

The second approach is also relatively straightforward. If we do not understand insiders as standing in relations of justice towards outsiders, then we need not worry about how outsiders are treated under, or affected by, the principles we adopt domestically. We might apply the same rules to outsiders, or we might discriminate against them. In either case, this will be determined by how our choices affect outcomes for insiders, who are the class towards whom justification is required. Because outsiders have no claims of justice, there are no conflicting claims to adjudicate.

The third approach, however, is more difficult. If we understand the claims of outsiders in Lockean terms, but those of insiders in Humean terms, then we are likely to struggle wherever insiders and outsiders participate in the same institutions. In the Humean mode, we will presumably support taxation of individual and corporate income, with revenues applied towards social goals. Yet, if outsiders' claims have a distinct, Lockean, form, then such taxation will constitute a rights violation towards them.[53] Similarly, while the property rights of insiders can be restricted for the benefit of others, such restrictions will not be justifiable vis-à-vis outsiders. We are thus led towards a two-tier structure, where outsiders enjoy additional protections beyond those claimed by insiders.[54] Such inequalities, where different classes of persons enjoy different legal rights and duties, will strike many as objectionable in themselves, but they also raise formidable practical challenges where insiders and outsiders interact and compete in the same markets.[55]

5 Justice and Institutions in a Global Economy

There seem, then, to be various reasons to reject the Lockean turn in international morality. First, insofar as it depends on an absence of cooperation, the Lockean approach is unmotivated. Second, insofar as it reflects doubts about international economic justice generally, Hobbesian skepticism seems a better response. And

[53] *See* Locke (1988 [1689]), p. 362; Nozick (1974), pp. 169–171 (on the limits of taxation in the Lockean mode). The Lockean might avoid this worry by suggesting that outsiders implicitly accept limits on economic rights, in line with those applied to insiders, as a condition of participation. The problem with this argument, however, is that it can be applied to qualify the Lockean position in any situation where two views conflict. The Lockean thus saves the structure of his view, but at the cost of any practical significance.

[54] Such two-tier protection is already evident, albeit for particular political and historical reasons, in investment treaties and the customary law of aliens' rights.

[55] Consider, for example, how a state's power to regulate particular property changes when transferred from insider to outsider and the perverse incentives this sets up.

third, whatever its merits at an abstract level, the challenges of applying it in practice make it unattractive. So where do we go from here? Given the deficiencies of the Lockean approach, the challenge must be to elaborate a plausible Humean alternative for international economic law, and, specifically, external and sovereign debt. It is to that task that I now turn, building from what I see as the best interpration of Rawls' theory of *Justice as Fairness*.[56]

Justice, as Rawls understands that concept in his domestic theory, is concerned with the evaluation of non-voluntary institutions that allocate basic rights and duties, and determine the distribution of the benefits and burdens of social cooperation.[57] The fact that we share the world with others, in whom we recognize some basic equality, and with whom we cannot avoid interacting, is sufficient to give rise to problems of personal morality. But when we solve the problems of our mutual interactions through the constitution of political institutions, through which the options open to some are made subject to the choices of others, we require a different category of principles, under which the restrictions imposed on individuals can be justified to them, through the mechanism of hypothetical consent in the original position. I may not in fact have consented to the rules subject to which I live, but my hypothetical consent means that those rules can at least be reconciled with my continuing claim to be regarded as free and equal. Therefore, it is with institutions that we begin.

The international economy is characterized by such non-voluntary institutions. These include formal international institutions, such as the IMF and WTO, to which states formally consent, but which, in practice, they have little choice but to accept;[58] they include informal international institutions, such as the globalized economy and the relations of trade, investment, and debt comprised therein;[59] and they include the political institutions of other states, which restrict the options of individuals and communities both within and outside their borders.[60] It is the existence of these non-voluntary institutions, and the fact that they play a distributive role across borders that creates the need for principles of distributive justice in the Rawlsian mode. Just as the institutions of the state require to be justified through the hypothetical consent of those insiders subject to them, so the plural institutions governing the international economy require to be justified to all of those, whether inside or outside, whose rights and entitlements they determine.[61] On this view, it

[56] While the argument is Rawlsian, it is not Rawls's own view. Rawls denies that questions of distributive justice arise in the international economy. Two assumptions drive that conclusion, both of which I reject: First, that productive cooperation is substantially limited to the state; and second, that the international system is not itself coercive. *See generally* Rawls (1999), pp. 105–120.

[57] Rawls (1999 [1971]), p. 6.

[58] Maffettone (2009), p. 243.

[59] Cavallero (2010), p. 16.

[60] Drezner (2007); Follesdal (2011), p. 46.

[61] The fundamental assumption that justification is owed to both insiders and outsiders is substantially cosmopolitan. But depending on how institutions and justification are understood, the prescriptions flowing from it may leave significant room for the autonomy of states as well as for inequalities between them.

is the fact of being subject to non-voluntary institutions that gives rise to claims of justice, and the fact of participation in socially productive cooperation that gives those claims a distributive character.[62]

While it is thus clear that there are non-voluntary institutions of the relevant kind, how exactly we specify these, and how we understand the relations between them, may have important implications for thinking about the justice thereof. There are at least two ways we might do this for the purpose of theory building.

First, we might understand the international economy as a single cooperative institution, albeit one with many different elements, in which all persons and peoples participate in an at least formally symmetrical manner. That institution comprises rules and practices that do not reduce to the rules and practices of individual states. States are themselves subject to those markets, having no choice but to respond to their demands. The relation in which peoples, and indeed persons, stand towards the international economy is thus analogous to that in which individual persons stand towards their own states; and the terms in which it falls to be justified are symmetrical as regards each people.

By argument parallel to that which Rawls deploys domestically, this suggests that the international economy *as a whole* should be organized so as to be to the greatest advantage of the least advantaged representative person or people.[63] A subsequent argument might determine whether the appropriate focus was on one or the other. Further, we might argue about the role that self-determination should play in that justification. Rather than emphasize access to economic advantage, as Rawls does domestically, we might argue that the international economy should maximize the capacity of individual peoples to pursue their own chosen paths.[64] Or, we might adopt a two-limbed principle, equalizing economic advantage subject to a self-determination side constraint. Regardless of how these questions are answered, we would require a justification that applies symmetrically to each people; it does not license preferring the interests of some over others.

Second, we might understand the international economy, and, in particular, international debt markets, as the convergence of a plurality of diverse economic and legal institutions, including various international institutions—the IMF, the Basle Committee, the European Union, etc.—and the domestic law and institutions of individual states, insofar as these affect or purport to govern outsiders. First among these will be states themselves. Debt obligations, after all, are governed by the national law of individual states, whether creditor state, debtor state, or a third state subject to whose law the debt contract is negotiated. There is some coordination among national rules, but to regard these as constituting a unitary whole seems implausible. Further, insofar as there are international rules, these are commonly

---

[62] Suttle (2014) develops in greater detail the points in the foregoing paragraphs.

[63] For two accounts that derive a global difference principle using this route, *see* Beitz (1979); Pogge (1989).

[64] For prominent approaches highlighting how self-determination might temper distributive equality, *see generally* Miller (2007); Rawls (1999).

mediated through domestic law, or reflect agreements amongst, or are reducible to decisions of, individual states.[65] This is not to deny the importance of international rules and institutions. These clearly play an important role, but that role does not eclipse the continued importance of states' domestic institutions.

We are not, on this second view, concerned with the justification of the international economy, or the international debt market, as a whole, because no such institution exists. Rather, there are plural institutions, each of which falls to be considered, and justified, separately. Depending on how we understand the basis of individuals' claims against institutions, this might not make a difference: We might think that justification is owed for national institutions to both insiders and outsiders in precisely the same terms, leading to the same outcomes as the first, unitary, model.[66] But, if we understand the demand for justification as contingent on the particular relation between agent and institution, then the different relations of insiders and outsiders towards particular institutions will likely lead to quite different justificatory demands.[67] Michael Blake, for example, suggests that this focus will lead us to understand the justification of states to insiders in egalitarian terms, while viewing the claims of outsiders in sufficientarian terms.[68]

These represent fundamentally different images of the international economy, with very different implications for what justice demands in its organization. How then can we adjudicate between them? This is not simply an empirical question. Rather, the answer turns on why we are interested in institutions in the first place.

One answer is that we focus on institutions because of the pervasive effects they have on individuals' lives.[69] It is these that make institutions objects of urgent moral concern. That the international economy, considered as a whole, has such pervasive effects on the lives of individuals seems hard to deny. No state can simply shrug off the international economy and chart its own course, except at prohibitive cost.[70] Nor can any other component institution assure particular outcomes independent of the others. The upshot, for many strong cosmopolitans, is that we should adopt the first, unitary, perspective, and in consequence that the international economy demands justification in globally egalitarian terms.[71]

There is, however, a danger in this approach. If we understand the object of moral criticism to be the international economy *as a whole*, we may struggle to find plausible prescriptions for its reform, or to apportion responsibility for implementing

[65] Freeman follows this line to argue that the institutions of the international economy "supervene upon" those of particular states, and that there is in consequence no institutional structure to which an international difference principle can be applied. *See* Freeman (2006), pp. 246–248.

[66] For an argument towards this view, *see* Abizadeh (2007), p. 318.

[67] *See generally* Suttle (2014).

[68] *See generally* Blake (2005).

[69] *See, e.g.*, Buchanan (2007), p. 18.

[70] It is disagreement on this point that leads Rawls to reject global egalitarianism. Rawls (1999), pp. 108–111.

[71] *See generally, e.g.*, Beitz (1979); Pogge (1989); Moellendorf (2001).

such prescriptions. The rhetoric of globalization and the eclipse of the state often leads, not to progressive critique, but to a sense of powerlessness. In the absence of a global political authority, focusing on an amorphous "global basic structure" may absolve more concrete agents and institutions of responsibility.[72]

This suggests a second way we might explain the focus on institutions, and, hence, choose between these perspectives.[73] Moral language is normative, in the sense of action guiding. It is not simply because particular institutions have significant effects that we focus on them, but because those effects are a function of political agency expressed through those institutions.[74] When we criticize an institution in terms of justice, we seek to guide those agents with power to change it. An obvious objection to the first, globalist, perspective is that there is no individual or collective agent with authority over the unitary global economy that it identifies. That economy is a human creation, but there is no particular person or persons in a position to reconstruct it *as a whole*, such that it can reliably deliver specific distributive outcomes. Simply put, the international economy is complicated. Its outcomes cannot be understood as a function of any specific intentionality. It seems unlikely that any institution lacking the bureaucratic and coercive capacities of the modern nation state could sustainably assure particular distributive outcomes to persons or peoples. It seems equally unlikely that any institution with those capacities could—or indeed should—be constituted on a global scale.[75] Yet, in the absence of such an institution, distributive principles for the global economy *as a whole* lack any plausible addressee.[76]

In contrast, the second pluralist perspective identifies not only the institutions that require to be justified, but also the agents to whom criticism is appropriately addressed. In the case of national institutions and legal systems, those agents will be national governments. In the case of formally constituted international institutions, they will be those with effective political control over them. Where informal institutions are subject to effective direction from one or a number of agents acting, or capable reliably of acting, jointly, then we can address questions of their

[72] For an analogous point, *see* Meckled-Garcia (2008), p. 245.

[73] This paragraph draws on arguments in Freeman (2007), pp. 290, 305–307, 314–317.

[74] Recall the suggestion above that justice is about situations where our options are subject to the *choice* of another: We do not enquire about the justice of the weather.

[75] This is important in pre-empting the following objection. We might accept that outcomes in the international economy, as presently organized, are not attributable to definite agents and so not directly criticizable in terms of justice. Yet this might suggest a duty to bring into being institutions that would make such criticism possible. Indeed, this would seem an obvious implication of Rawls's duty "to further just arrangements not yet established." Rawls (1999 [1971]), p. 99. But if, as Rawls himself holds, a global state is implausible or undesirable, then there can be no duty to bring such an institution into being. Rawls (1999), p. 36.

[76] Some might object that this function can be fulfilled by one or a subset of leading states, coordinated through formal or informal international organizations. I do not deny that such coordinated action is possible in particular instances. But there clearly is not, nor is there likely in the foreseeable future to be, any individual or collective agent able to determine outcomes in the international economy, or international financial markets, as a whole.

justice to them. Rather than asking who is responsible for the justice of international financial markets as a whole, we ask a more tractable question: Who is responsible for the justice of each of the specific national, regional, and international institutions whereby those markets are constituted?[77] And rather than asking whether the outcomes of the economy, all things considered, are just, we inquire whether the impacts specific institutions have on those outcomes are justifiable to those on whom they are imposed.[78] By focusing on agency, we are thus led to prefer the second, pluralist, perspective on the institutions of the international economy.

A further benefit of this pluralist approach is its flexibility. We do not assume that there is a single institutional scheme to which a set of independent standards may be applied. Nor do we assume that outcomes are exclusively a function of states themselves. Rather, we examine the institutions that in fact exist and affect outcomes in a particular domain, the extent to which these are a function of responsible moral agents, and how they do and should affect outcomes in order to be justifiable to those persons and peoples subject to them. This allows us to accommodate not only global institutions, such as the IMF and the Basel Committee, and national institutions, such as particular countries' systems of financial regulation and private law, but also intermediate institutions, such as the European Council, Eurozone, and ECB, which may exhibit both varying degrees of agency, and varying relations with diverse persons and peoples.

To see this flexibility in action, consider the case of the European Union (EU). It seems plausible that, at least in some fields, the EU has substantial agency. It has highly developed decision-making processes. Its decisions enjoy a high level of compliance among those to whom they are addressed. As a consequence, without aspiring towards unitary political authority, it constitutes an effective mechanism for solving collective action problems and assuring particular outcomes from the various legal and economic institutions over which it exercises authority.[79] We can thus demand justification for those institutions.

The form that justification takes will depend on the ways those institutions affect morally relevant outcomes in the international economy, and the relation in which the EU stands to those affected thereby. This will include European citizens and

---

[77] A similar point might be made in the language of positive and negative responsibilities. For such a strategy, albeit applying quite different standards, *see* Pogge (2011), p. 2.

[78] This does not mean coordination problems are entirely avoided. Clearly, to judge whether a given institution is just, we must consider how its effects interact with those of other institutions; and we might conclude there were duties on various institutions to coordinate, including potentially by constituting new overarching institutions. But we will in all cases be working outwards, from existing institutions and *loci* of political authority, rather than beginning with a set of desirable outcomes and imagining into being institutions capable of bringing these about.

[79] Obviously, in many cases political constraints in individual countries will preclude any effective action. But such cases reflect a failure of will, rather than an absence of agency. Assuming we can identify the changes that are required to the relevant institutions, no agent can claim that they do not know what they must do to bring these about, or that they lack assurance that others will play their part if they do themselves. This analysis would obviously be quite different if members' respect for EU law were substantially to decline.

residents, and European peoples, but also outsiders, whether individuals or groups. These relations may be in some ways analogous to those between a national government and its citizens and foreigners respectively. But, the intervening institutions of European states are likely significantly to complicate the analysis, including, in particular, the content and currency of their justification. Individuals have many identities, and are commonly members of multiple and overlapping groups; but the liberal state relates to each simply as a citizen, with rights and claims identical to those of other citizens.[80] Yet, from the perspective of European institutions, it may be appropriate to act towards individuals not only in their capacity as Europeans, but also in their capacities as Irishmen, Germans, or Greeks.[81] This might manifest in the kinds of distributive claims that individuals can make against those institutions. It might also, and relatedly, manifest in claims made by groups, that in turn affect the claims of their members. Most obviously, standard models of the liberal polity include nothing analogous to the claims to self-determination that individual European peoples might have against European institutions. Indeed, the salience of self-determination may mean that the justifications European institutions owe towards insiders have much in common with the justifications national institutions owe towards outsiders who are similarly organized in, and make claims in their capacity as, peoples.

Much more might be said about the EU in terms of relevant features. The key point, for my purposes, is that beginning with particular institutions, and the particular agents with authority over them, allows us to acknowledge and accommodate these diverse features more effectively than if we simply assumed a unitary structure and symmetrical relations.

6 One Humean Take on Eurozone Sovereign Debt

The discussion up to this point has been quite schematic. The reader could be forgiven for wondering what the practical implications are for thinking about sovereign and quasi-sovereign debt restructuring in the Eurozone. Before developing these, it may be helpful to recall the argument so far.

I have argued for a number of claims. First, I outlined the distinct Humean and Lockean approaches to economic justice, arguing that the former was the dominant mode of understanding domestic economic questions, while the latter played a prominent role in discussions of cross-border and especially sovereign and quasi-sovereign debt. Second, I considered and rejected what seemed like the most plausible principled explanation of this disconnect, namely the claim that international

[80] Of course, in practice, many states are not unitary and many ostensibly liberal states act towards their citizens as members of groups. Whether this constitutes a failure of liberal theory or political practice is beyond the scope of this chapter.

[81] Communitarian critiques of liberal neutrality might offer inspiration here.

debt was not cooperative in the required sense. I also highlighted the extent to which arguments for limiting the scope of justice to the state motivated, not the Lockean morality of debt, but rather a Hobbesian international moral skepticism, as well as the practical problems of combining Lockean and Humean elements in a single scheme. This led me to reject the Lockean approach, focusing instead on elaborating the Humean approach internationally.

The goal of these earlier sections was to clear away the conventional wisdom of cross-border debt in order to open space for an alternative analysis. Those already working within a Humean framework might find these earlier sections unnecessary, but the prominence of Lockean perspectives in practice means they at least need to be addressed. This done, in the previous Section I began my constructive project, inquiring how an approach focusing on institutional justification should translate to international financial markets, and suggesting that we recognize the plurality of international economic institutions, rather than seeking to apply any single principle of justice to the global economy as a whole.

This Section continues that constructive project, elaborating its implications under one specific account of international economic justice, which I label Equality in Global Commerce (EGC).[82] I contrast the prescriptions of EGC with the Lockean view criticized above. While I do not find that Lockean perspective plausible, contrasting its prescriptions with EGC highlights the implications of taking seriously the international implications of our domestically entrenched Humean commitments.

6.1 From Equality in Global Commerce …

EGC is broadly Rawlsian in its content and methods, drawing on elements from Rawls's domestic and international theories. It understands justice in terms of the hypothetical consent of both persons and peoples. Persons are modeled as concerned with individual freedom, operationalized in terms of basic liberties, and access to economic advantage. Peoples are modeled as concerned with collective self-determination, operationalized in terms of their capacity effectively to determine the course of their shared lives, to pursue valued projects, and to realize their domestic conceptions of justice.

As regards national institutions, the upshot is that these are domestically just—they satisfy the justice claims of insiders—to the extent they comply with Rawls' two principles of justice, including the difference principle, which identifies the extent of permissible inequalities. They are, in most cases, internationally just—they satisfy the justice claims of outsiders—provided they do not undermine basic rights or the capacity of other peoples to become or remain self-determining in the sense sketched above. But, where peoples, through their national institutions, pursue goals specifically through their effects on the international economy, these

[82] For a detailed account of the arguments supporting EGC, *see generally* Suttle (2014).

require more stringent justification, in globally egalitarian terms, or in terms of the protection—as opposed to the exercise—of self-determination. For our purposes, the key distinction is that in the case of most domestic measures, states are free to focus on their domestic priorities, provided they do not jeopardize the capacity of others to do the same. Where their domestic institutions are outward-oriented, however, justification must be symmetrical between insiders and outsiders.

As regards international institutions with universal or near-universal membership, justification will necessarily be symmetrical. It will focus, in the first instance, on preserving the self-determination, as sketched above, of each people subject thereto. To the extent that an institution could take one of a number of forms, each of which will effectively preserve that self-determination, it will select among these to maximize the economic position of the economically least advantaged people, with a view to in turn maximizing the economic advantage of less advantaged persons therein.

In the case of regional or other non-universal international institutions, the position is somewhat complicated. Among members, justification will take the same form as universal institutions. But this will be subject to the same side constraint, as to the self-determination of outsiders, as applies to national institutions. The self-determination of peoples, both insiders and outsiders, thus constitutes the first criterion for assessing the justice of such institutions. As with universal institutions, however, where a number of candidate institutions meet this threshold, EGC mandates choosing among these based on their impact on the economic position of the least advantaged people directly subject thereto. This will, in the normal course, mean the least advantaged member country. This standard differs from universal institutions in applying this criterion over the set of member peoples only.

It is worth highlighting one limit on this approach: It is an account of the justification of *non-voluntary* institutions. The voluntariness or otherwise of institutions is a relational quality; an institution may be voluntary from the perspective of some agents, but not of others. It seems plausible, for example, that many institutions are, in their early years, voluntary from the perspective of their members. States choose for themselves whether to participate in such institutions. Where they choose to do so, we may regard this as a free choice and an exercise of their self-determination. The goals states pursue through international cooperation are diverse, so the goals of international institutions are similarly diverse. In particular, nothing in EGC denies that states are free to bind themselves in pursuit of goals other than those of individual freedom and collective self-determination.[83] In the case of such institutions, where membership is genuinely voluntary, EGC has little to say about the relations among members. It will, however, highlight the ways these voluntary institutions are experienced by *non-members* as non-voluntary. Where two states choose freely to coordinate their policies in a particular area, third states experience

[83] What exactly those goals are is an open question, the answer to which will depend on the domestic theory of justice adopted. If that domestic theory is Rawls's political liberalism, then the list will be very short. Rawls (1999), pp. 34–35.

this coordination as a non-voluntary—and potentially very significant—feature of the environment in which they must now act. For this reason, even genuinely voluntary institutions will be subject to the same side-constraint as to their effects on the self-determination of outsiders.[84] And where initially voluntary institutions become non-voluntary over time, EGC will come to apply among their members.

This point is well illustrated by the EU. In its early years, the then European Communities plausibly constituted a voluntary membership institution. At least from the establishment of the EEC Customs Union, however, it was non-voluntary from the perspective of outsiders, for whom the reorganized European economy was an objective feature of their economic environment.[85] Over time, its voluntariness for members also receded, as European institutions achieved greater salience for members and their citizens. Among long-standing members, the EU today is non-voluntary, in the sense that the costs of exit are prohibitive, particularly where other members remain.[86] For more recent members, including especially post-Communist states, it is non-voluntary in the sense that for these states' membership was an important step in constituting and securing their democratic transitions, and, to that extent, giving substance to their self-determination.[87] Similarly, arguments might be made for the earlier democratic transitions in Spain, Portugal, and Greece.[88]

6.2 … *To the Justice of Sovereign Debt*

These, then, are the principles I label EGC, as they apply to national, international, and non-universal or regional institutions. How do we apply these to the case of sovereign and quasi-sovereign debt restructuring?

First, recall that no institution, whether national or international, will be just if it undermines self-determination, understood as a people's capacity effectively to determine the course of their shared lives, to pursue valued projects, and to realize their domestic conceptions of justice. Clearly, where a state's debts can be serviced only through politically constraining and economically debilitating taxation and austerity over decades, that state's self-determination is substantially impaired.

[84] We need not identify this as a separate obligation. Insofar as such institutions coordinate the policies of individual states, the side-constraint on national institutions translates into a side-constraint on non-universal international cooperation. Insofar as non-voluntary institutions have their own executive capacities, the reasons for imposing this side-constraint on national policies will apply equally to international executive capacities.

[85] Consider, for example, the ways trading relations with colonies and former colonies were reorganized on a community-wide basis.

[86] These costs and uncertainties are painfully illustrated by the UK's exit vote.

[87] On some connections between EU membership and democratization, *see* Dimitrova and Pridham (2004), pp. 5, 91–112.

[88] On the complexities of the Iberian cases, *see* Fishman (2003), pp. 31–46.

Constraints on economic policies may preclude the state from realizing its domestic conception of economic justice, or from vindicating the basic rights of its citizens, for example to healthcare. The external oversight of economic policies that commonly accompanies such circumstances may prevent a people from taking effective charge of their shared life, or from making decisions of any importance about how their community develops. No institution that avoidably brings about such consequences can be regarded as just.

This implies the need for a mechanism for restructuring sovereign debt in such circumstances, allowing peoples to disclaim unsustainable debts, and thereby to regain effective control over their own institutions, and over their shared lives. The only justification for opposing such restructuring would be that this would lead to worse outcomes in terms of the value—self-determination—that is at issue. Empirical questions arise at this point; but given the fact of sovereign defaults in the past, it seems implausible that any particular default would undermine other states' capacity to become or remain well-ordered. The fact—as does seem plausible—that it might increase the financing costs of other states in similar positions cannot justify sacrificing the self-determination of some peoples for the benefit of others.[89]

Where does this argument locate the relevant restructuring mechanism? This depends on where we locate the threat to self-determination. Insofar as we are concerned with national institutions and the ways the institutions of one state—the creditor, market, or governing law state—may undermine the self-determination of another—the borrower—it suggests that states should provide, in their national laws, mechanisms for other states to restructure debts subject to those laws. To take a prominent example, the laws of New York should provide mechanisms for states issuing bonds in New York, and subject to New York law, to restructure the resulting debts. States should also ensure their laws are not used to enforce debts that a borrower has a good claim to restructure, even where the debts themselves are not issued subject to those laws. They should, for example, decline to enforce orders in respect of such debts against property within their jurisdictions.[90]

A similar obligation to facilitate restructuring will arise for formal regional and international institutions, and for national institutions that are oriented towards the international economy. A further complication arises here, however. In the case of genuinely domestic institutions, I have suggested that states should apply as their principal yardstick their own domestic conceptions of justice, subject to a

---

[89] The assumption here is that arguments invoking the systemic effects of restructuring and the effects on the financing costs of others involve sacrificing the interests of the already disadvantaged for the benefit of those more advantaged. It does not mean that restructuring cannot be made conditional on policies to ensure it, in fact, leads to the borrower's effective self-determination. The creditor's obligation is to facilitate the borrower's self-determination, not simply to forgive the debt. Concerns for self-determination will also be relevant in deciding how far lenders or the international community can dictate the specific content of the required reforms. This further suggests that, where restructuring is contingent on domestic reforms, we carefully examine whether these are for the long-term benefit of the borrower, or rather serve to deter future defaults by others or to maximize recovery by creditors.

[90] On the various mechanisms whereby sovereign debt is enforced, *see* Panizza et al. (2009), p. 651.

self-determination side-constraint. Outsiders have a different, and secondary, moral status in considering such institutions. In contrast, when it comes to outward-oriented national and formal international institutions, their claims are symmetrical. We can thus inquire, in respect of such institutions, whether they are themselves organized and act so as to equally vindicate the self-determination of all states subject to them, and to the extent they do so, whether they further seek to maximize the economic position of the least advantaged such state. We might ask, for example, not only whether the IMF's lending vindicates the self-determination of heavily indebted countries, but also whether it facilitates less advantaged countries' access to finance on the most favorable terms possible. We might judge the ECB's monetary policies not only in terms of price stability, which is plausibly a pre-requisite to effective self-determination for all, but also in terms of growth effects on the least advantaged Eurozone states. How we identify when national institutions are outward-oriented is not straightforward. But, to the extent we can identify national institutions designed to facilitate international—as opposed to domestic—debt markets, we might conclude that these were outward-oriented in the relevant way, and so subject to this additional requirement.[91]

A further upshot of this approach merits mention. The story that I have told is about unsustainable debt as a threat to the effective self-determination. It is not about the relative economic positions of borrowers or lenders. It does not claim, as more straightforwardly egalitarian cosmopolitans might, that economically less advantaged peoples should be entitled to default on debts to more advantaged peoples, because it does not assume that those more advantaged peoples have any general obligation, through their own institutions, to maximize the economic position of the globally least advantaged. Rather, it assumes that the more advantaged pursue their own goals through their own institutions, and that the effects these have on outsiders are justified provided they allow those outsiders to do the same. It is not because I am poor, but because my debts undermine my self-determination, that I have a claim to default on them. That may happen at high or low levels of national income. The corollary is that, in many cases, those economically less advantaged may need to facilitate restructuring by those more advantaged: The poor may have to bail out the rich.[92] This may seem perverse, but it is a function of understanding

[91] We might thus distinguish states that have organized their capital markets and private law with an eye to becoming global centers from those for whom participation in international debt markets is largely limited to offering the state's own debt, currency reserve activities, and citizens' purchasing of domestic and foreign bonds.

[92] A parallel might be drawn to personal bankruptcy laws, which do not necessarily reduce bankrupts to the lowest acceptable economic position but rather allow them to retain many economic advantages, such as tools of trade. If the function of bankruptcy is to give individuals back control of their own lives, which are continuous both before and after bankruptcy, then it may be necessary to allow them to keep some of the advantages that accrued to them in their "former" life. To do otherwise might be to irreparably disrupt whatever ongoing projects they had, which are central to their continuing agency/identity. Of course, economic rationales can also be offered for these provisions.

self-determination and economic advantage as distinct categories of good, and subordinating the latter to the former.[93]

The relation between self-determination and economic advantage also matters for answering the obvious objection, that this approach will increase financing costs for borrowers, without giving them any greater freedom of action. They could, after all, issue debt in their own currencies, and make such debts subject to their own laws if they wanted to protect their freedom to restructure. That they do not do so suggests that they prefer to accept greater discipline in exchange for lower interest rates.

This may be true,[94] but it mistakes the reasons why, as Humean liberals, we value states' freedom to contract debts and constitute institutions under which those debts are repayable. We do not do this because we regard either debt or contracting as expressions of an intrinsic moral power. Rather, we value them as elements in a scheme that realizes particular valuable goods—in this case, self-determination and economic advantage. Now let us imagine a state seeking to borrow money. Assuming restructuring terms affect financing costs, the state has two options: First, the state could borrow under a regime requiring strict enforcement in all circumstances, at an interest rate of x. Second, it could borrow under a regime permitting restructuring where necessary, at a rate of $x + y$. y is thus the price that the borrower pays for the restructuring option. Now consider two scenarios: y might be the difference between the borrower being able or unable to borrow funds necessary for it to become or remain effectively self-determining. In this case, requiring an interest rate of $x + y$ would itself undermine the borrower's self-determination. Yet, the borrower has a good claim in justice against the institutions of the international financial market to the vindication of its self-determination. We might reasonably inquire how that duty should be vindicated[95] but it cannot be done by requiring restructuring terms that will themselves undermine that self-determination.[96] If, on the other hand, y is simply the difference between the borrower achieving a higher or lower level of economic advantage, then advocating the strict enforcement regime requires sacrificing a good with greater priority—self-determination—in pursuit of one with lesser priority—economic advantage.

---

[93] The priority of self-determination over economic advantage is a function of conceiving self-determination as extending to economic choices. If economic advantage took priority, the upshot would be continuous redistribution from more- to less-advantaged and a consequent denial of any meaningful economic self-determination; *see* for this problem Miller (2007), p. 68 and Rawls (1999), p. 117.

[94] While plausible, this objection finds little empirical support. Bond prices seem largely unaffected by including restructuring clauses. *See* Becker et al. (2003), pp. 127–161.

[95] For a further discussion, *see infra* Sect. 7.

[96] The objection here recalls Joan Robinson's observation that "the misery of being exploited by capitalists is nothing compared to the misery of not being exploited at all." Robinson (1962), p. 46. It is no objection to a proposal to say that it would make it more difficult for states to obtain financing, if their needing that financing itself constitutes an injustice for which those in whose name the objection is raised are themselves responsible. Some might object to this allocation of responsibility, but a plausible reply highlighting states' dependence on international markets, and others' constitution of those markets through their domestic institutions, supports it.

It might here be further objected that it is the borrowing state that is making that choice. Three replies occur: First, the mere fact of prior choice does not necessarily license imposing on an agent all the consequences of that choice; the extent to which we bear consequences depends on a subsequent argument about the normative extent of responsibility.[97] Second, allowing some borrowers this choice may impose significant negative externalities on others; where there is an option to borrow on strict terms, lenders may be less willing to lend on terms that allow restructuring, as compared to a situation where all lending must allow restructuring.[98] Third, the issue is not the borrower's freedom to agree to strict terms, but rather whether non-voluntary institutions should enforce such agreements. Thus, at the stage of enforcement, it is a question of some undermining the self-determination of others.[99]

The role of choice highlights the difference between the Humean and the Lockean account of sovereign debt. For the Lockean, the promise to repay constitutes a free-standing moral obligation grounded in the joint choice, and the joint self-ownership, of borrower and lender. It is neither here nor there, on this view, that repayment may substantially undermine the good of the borrower, including the fundamental good of the self-determination of peoples. To the extent the Lockean acknowledges the good of self-determination, he is likely to find its expression in the choice to borrow, rather than the consequences of repayment. In contrast, the Humean understands debt, and the duty to repay, as internal to, and dependent on, a scheme of institutions which themselves require to be justified in terms of the good of those subject to them. The moral obligation of debt is thus limited to the extent such limitation in turn facilitates the realization of that good.

Two questions arise at this point about the role of non-market lending, in the form of "bail-outs" by states or regional or international institutions. The first is whether there is a duty to provide such bail-outs. The second is whether the resulting debts have a different moral status to commercial debts.

The answer to the first question will depend on what is required to prevent an institution undermining the effective self-determination of a borrowing state. Where a distressed borrower—notwithstanding reasonable steps to reform a dysfunctional economy—is running a primary budget deficit, or requires to recapitalize a financial system, or otherwise requires access to additional short-term funds in order to become or remain effectively self-determining, an institution that denied access to those funds, on terms themselves compatible with the borrower's self-determination, would be unjust.[100] If we understand the cross-border debt relation as—at least in part—a function of the political institutions of the creditor or market state, then

---

[97] For this point in another context, *see* Olsaretti (2009). We might further emphasize that, for Humean liberals, economic choice is valued for the goods it in turn realizes. To the extent that imposing the consequences of a choice undermine those goods, the mere fact of being chosen is no argument for it.

[98] But *see supra* note 94 (discussing contrary empirical evidence).

[99] For the analogous argument against slavery contracts, *see* Freeman (2001), p. 105.

[100] This is the scenario anticipated in the text accompanying *supra* note 95.

the justification of those institutions will extend not only to facilitating the denunciation of debts to the extent necessary, but also to the provision of funds where necessary to address the negative effects that interaction with those institutions has had for the borrowing state.[101] Viewing the bail-out obligation as an aspect of the justification of the institutions of the lending state has the additional benefit of providing a clear basis for allocating that obligation to specific agents. This does not mean, of course, that those agents cannot themselves delegate that responsibility to, for example, the IMF.

As to the second question, we might wonder whether the moral status of bail-out loans, *ex hypothesi* provided otherwise than for commercial gain, is different from commercial loans. As a matter of practice, international institutions financing sovereign bail-outs, including the IMF and European institutions, insist that their loans have priority over commercial loans, and cannot be subject to restructuring.[102] Certainly, the stories told above about the relation between debt, interest, and cooperation do not easily map onto bail-out loans. But two slightly modified stories can be told, which suggest these loans are equally subject to justification in distributive terms.

First, note that while bail-out loans may be provided for moral rather than commercial reasons, the moral obligation to provide them is itself contingent on the lending people's constitution of, or participation in, institutions through which that people pursues cooperative gains. The provision of these loans, just like the cost of default when it occurs, is thus a cost of mutually beneficial cooperation through international financial markets. States, rather than lenders, bear the cost, but that is simply a function of the lending people's organization of its own economy. There is nothing to stop the lending state from passing it on to lenders through a suitable financial sector tax.

Second, note that bail-outs are—at least sometimes—provided for the benefit of lending institutions, or to protect the stability of the international financial system, rather than simply for the benefit of the borrowing state. This was very clearly the case in Eurozone bail-outs, which served in part to isolate international financial markets from the risk of default by distressed sovereigns and banking systems. The loans thus served to protect, for the benefit of lending states, the scheme of mutually beneficial international cooperation. Thus, again, these loans appear as simply one more cost of that mutually beneficial cooperation.

The upshot is that bail-out loans cannot claim any privileged moral status over and above that due to commercial loans. This does not of course answer whether they should be accorded a higher legal or political status. I suggested above that it

[101] The claim here is that the creditor has facilitated the debtor's reliance on international funding, and cannot simply withdraw that funding without allowing the debtor some reasonable period to restructure its economy away from that reliance. *Cf. generally* James (2012), (for an account of the international economy as a practice of mutual reliance on common markets).

[102] Although for doubts about how far this insistence translates into practice, *see* Bulow et al. (1992), pp. 195–234.

was implausible to assume facilitating sovereign defaults posed a greater threat to the self-determination than enforcing unsustainable debts. It seems more plausible, however, that facilitating default on non-commercial bail-out loans, other than in the most extreme of circumstances, would undermine the continued availability of such loans. Witness the political opposition in Eurozone lender countries to repeated bail-outs. It may be that a creditor government, called upon to lend good money after bad or to recapitalize an international financial institution tasked with doing so, would face insuperable domestic political opposition, notwithstanding any moral obligation to act in these circumstances.[103] It may therefore be necessary, for practical reasons of incentives and political will, to treat such loans as a legally privileged category.

7 From Relations of Justice to the Scope of Democratic Community

My focus thus far has been questions of justice. I want, in this final section, to shift that focus somewhat, to highlight the implications of this approach for thinking about democracy in financial markets, and specifically in respect of sovereign debt restructuring. In recent debates, different players have advanced as self-evident a range of claims about what democracy demands in the context of debt restructuring. On examination, many of these reflect an underlying commitment to one or other of the perspectives discussed above.[104] With a view to making those commitments explicit, I develop in this section the implications for democratic choice of three perspectives: The Lockean received wisdom, Hobbesian international moral skepticism, and EGC.

Because it understands property, contract, and debt as prior to political institutions, the Lockean approach suggests a quite limited role for democratic choice. The lender has a right to repayment of the debt, and no democratic choice on the part of any other person can license depriving him of it. Democracy might play a role in circumstances, such as the current Greek case, where the lender is itself a democratic political community. If there is any question, this view suggests, of releasing the Greek polity from an obligation that is owed to Finland or Germany—taking two particularly vocal examples—then it is a matter for the Finnish and the German polities to decide. Debts are rights, and rights can be waived, but only the right holder gets to make that decision.

A complication arises where, as again appears in the Greek case, debts are owed to international institutions at whatever level. A question arises as to which polities

[103] Whether such constraints fall properly under the concept of justice is not a question I propose here to explore. *See generally* Cohen (2008).

[104] For an example including elements of each, *see* Buttonwood (2015).

are to make decisions about waiving such liabilities. There are at least three stories we might tell here. The first "looks through" the relevant institutions, understanding their claims as delegated from their sponsoring states, and hence looking to those states, as distinct polities, to authorize any waiver. The second relies on decision-making procedures in the relevant institutions. This conventionalist response has obvious weaknesses as an answer to questions of political morality, as opposed to legal formality. To the extent it is normatively attractive, it depends on a combination of normative legal positivism and an implicit commitment to the first, look-through, story. A third alternative understands the unit of political choice as the whole of the sponsoring community. Subsequent questions, about the units whereby democratically expressed choices fall to be aggregated, whether at the level of individuals or peoples, would need to be addressed. But at a minimum, this third story suggests little reason for demanding democratic authorization at the level of individual lending states.

The Hobbesian moral skeptic, like the Lockean, will emphasize democratic choices of lending states. But this approach also sees room for democracy in the borrowing polity. Recall, the Lockean sees no role for borrower democracy because he does not perceive any choice that falls to be made by the borrower. The borrower must pay his debt unless the lender chooses at his sole discretion to waive it. In contrast, the skeptic denies that any such obligation exists. Whether to pay is always a matter of political choice for the borrower. Importantly, however, the borrower has only a liberty right to make that choice; lenders are under no obligation to accept it. Just as the borrower is free to default, the lender is free to reject that default and to press for repayment using whatever means are at its disposal. There may be many reasons the borrower might choose to repay, notwithstanding this free choice. At a minimum, he can expect to pay a penalty for default in the form of exclusion from international debt markets for some period of time.[105] What is important for my purposes, though, is that the skeptic must counsel a borrower to weigh the likely consequences of these various factors for the borrowing people itself, in accordance with the principles of political morality properly applying domestically. The effects of this choice—to repay or default—for outsiders are relevant only insofar as they affect likely outcomes for insiders, as it is only insiders who have moral claims on the state's decision. Similarly, the lending state's democratic choice about whether to accept a default and to agree an orderly reorganization of the borrower's debts, falls to be made in terms of its interests, and the claims of political morality made by its citizens. In a highly integrated international financial market characterized by ongoing interaction and cooperation, it may be rational to facilitate reorganization,

[105] In the pre-charter period, the prospect of gunboats in their harbors, foreign seizure of assets and revenues, and similar "super-sanctions" might deter borrowers. In the Eurozone context, unpredictable consequences for the stability of the defaulter's banking system and their continued membership in the currency union provide further disincentives.

but rationality here is the self-interested instrumental rationality of the lender, giving no independent weight to the interests of the borrower.

The third—Humean—approach does not so easily generate an account of the constituencies entitled to make choices affecting international debt and debt markets. That outsiders have claims of justice against states' institutions implies that national democratic choice alone cannot legitimize those institutions towards them.[106] The role of self-determination in this story, however, suggests national democracy should continue to play a central role. Perhaps the most plausible response is that decisions fall to be made by the individual polities concerned, but that they should make those decisions with due regard for the justice-claims of outsiders.[107] In the same way the Lockean sees the borrower's choice as constrained by the duty to repay, the Humean sees the lender as constrained from seeking to enforce their debt, or in appropriate circumstances from refusing to advance further loans.[108] This mismatch—between those making choices and those with claims on those choices—might lead us to seek institutional innovations that might improve the quality of such decisions, making them more likely accurately to track the reasons of justice that apply. Giving outsiders voice in the community's political process is one obvious suggestion. Another is to create impartial expert agencies, whether judicial or non-judicial, authorized to find the relevant economic facts, and perhaps to articulate the relevant duties of justice.[109] We might go further, advocating binding international legal obligations in this regard. But the obvious difficulties in specifying the exact content of those obligations, in a form susceptible to judicial application, and the substantial epistemic resources required to determine with any certainty whether and to what extent they arise in a particular case, might lead us away from that suggestion, particularly given its implications for the self-determination of creditor/market states. I do not claim to have good answers to these questions of institutional design. The foregoing discussion, however, should at least give the reader an idea of the kinds of considerations that should be relevant to it.

[106] For a similar point, albeit invoking a different account of economic justice, *see* Kumm (2013), p. 605. *Cf. generally* Goldmann and Steininger, chapter "A Discourse Theoretical Approach to Sovereign Debt Restructuring: Towards a Democratic Financial Order".

[107] Incorporating such moral constraints on democratic choice is not a novel suggestion. *See, e.g.*, Waldron (1990), p. 44; Rawls (1996), p. 216.

[108] We might express the same idea by suggesting that decisions by national polities may be internationally legitimate, given available alternatives, without being internationally just. This problem of democratic mismatch is not limited to whether to facilitate default but also such questions as what conditions, as to domestic reforms, can appropriately be attached to bail-out lending.

[109] This raises similar problems of democratic legitimacy to judicial review under human rights treaties and domestic constitutions. That said, if we accept these latter practices, I see little reason in principle to exclude similar review against principles of global economic justice.

8 Conclusion

I began with a puzzle and two questions. The puzzle was that the discourse of sovereign debt seemed to express a fundamentally different view about the structure of moral obligation in economic affairs to that found in liberal domestic polities. The first question was whether there were good principled explanations for this divergence. The second was whether we could construct an account of the morality of sovereign debt that was a better fit with the ways we think and talk about economic morality domestically. In Sect. 3 and 4, I answered the first question in the negative. In Sect. 5 and 6, I advanced an answer to the second question, deriving from the principles that I label Equality in Global Commerce, and emphasizing the relation between self-determination and economic advantage in the justification of international economic institutions. I argued that taking seriously our commitments in the domestic context required facilitating orderly defaults on unsustainable debts and more liberal bail-out lending, where this was necessary to vindicate the self-determination of borrowing countries. Finally, in Sect. 7, I examined the different implications that the various approaches to international economic justice canvassed in earlier sections have for questions of democratic choice, including in particular who should decide the terms of any restructuring of sovereign debt. I contrasted the simplistic answers of the Lockean and the Hobbesian, with the more nuanced, and in consequence more institutionally challenging, implications of EGC.

Much more might be said about liberal justice and sovereign debt. For example, I have said nothing about historic injustices or non-democratic borrowing governments as alternative grounds for denying the moral force of international debt. These were prominent concerns in earlier debt crises, but they seem less relevant to contemporary problems in the Eurozone. More relevant for my purposes are questions about the forms that institutions might take to vindicate the demands of the Humean perspective, both as to substantive outcome and democratic control. It may be that these concrete questions of institutional design and political possibility are where the real challenge lies. But meeting that challenge at least requires identifying the kinds of demands we should make of those institutions. It is towards clarifying that question that this chapter is offered.

Acknowledgements I am grateful for valuable comments from the editors of this volume, from participants in the workshop from which it derives, including, in particular, Jen Hendry, and from Robert Burrell, and Sagar Deva, who kindly read and commented on earlier drafts.

References

Abizadeh A (2007) Cooperation, pervasive impact, and coercion: on the scope (not site) of distributive justice. Phil Pub Aff 35:318

Barry B (1982) Humanity and justice in global perspective, nomos: ethics. Econ L 24:219

Becker T, Richards A, Thaicharoen Y (2003) Bond restructuring and moral hazard: are collective action clauses costly? J Int Econ 61:127–161

Beitz C (1979) Political theory and international relations. Princeton University Press, Princeton
Bentham J (1843) Principles of the civil code (ed: Dumont É). William Tait, Edinburgh
Blake M (2005) Distributive justice, state coercion, and autonomy. Phil Pub Aff 30:257
Buchanan A (2007) Justice, legitimacy and self-determination: moral foundations of international law. Oxford University Press, Oxford
Bulow J, Rogoff K, Bevilaqua AS (1992) Official creditor seniority and burden-sharing in the former Soviet Bloc. Brookings Pap Econ Act 1:195–234
Buttonwood (2015) More on debt and democracy. Economist, 20 Feb 2015. http://www.economist.com/blogs/buttonwood/2015/02/greece-and-eu. Accessed 24 Jan 2018
Caney S (2005) Justice beyond borders. Oxford University Press, Oxford
Cavallero E (2010) Coercion, inequality and the international property regime. J Pol Phil 18:16
Cohen GA (1981) Freedom, justice and capitalism. New Left Rev 126:1
Cohen GA (2008) Rescuing justice and equality. Harvard University Press, Cambridge
Dimitrova A, Pridham G (2004) International actors and democracy promotion in central and Eastern Europe: the integration model and its limits. Democratisation 11(5):91–112
Drezner DW (2007) All politics is global: explaining international regulatory regimes. Princeton University Press, Princeton
Dworkin R (2000) Sovereign virtue: the theory and practice of equality. Harvard University Press, Cambridge
Fishman RM (2003) Shaping, not making, democracy: the European Union and the post-authoritarian political transformations of Spain and Portugal. South Euro Soc Pol 8:31–46
Follesdal A (2011) The distributive justice of a global basic structure: a category mistake? Pol Phil Econ 10:46
Freeman S (2001) Illiberal libertarians: why libertarianism is not a liberal view. Phil Pub Aff 30:105
Freeman S (2006) Distributive justice and the law of peoples. In: Martin R, Reidy DA (eds) Rawls's law of peoples: a realistic utopia. Blackwell Publishing, Oxford, pp 243–260
Freeman S (2007) Justice and the social contract. Oxford University Press, Oxford
Friedman M (2002) Capitalism and freedom. University of Chicago Press, Chicago
Garcia FJ (2003) Trade, inequality and justice: toward a liberal theory of just trade. Brill, Leiden
Gauthier D (1986) Morals by agreement. Oxford University Press, Oxford
Goldsmith J, Posner EA (2007) The limits of international law. Oxford University Press, Oxford
Graeber D (2011) Debt: the first 5,000 years. Melville House, New York
Hobbes T (1996 [1651]) Leviathan (ed: Tuck R). Cambridge University Press, Cambridge
Hollande F (2015) France to stand by Greece to lighten debt burden. France 24, 23 Oct 2015. http://www.france24.com/en/20151023-france-grece-hollande-tsipras-support-renegotiate-bailout-terms-creditors. Accessed 24 Jan 2018
Hume D (2000 [1738]) Treatise on human nature (eds: Norton DF, Norton MJ). Oxford University Press, Oxford
Ipsos European Pulse (2015) EU citizens hold Greek government responsible for debt crisis, 28 Aug 2015. https://www.ipsos-mori.com/researchpublications/researcharchive/3616/EU-citizens-hold-Greek-government-responsible-for-debt-crisis.aspx. Accessed 24 Jan 2018
Ipsos Public Affairs (2015) The crisis in Greece. https://www.ipsos-na.com/download/pr.aspx?id=14813. Accessed 24 Jan 2018
James A (2012) Fairness in practice: a social contract for a global economy. Oxford University Press, Oxford
Kant I (1991 [1793]) Kant: political writings (ed: Reiss HS), 2nd edn, Cambridge University Press, Cambridge
Kant I (1999) Doctrine of right. In: Gregor Mj (ed) Practical philosophy. Cambridge University Press, Cambridge, pp 421–432
Kennan GF (1985) Morality and foreign policy. Foreign Aff 64:205
Keynes JM (2015 [1926]) The end of Laissez Faire. In: Skidelsky R (ed) The essential Keynes. Penguin, London
Kumm M (2013) The cosmopolitan turn in constitutionalism: an integrated conception of public law. Indiana J Global Legal Stud 20:605

Kymlicka W (2002) Contemporary political philosophy: an introduction, 2nd edn, Oxford University Press, Oxford
Locke J (1988 [1689]) Two treatises of government (ed: Laslett P). Cambridge University Press, Cambridge
Maffettone P (2009) The WTO and the limits of distributive justice. Phil Soc Crit 35:243
Mearsheimer JJ (2014) The tragedy of great power politics, 2nd edn, WW Norton & Co, New York and London
Meckled-Garcia S (2008) On the very idea of cosmopolitan justice: constructivism and international agency. J Pol Phil 16:245
Merton RC (1974) On the pricing of corporate debt: the risk structure of interest rates. J Fin 29:449
Miller D (2007) National responsibility and global justice. Oxford University Press, Oxford
Miller D (2009) Justice and boundaries. Pol Phil Econ 8:291
Modigliani F, Miller MH (1958) The cost of capital, corporation finance and the theory of investment. Am Econ Rev 48:261
Moellendorf D (2001) Cosmopolitan justice. Westview Press, Boulder
Morgenthau HJ (1966) Politics among nations: the struggle for power and peace, 4th edn, Alfred A Knopf, New York
Nagel T (2005) The problem of global justice. Phil Pub Aff 33:113
NozicK R (1974) Anarchy, state and utopia. Basic Books, New York
Olsaretti S (2009) Choice, Circumstance and the cost of children. In: De Wijze S, Kramer MH, Carter I (eds) Hillel Steiner and the anatomy of justice. Routledge, New York and Abingdon
Panizza U, Sturzenegger F, Zettelmeyer J (2009) The economics and law of sovereign debt and default. J Econ Lit 47:651
Piketty T (2015) Germany has never repaid its debts. It has no right to lecture Greece. Wire, 8 July 2015. http://thewire.in/5851/thomas-piketty-germany-has-never-repaid-its-debts-it-has-no-right-to-lecture-greece/
Pogge TW (1989) Realizing Rawls. Cornell University Press, Ithaca
Pogge TW (1994) An Egalitarian law of peoples. Phil Pub Aff 23:211
Pogge TW (2011) Are we violating the human rights of the world's poor? Yale Hum Rts Dev J 14:2
Rawls J (1996) Political liberalism. Columbia University Press, Ithaca
Rawls J (1999 [1971]) A theory of justice, rev. edn, Harvard University Press, Cambridge
Rawls J (1999) The law of peoples with the idea of public reason revisited. Harvard University Press, Cambridge
Rawls J (2001) Justice as fairness: a restatement (ed: Kelly E). Harvard University Press, Cambridge
Risse M (2012) On global justice. Princeton University Press, New Haven
Robinson J (1962) Economic philosophy. Routledge, Abingdon
Ruggie JG (1982) International regimes, transactions, and change: embedded liberalism in the postwar economic order. Int Org 36:379
Sangiovanni A (2007) Global justice, reciprocity, and the state. Phil Pub Aff 35:3
Singer P (1972) Famine, affluence, and morality. Phil Pub Aff 1:299
Steward H, Smith H (2015) Greek and German Finance Ministers Clash at debt relief talks. Guardian, 5 Feb 2015. http://www.theguardian.com/business/2015/feb/05/greek-german-finance-ministers-clash-debt-relief-talks. Accessed 24 Jan 2018
Strupczewski J (2015) Greek bid for debt relief faces Euro zone skepticism. Reuters, 7 June 2015. http://www.reuters.com/article/us-eurozone-greece-debt-idUSKBN0ON0QW20150607. Accessed 24 Jan 2018
Suttle O (2014) Equality in global commerce: towards a political theory of international economic law. Eur J Int L 25:1043
Tan K-C (2000) Toleration, diversity, and global justice. Pennsylvania State University Press, University Park
Valentini L (2012) Justice in a globalized world: a normative framework. Oxford University Press, Oxford
Von Hayek F (2001) The road to serfdom. Routledge, Abingdon

Waldron J (1990) Rights and majorities: Rousseau revisited. In: Nomos: majorities minorities, vol 32, NYU Press, New York, p 44
Walzer M (1983) Spheres of justice: a defense of pluralism and equality. Basic Books, New York

Oisin Suttle is a Lecturer at the School of Law of Queen's University Belfast.

The Financial Crisis as a Crisis of Democracy: Towards Prudential Regulation Through Public Reasoning

Matthias Goldmann

Abstract The financial crisis challenges our understanding of democracy. Before the crisis there was a widespread conviction that democracies were not only morally superior to authoritarian forms of government, but were also better positioned to deal with severe economic and financial turmoil. Systemic events that exceed purely cyclical ups and downs were believed to be confined to the less democratic parts of the world. The crises in Asia and the post-soviet states of the 1990s seemed to confirm this.

The recent financial crisis, however, has been a crisis in and of the West, while some authoritarian regimes have done much better. It raises the question whether democracy can really produce outcomes that are superior to those of other forms of governance and create a just society.

To explore this question, the paper chooses as a starting point Amartya Sen's comparative theory of democracy that combines output and input oriented aspects. Sen considers "public reasoning" as the key mechanism through which democracies achieve better outcomes than authoritarian regimes. The paper then looks into some of the causes of the crisis that have been identified in the literature. It shows that each of these causes can be understood as a lack of public reasoning. Indeed, I claim

Revised version of the original published chapter "The Financial Crisis as a Crisis of Public Reasoning" by Matthias Goldmann, in Democracy and Crisis. Democratising Governance in the Twenty-First Century, edited by Benjamin Isakhan and Steven Slaughter. Palgrave Macmillan, Basingstoke 2014, pp. 71–87

M. Goldmann (✉)
Goethe University Frankfurt, Frankfurt a.M., Germany
e-mail: goldmann@jur.uni-frankfurt.de

M. Goldmann, S. Steininger (Eds.), *Democracy and Financial Order: Legal Perspectives*, Beiträge zum ausländischen öffentlichen Recht und Völkerrecht, https://doi.org/10.1007/978-3-662-55568-2_7

that there is an intrinsic relationship between the prudential regulation of financial markets and public reasoning. Public reasoning is able to optimize decision-making under conditions of uncertainty, which is exactly what prudential regulation is about. This insight has important consequences for the design of the regulatory architecture of financial markets and the interpretation and application of the relevant domestic and international law.

1 The Financial Crisis as a Crisis of Democracy

The financial crisis which inflicted large parts of the world in 2007 has shattered the political landscape in Western democracies. The political parties that epitomized the post-war amalgamation of market liberalism with the welfare state have come under threat by right-wing populist movements which profoundly question the desirability of liberal democracy and seek to replace it by more authoritarian forms of government. Their message resonates with many people who doubt that liberal democracy will help them improve their economic, social and cultural status. One could therefore say that the financial crisis has meanwhile ended in a crisis of democracy.

Popular support for liberal democracy, as I argue in this contribution, depends on the capacity of democratic systems of government to achieve social justice (Sect. 2). This view relies on Amartya Sen's theory of democracy. Sen believes that the comparatively superior performance of democratic states in achieving social justice, and in particular their capacity to protect citizens against remediable disasters, is related to the fact that they enable public reasoning.[1] Public reasoning allows democracies to determine what kind of social justice they would like to achieve, and to ensure that this outcome is actually achieved. Sen's foremost exhibit corroborating his thesis is the fact that famines in rural India virtually disappeared with the end of colonial domination. Free media, free flows of information, and responsible leadership facilitated public reasoning, prompting governments to adequately calculate the needs of the population and to take measures against potential shortages.[2]

The financial crisis, however, seems to have challenged this understanding. There is evidence that it had a negative impact on social justice, especially on the economic well-being of the more vulnerable segments of the population in the most affected states. This comes on top of the news that equality in the distribution of wealth has been declining over the past decades, calling into question the idea of "trickle down" economics according to which economic growth should benefit all segments of the population.[3] The latter seems to result from the fact that economic power comes with a huge impact on democracies, whether through campaign finance, media power, or power over jobs and other production factors crucial for the life

[1] Sen (2009), pp. 321 f.

[2] *Id.*, pp. 338 f.

[3] Piketty (2014).

of a state. Some argue therefore that market liberalism and liberal democracy are incompatible antagonists.[4] One empirical study even claims that democracies are more likely to suffer from financial crises than autocratic regimes[5].

This contribution seeks to refute the contention about the antagonism of liberal democracy and market liberalism. On the basis of Sen's understanding of democracy as being essentially about public reasoning, I analyze some of the factors which contributed to the banking crisis following the burst of the housing market bubble in 2007, and to the ensuing sovereign debt crisis in Europe. It turns out that many of these factors can be understood as deficits in public reasoning. Thus, democracy is not necessarily incompatible with a stable, market-based financial order. Rather, the crisis might have been caused by a lack of democratic institutions and procedures necessary for proper public reasoning (Sect. 4). This insight has important consequences for the design of global financial regulation (Sect. 5).

2 The Promise of Democracy

What exactly is the promise of democracy which the financial crisis seems to have challenged? This has been the subject of quite some debate confronting input and output-oriented theories of democracy (Sect. 2.1). I adopt here the concept of Amartya Sen's theory of justice, which in my view avoids some common problems of output-oriented theories. This theory claims that democratic systems of government are better able to ensure for every citizen the effective enjoyment of an acceptable level of capabilities (Sect. 2.2). The reason for this lies in democracy's conduciveness to public reasoning.

2.1 Two Perspectives on Democracy: Input and Output

Since the era of the enlightenment, one can distinguish two different, but related theoretical approaches to the question why democracy is a preferable system of government. The first approach focuses on the input aspect of politics: Democracy is preferable as a system of government because it establishes a morally just institutional framework for the exercise of public authority. The second approach emphasizes the outcomes of politics: Democracy is preferable for instrumental reasons, because it facilitates the advancement of public welfare.

[4] Streeck (2011b).

[5] Lipscy (2011).

The first, input-oriented approach to democracy considers democracy as a superior form of government for transcendental reasons. Accordingly, only democracy is able to guarantee the autonomy of the individual. Immanuel Kant and Jean-Jacques Rousseau are among the patron-saints of this theoretical tradition. In their view, democracy establishes a system of government by reason, i. e. by decisions to which every reasonable person should be able to agree.[6] Today, such a steadfest belief in reason seems no longer possible. The disenchantment of objectivity and rationality since the last third of the 19th century prevent the further sanctification of reason. Unless one discards the idea of reason altogether, one has to accept that it is possible to reasonably disagree on most issues, especially in politics.[7] Contemporary proponents of input-oriented approaches base their theories on much less substantive, much more modest understandings of reason which emphasize its contingency and usually argue that reason follows from a particular kind of communicative rationality, from a particular way of arguing and decision-making process, rather than from the substantive content of a decision.

Such an idea of communicative rationality underpins John Rawls's concept of "public reason". Accordingly, in order to ensure that democratic decision-makers do not act in their self-interest, they need to justify their actions by reasons acceptable to all (public reasons), i. e. non-egoistic, non-idiosyncratic arguments of a moral, ethical, or pragmatic nature, such as common sense or widespread scientific insights. Also, they have to grant a right to be heard to those affected by the decision.[8]

Jürgen Habermas has given a more elaborate account of communicative reason in the political field. According to him, even though people might disagree on many aspects of the organization of society, everyday language devises a way for the integration of diverging views in societies: It enables communicative action.[9] Communicative action takes place when the participants in a conversation put forward public reasons in a Rawlsian sense. In an ideal setting, i. e. under the conditions of a fair, sincere discourse free from domination, such a conversation should lead to decisions that are rationally acceptable to everyone.[10] In the context of political decision-making, this approach requires societies to agree on an institutional framework that ensures deliberation and guarantees fundamental and participatory rights, while also allowing for bargaining and pragmatic compromise. The constitutional arrangements of liberal democracies which comprise professional parliaments, law-abiding administrations and judicial review (including judicial review of the acts of parliament) usually satisfy these conditions.[11]

---

[6] Kant (1797), § C [Introduction to the Doctrine of Right]; Rousseau (1762), liv. II, chap. III. In the terminology of Suttle, chapter "Debt, Default, and Two Liberal Theories of Justice", this would be categorized as a Humean approach to justice.

[7] On such limits of rationalism, *cf.* Albert (1991), pp. 35 f.

[8] Rawls (1993), pp. 212 f.; Rawls (1997), pp. 765–807.

[9] Habermas (1996), pp. 1–3. *See* Goldmann and Steininger, chapter "A Discourse Theoretical Approach to Sovereign Debt Restructuring: Towards a Democratic Financial Order".

[10] *Ibid.*, p. 43. This draws on Habermas (1981), pp. 384 f.

[11] Habermas (1996), chapter 4, in particular pp. 168 f.; *see also* chapter 9, pp. 430 f.

However, this account of modern input-oriented theories of democracy reveals some of their difficulties. First, they are based on a number of idealizations which seem to be at odds with social reality. For example, they assume that people act rationally and proffer non-egoistic justifications for certain political decisions.[12] Behavioural economics teaches that the presumption of rationality does not always hold true.[13] Second, these theories idealize the model of parliamentary representation. In reality, however, people usually only have one vote in order to express their preferences on a vast array of issues.[14] Third, input-oriented theories have a difficult time to achieve what would count as global justice by their own standards. As there is no parliamentary democracy at the global level, decisions acceptable to everyone might not come along.[15] Fourth, by focusing on the input aspects of political systems, those theories turn a blind eye on the actual outcomes of political decisions. They do not even provide a standard by which such outcomes could be measured.[16] One might find it difficult to convince the myriads of disenfranchised, socially disadvantaged people on the globe of the desirability of democracy if its theory does not show sufficient concern for their most fundamental needs.

In contrast to input-oriented approaches, output-oriented theories (also called consequentialist or comparative theories) do not risk the same level of idealizations or ignore the practical effects of policy-making. These theories argue that institutional arrangements should be made in order to maximize the aggregate outcome for society as a whole. The institutional arrangements suggested for this purpose often amount to some form of democracy. For Jeremy Bentham, measuring the aggregate outcome implied giving everyone's benefit equal weight.[17] John Stuart Mill also considered democracy as necessary for the maximization of aggregate happiness, which is his measure for outcomes. Democratic processes would be useful for determining what happiness is in the first place, which Mill considered a difficult task that presupposed freedom of opinion.[18]

Critics of such theories, however, point out that it is highly difficult to assess outputs. Whatever this concept may be, whether it is called happiness,[19] satisfaction,[20] or wealth-maximization,[21] it defies objective definition. Everything else would be paternalistic.[22] Interestingly enough, this problem has led to controversies

---

[12] For a fatal example of such optimism, *see* Heller (1930), p. 448 f.

[13] *Cf.* Jolls (2007).

[14] Sen (2009), pp. 91 f. with reference to social choice theory.

[15] *Id.*, pp. 67 f.

[16] The difference principle advanced by Rawls (1972), p. 60, does not provide a standard which would allow a decision as to which one of different policy options is better. It only narrows down the range of possible decisions. *See* Sen (2009), pp. 96 f.

[17] The principle of utility is defined in Bentham (1823 [repr. 1907]), p. 2.

[18] Mill (1859 [2006]), pp. 71 f.

[19] Bentham (1823 [repr. 1907]).

[20] Hourani (1956).

[21] Posner (1979), pp. 103–140, 103 f.

[22] Möllers (2008), p. 22.

even within the comparative camp. Thus, Karl Marx accused Bentham of a lack of consideration for the difficulties involved in establishing what people really want[23]—only to end up with an even more paternalistic theory. Mill's theory advocates freedom of expression for exactly that reason,[24] while Hayek expressed scepticism about the possibility to reconcile democracy and economic liberalism.[25]

2.2 A Compromise? Amartya Sen's Capabilities Approach

Given the difficulties implied in either of the two mentioned perspectives, it seems tempting to produce a theory of democracy that combines the strengths and avoids the flaws of both strands of theory. In his 2009 book on "The Idea of Justice", Amartya Sen advocates an approach that is grounded in the output-oriented tradition, but adopts ideas about the relationship between justice, communicative reasoning and democracy which have been developed in the transcendental camp, namely by Rawls and Habermas.

In order to measure and assess outcomes, Sen proposes the concept of capabilities. Capabilities describe the *actual* opportunity of individuals to pursue their objectives, not only the mere theoretical possibility to do so—which matters for liberal, input-oriented theories.[26] This is what Sen calls the "opportunity aspect" of freedom. Further, capabilities stand for the actual capacity to choose between different objectives. Individuals should have an effective choice between different objectives. They do not have an effective choice between different objectives if the only option available is the one they would have chosen anyway. This is what Sen calls the "process aspect" of freedom.[27] The concept of capabilities thus provides an outcome measure, but one which is focused on the idea of individual autonomy. This aspect of Sen's theory addresses the most serious criticism of comparative approaches, that of paternalism. At this point, Amartya Sen disagrees with Martha Nussbaum's concept of capabilities.[28] Instead of some notion of basic human entitlements, Sen's starting point is individual autonomy, which he considers an *a priori* value.[29] Capabilities are to be understood as open-textured measures for outcomes defined on the basis of individual autonomy.

---

[23] Marx (1887), chapter 24, section 5. Marx makes this point quite clear by calling Bentham "that insipid, pedantic, leather-tongued oracle of the ordinary bourgeois intelligence of the 19th century" (*id.*).

[24] Mill (1859 [2006]).

[25] Sceptical: Hayek (1979 [ed. 2003]), pp. 404 f. (chapter 16); on this complex issue, *see* Iversen (2006), pp. 601–623.

[26] *E.g.* the concept of primary goods in Rawls (1972), p. 62. On the difference, *see* Da Silva (2012), pp. 54–66, 57–58.

[27] Sen (2009), pp. 228 f.; Sen (2005), pp. 151–166.

[28] Nussbaum (2004), pp. 3–18.

[29] Sen (2009), p. 299.

Sen claims that democracies are conducive to the enjoyment of capabilities because they enable and foster public reasoning. This argument proceeds in three steps.

First, Sen argues that public reasoning is indispensable in order to agree on the capabilities a given society should guarantee and how they should be weighted.[30] In contrast to Nussbaum's concept of capabilities[31] and to Rawls' concept of public goods,[32] Sen does not provide a fixed list of capabilities, which would be tantamount to a one-size-fits-all concept of distributive justice. He recommends keeping the issue deliberately open and to submit it to democratic decision-making based on public reasoning.[33] That would ensure that such distributive decisions are ethically acceptable in pluralistic societies. As concerns decisions whose effects transcend borders, the process of public reasoning needs to include the views of all those affected by them, whether they are members of a given society or not.[34] Such an open, deliberative process would also reduce the risk that vested interests tilt the decision in their favour.[35] In all these respects, Sen's theory comprises an idea of ideal discourse. This brings it into close proximity of Habermas's discourse theory and serves as a reminder that that one should probably not overstretch the difference between transcendental and comparative approaches.[36] Nevertheless, Sen shows more awareness of the limits of institutional design. He therefore prefers flexible stakeholder participation over representative institutions.[37]

Second, once it has been decided which capabilities are desirable, Sen argues that public reasoning enhances the realization of these capabilities. Although public reasoning does not necessarily lead to the complete realization of all capabilities, it might at least prevent severe, "clearly remediable injustices".[38] By way of example, Sen recalls that famines in rural India (as well as in other parts of the world) disappeared with the establishment of democratic government and public reasoning.[39] He attributes this effect to various virtues of public reasoning: Public reasoning requires *transparency* and ensures that crucial information about risks for, or the preferences and needs of, different groups of society gets passed on to the decision-makers.[40] It also fosters the *accountability* of governments which need to publicly justify their decisions, whether or not they face re-election. Further, the *media* and educational institutions may increase the quality and reach of public reasoning.[41]

---

[30] *Id.*, pp. 17, 241 f., 326.

[31] Nussbaum (2004).

[32] Rawls (1972), p. 62; Da Silva (2012).

[33] Sen (2009), p. 233.

[34] *Id.*, pp. 124 f., 155 f.

[35] *Id.*, pp. 39 f., 122; Sen (2005), pp. 151–166, 163.

[36] In this sense, *see* Biondo (2012), pp. 555–577.

[37] For an interesting theory on how to realize the participation of stakeholders, *see* Macdonald (2008), pp. 139 f.

[38] Sen (2009), p. ii.

[39] *Id.*, pp. 338–343.

[40] *Id.*, p. 232.

[41] *Id.*, pp. 37, 335 f.

Although Sen developed this line of reasoning with respect to developing countries, there is no reason to assume that it would not apply universally. Rather, it resonates with theoretical studies which emphasize the importance of public reasoning or of the synonymous concept of deliberation for economic regulation.[42]

Third, as the previous step already reveals, there is an innate connection between public reasoning and democracy. Proper public reasoning which enables both the determination of capabilities in ways that respect individual autonomy, and their protection against remediable catastrophes, requires a society which is based on transparency, participation and meaningful dialogue involving all parts of society. Sen believes that such public reasoning is only possible in democracies.[43] One might add that democracies usually also endorse the idea of freedom that underlies the very idea of capabilities. Democracy is therefore a preferable form of government. Sen goes to great lengths to demonstrate that democracy and public reasoning are not as culturally contingent as one might think.[44]

While I do not pretend that Sen's theory is the better way, or the only one, of understanding democracy and its relationship with social justice, this approach devises a useful and defensible theory about the relationship between democracy and people's actual living conditions. Since this is the central interest of this contribution, Sen's theory seems to be a promising pick.

3 Doubts About the Performance of Democracies

The recent global financial crisis provides the opportunity to carry out a reality check on the optimistic account of democracy as a capability-enhancing system of government. The crisis likely has led to a decline in the level of capability enjoyment of certain segments of the population in the democracies most affected by it, including the United States and certain parts of Western, Central, and Southern Europe, such as Greece, Ireland, Italy, Spain, Portugal, but also France, Germany, and the UK. At first sight, such a hypothesis seems plausible given the manifold anecdotal evidence about foreclosures, layoffs, and the severe consequences of austerity in states facing precarious debt levels as a consequence of the crisis. To prove the decline in capabilities empirically, however, would require an enormously complex research methodology, both conceptually and with regard to the necessary econometric data. This would exceed the scope of a contribution which is in the first place theoretical. The following lines therefore only attempt to corroborate the hypothesis about a widespread capability decline in the wake of the crisis and to elaborate on some conceptual issues in this regard, not to prove it in strictly causal terms.

A first conceptual hurdle relates to the definition of capabilities. How do the states most affected by the crisis define their desired level of capability enjoyment?

---

[42] Black (2000), pp. 597–614; Black (2001), pp. 33–58; van Aaken et al. (2004).

[43] *Id.*, p. 326.

[44] *Id.*, pp. 327 f.

Constitutions define freedoms and liberties predominantly in negative terms. Exceptions are the economic, social, and cultural rights guaranteed by the respective International Covenant. Also, some states guarantee their citizens a minimum income at subsistence level.[45] However, while the right to education enjoys wide acceptance,[46] the actual provision of educational services by states and their quality varies widely.

Despite these definitional issues, the enjoyment of capabilities in liberal, market-oriented economies seems to depend by and large on a number of decisive factors, no matter how one defines capabilities in detail. A first crucial factor is employment. It enables people to care for themselves. Second, official resources enable the government to secure a high level of capability enjoyment to their citizens. Third, per capita GDP provides at least a rough estimate of both private and public resources, hence of the level of capabilities enjoyment. Amartya Sen has rightly pointed out the risks involved in overreliance on GDP, in particular because it has no sensitivity for distributional inequalities. It therefore needs to be complemented by distributional data like the Gini coefficient. Fourth, rising sovereign debt levels over the economic cycle indicate decreasing official resources in the long run, leading to decreasing resources for the provision of capabilities to the disadvantaged parts of society, unless offset by long-term increases in growth.

On the basis of these indicators, the financial crisis turns out to be an event which has most likely reduced the level of capabilities enjoyment in the most affected states. The decline in respect of the mentioned factors exceeded normal cyclical downturns and in some respects has been worse than any other event since the Great Depression. Many states like the US and certain parts of Europe have experienced protracted increases in unemployment.[47] More countries than in any other crisis experienced significant GDP declines in the two years subsequent to the 2007 banking crisis.[48] At the same time, data on wealth distribution shows that, after a short decline in 2008, the well-off have increased their fraction of the entire wealth in most affected states during the last years.[49] At the same time, sovereign debt has

---

[45] Art. 11, International Covenant on Economic, Social and Cultural Rights; Bundesverfassungsgericht [BVerfG] [Federal Constitutional Court], Case No. 1 BvL 14/76, 45 Entscheidungen des Bundesverfassungsgerichts [BVerfGE] 187, 228 (21 Jun 1977).

[46] Art. 13, International Covenant on Economic, Social and Cultural Rights; Art. 2, First Protocol to the European Convention for the Protection of Human Rights and Fundamental Freedoms.

[47] *E.g.* Eurostat (2017); Bureau of Labor Statistics (2017).

[48] Reinhart and Reinhart (2010), pp. 10–11.

[49] Piketty (2014), tables on pp. 430 f; OECD (2014). Wealth distribution is measured by Gini coefficients, whereby a coefficient of 0.0 stands for full equality and a coefficient for 1 for a state in which one single person owns all wealth. In 2000, Gini coefficients for wealth distribution in developed countries were rarely below 0.6 (Davies et al. 2006, p. 50). In the United States, inequality in wealth distribution decreased from about the Great Depression until the 1970s. It has increased since then, particularly during the 1980s (Cagetti and De Nardi 2008, pp. 285–313, 291–292). In Germany, the Gini coefficient for wealth inequality rose from 0.777 in 2002 to 0.799, or, depending on the calculation method, to 0.8092 in 2007 (Bach et al. 2011, p. 11). For an analysis of rising inequality in post-crisis Germany, *see* Wehler (2012), pp. 65 f. For a Europe-wide analysis of current high levels of wealth inequality, *see* Skopek et al. (2011).

reached almost unprecedented levels in the US and numerous European states. With little hope for this debt to be offset by an equivalent growth level at least in the near future, one may tentatively conclude that the financial crisis and the debt crisis have endangered the enjoyment of capabilities by the less advantaged citizens in the most affected democracies.

Thus, contrary to Sen's assumption, democracies do not seem to have fared better during the crisis. More than that, the crisis might reveal a structural conflict between democracy and a free market economy. On a theoretical level, this has prompted Wolfgang Streeck to suggest that "democratic capitalism" is impossible because it leads to continuous struggle between interest groups, either ending up in a non-democratic market economy serving the interests of the rich, or in a democratic welfare state violating the rules of the market economy. In the decades preceding the recent financial crisis, he argues, the pendulum swung towards non-democratic neoliberalism which evoked policies of fiscal austerity and deregulation. This compelled the working classes to turn to commercial credit in order to finance their standard of life, thereby creating first a private debt crisis and later a public debt crisis because of government bailouts.[50]

Philip Lipscy even goes as far as to claim that there is a significant correlation between democratic regimes as defined by the Polity IV database[51] and the propensity of banking crises.[52] Accordingly, between 1800 and 2009, states classified as democratic in the Polity IV database experienced a banking crisis on average every 18 years, autocracies only every 65 years.[53] Lipscy tests these results for certain explanatory factors, namely the ability of democratic regimes to borrow more cheaply, thereby creating bubbles more easily; a higher level of transparency which might trigger bank runs; shorter time-horizons of government executives which might incentivize risky policies; greater liberalization of financial markets because it serves the idea of liberty; and contagion trough open markets.[54] Only financial liberalization and open markets emerge as significant factors explaining the propensity of democracies for the onset of financial crises.[55] Thus, there are fundamental empirical and theoretical challenges for Amartya Sen's thesis.

[50] Streeck (2011a), pp. 5–29; Streeck (2014). *See also* the contributions in Schäfer and Streeck (2013), especially the concluding chapter. For a related approach that focuses on the transformations of political parties in the wake of democratic capitalism, *see* Crouch (2004).

[51] *Cf.* http://www.systemicpeace.org/polity/polity4.htm.

[52] Lipscy (2011), p. 30 (table 2).

[53] *Id.*, p. 18.

[54] *Id.*, pp. 7 f.

[55] *Id.*, p. 34.

4 The Crisis as a Result of Deficient Public Reasoning

4.1 Hypothesis: Correlation Between Financial Crises and Deficient Public Reasoning

The findings about the weak performance of democratic states send an alarming signal. They challenge the promise of democracy according to Sen. Is democracy after all not able to hold its promise to safeguard capabilities better than autocracies? I suppose that the contrary is true. My optimism about the capacity of democracy has to do with Sen's idea of democracy as a system of government that allows for public reasoning. If this is taken seriously, there is little reason to doubt the value of democracy to fend off financial crises. Having set out the theoretical argument for democracy understood as public reasoning, this part is mainly empirical. I first reject Lipscy's argument before I set out how I want to empirically corroborate my claim by a numer of qualitative arguments.

First, as regards Lipscy's skepticism about the performance of democracies, it relies on a highly problematic definition of democracy that ignores the role of public reasoning. Lipscy uses the concept of democracy as it has been defined by the Polity IV project. This definition emphasizes formal elections, political participation and US-style executive constraints as the main characteristics of democracies. By contrast, the Polity IV ratings do not take into account data on civil liberties, and blatantly ignore the influence of international and regional human rights courts,[56] although both might be crucial factors for the possibility to engage in public reasoning. The results of Polity IV bespeak the questionable wisdom of its methodology. Thus, Polity IV rates Greece and Italy as "full democracies", while countries as different as Brazil, France, Ukraine and Kenya find themselves in the inferior category of "democracies". The United States, by contrast, reached the status of a "full democracy" in 1871 and has held it ever since, no matter the lack of universal suffrage and the situation of African Americans at the time, the dire situation of the working class during the Lochner era, or the fact that election fraud was commonplace up until the New Deal era.[57] Those looking for an explanation for the classifications in the country specific assessment reports published on the Polity IV website will be disappointed by short texts containing rough descriptions of the political system and brief summaries of recent political gossip instead of reasoned decisions as to why political participation in a specific country was rated with, say, 9 instead of 10 points.[58]

Second, to state that Lipscy's findings are problematic of course does not automatically imply that Sen's assumptions are true. One needs to prove them, or at least show their empirical plausibility. The remainder of this chapter attempts to

[56] Polity IV Project (2016), pp. 12 f.

[57] P. Krugman (2007), pp. 21 f.

[58] *Cf.* the country reports included in the Polity IV Project (2010).

provide some qualitative support for Sen's assumptions. While it is difficult to show a relation between democracy and the non-occurrence of crises, as non-events are impossible to measure, it is far easier to investigate a relation between the crisis and deficits in public reasoning. In fact, a number of well-established, important factors for the banking crisis starting in 2007 can be understood as instances of insufficient public reasoning (Sect. 4.2). Likewise, deficits in public reasoning contributed to the sovereign debt crisis in Europe which followed the banking crisis (Sect. 4.3).

Again, some caveats are in order. The following analyzes only the financial crisis beginning in 2007. It therefore does not entail a general claim that financial crises result from insufficient public reasoning. Also, my analysis is qualitative, not quantitative, i. e. it is impossible to make broad generalizations on that basis. It only provides some clues why Sen might not have been wrong.

4.2 Public Reasoning and the Banking Crisis of 2007

By now, the causes of the banking crisis which started in 2007 with defaults in the money market and reached its peak in September 2008 with the insolvency of Lehman Brothers have been studied extensively. Certain root causes have been identified, with liberalization, unethical behavior, overly accommodating monetary politics[59] or irresponsible regulatory decisions allowing poor people to take out loans which they could not afford being among the more frequently mentioned candidates, although their precise interplay might still leave some questions open. Also, the reasons why the crisis hit so hard and spread so far and so quickly are relatively well understood.[60] I argue that some important factors that have been identified as responsible for the spread of the crisis can be understood as deficits in public reasoning.

4.2.1 Simplifying Indicators for Financial Regulation

In the years prior to the crisis, financial regulation and supervisors made broad use of simplifying indicators. As a consequence, supervisors took important decisions on the basis of insufficient information. In particular, supervisors relied excessively on microprudential indicators which aggregate complex fact-patterns into crude binary or numeric figures. Examples include capital requirements under the Basel II framework as well as the indicators used to calculate and verify them, such as credit ratings, stress tests, and accounting standards.

The minimum capital requirements concerning credit, market and operational risk stipulated in pillar 1 of Basel II are important tools for prudential supervision.

---

[59] *E.g.* Taylor (2008), pp. 1–18.

[60] *See, e.g.*, National Commission on the Causes of the Financial and Economic Crisis in the United States (2011); Acharya et al. (2009), pp. 1–56.

They provide a global minimum standard and establish a level-playing field. Nevertheless, they are only as good as the data which is used for their calculation. Under the so-called standardized approach, credit risk is measured on the basis of credit ratings.[61] Numerous studies have revealed not only the conflicts of interest inherent in the business model of rating agencies, but also the methodological problems undermining many ratings.[62] Non-impartial, intransparent and insufficiently granular credit ratings in turn led to serious misjudgments about the regulatory capital necessary for certain assets such as mortgage-backed securities. Thus, serious flaws in one indicator infected another indicator, leading in the end to financial supervision that lacked the public reasoning necessary to properly discharge of its task.

One might object to this conclusion that pillar 2 of the Basel II framework urges supervisors to go beyond the mere mathematical calculation of regulatory minimum capital under pillar 1 and examine exposure to risks which pillar 1 does not, or does not fully, take into account.[63] For example, capital requirements for banks under pillar 1 of Basel II did not include provisions against liquidity risk. This was entirely left to pillar 2.[64] However, in apparent reliance on the wisdom of the market, supervisors turned a blind eye on such risks and did not properly double-check for liquidity risks, amongst others. Again, supervisory decisions suffered from a lack of information that made them unaware of risks for the public interest. The consequences were fatal. Some authors claim that Northern Rock, Bear Stearns, and Lehman Brothers would not have experienced the sort of difficulties they did had their liquidity risks been taken better care of.[65]

Internal models for the calculation of regulatory capital and stress tests are another instance of indicators which simplify the information available to supervisors and hamper public reasoning. The Basel II framework partly "privatized" supervision by allowing certain banks to use their own, internal risk assessment for the calculation of capital requirements relating to certain risks.[66] Despite their mathematical sophistication, such internal models suffer from historical bias. Most of these models use econometric assumptions, such as value-at-risk, which projects capital requirements on the basis of past losses. However, such models use only a limited amount of historical data for downside events, which might not go back far enough in order to cover rare events of exceptional distress ("fat tails").[67] For this reason, Basel II obliges banks to carry out stress tests as an antidote against the shortcomings of internal models, as well as potential self-interested abuse.[68]

---

[61] Basel Committee (2006), para. 50 f.

[62] *E.g.* Altman et al. (2011), pp. 443–467.

[63] Basel II, para. 719 f.

[64] Basel II, para. 741.

[65] Hanson et al. (2011), pp. 3–28, 12–13.

[66] Basel II, para. 211 f. (regarding the Internal Ratings Based Approach to credit risk); *id.*, para. 718(lxx) f. (regarding the Internal Models Approach to market risk).

[67] In more detail Aragonés et al. (2001), pp. 44–49.

[68] Basel II, para. 434 f. (concerning the Internal Ratings Based Approach to credit risk); Basel Committee (2011), para. 718(lxxvii) f. (concerning the Internal Models Approach to market risk).

In a stress test, a financial firm calculates the value of a given asset portfolio under adverse economic and financial conditions which are unlikely to occur, but not entirely unrealistic. Ironically, though, those stress tests often fell victim to similar problems.[69] For example, financial firms used stress test scenarios that were not adverse enough. They simulated past crises based on limited historical data and ignored the possibility that future crises might look differently, in particular because of financial innovation.[70] Thus, internal models and stress tests led to supervisory non-intervention on the basis of highly problematic information. While these tools were destined to make supervision more effective by delegating it to those who were supposed to know the risks best, it hid those risks from supervisory scrutiny and discouraged supervisors from second-guessing the results of internal risk calculations and stress tests. That allowed regulated institutions to hold less capital.

Off-balance sheet items caused further deficits in public reasoning. Once financial firms removed assets from their balance sheet and packed them into so-called special purpose vehicles or conduits, they received capital relief. Basel I required zero regulatory capital for off-balance sheet vehicles, whereas under Basel II, relaxed capital requirements applied, sometimes amounting no more than a risk weight of 20 %.[71] However, those reduced requirements did not take sufficiently into account the fact that financial firms usually extended liquidity and credit enhancement to their off-balance sheet vehicles. This improved the ratings of the vehicles, but it also involved risks, namely the risk that the assets would return to the balance sheet of the financial firm in case the vehicle came into trouble.[72] This is what happened during the crisis, sometimes merely on the basis of implicit guarantees which banks as the sponsors of a vehicle could not escape for reputational reasons.[73] Again, the chosen indicator was misleading. Balance sheets were supposed to provide accurate information about a bank's liabilities, which they fell short of.

Thus, the domestic and international legal frameworks for financial regulation as well as the approach chosen by many supervisors relied heavily on sometimes crudely simplifying indicators for the assessment of complex fact patterns. The information thus retrieved was incomplete, misleading, purporting a situation of financial stability that discouraged closer supervisory scrutiny. The ensuing decisions suffered from a lack of public reasoning. A broad look behind these indicators and formal requirements at additional risks not reflected in them might have revealed some of the risks.

The contrasting example of Canada underlines the crucial role of public reasoning: Despite international pressure for liberalization, Canadian regulators and supervisors exercised tight oversight over their banks since the early 1990s, second-guessing their internal risk calculations in in-depth examinations including the

---

[69] On analogous problems in the context of supervisory stress tests, *see* Goldmann (2012b).

[70] Basel Committee (2009), pp. 8 f.

[71] Basel II, para. 82 f; for credit risk mitigation through collateral, insurance, or else, *see also* para. 109 f.

[72] Acharya and Schnabl (2009), pp. 83–100, 85–87.

[73] Richardson et al. (2011), pp. 469–489, 473.

board and all supervisory authorities. This comes very close to the ideal of public reasoning, which does not have to be carried out "in the public", since business confidentiality needs to be respected, but which should include representatives of all those affected and exclude decisions justifiable only by self-interest. In the case at hand, it provided Canadian banks with qualitatively better capital and made them very resilient against the 2007 crisis.[74]

4.2.2 Non-inclusive Decision-Making: Fragmented Regulation and Supervision

While financial markets became more and more integrated during the decades preceding the recent crisis, the regulatory and supervisory framework remained characterized by territorial, horizontal and vertical fragmentation. This led to decisions that did not include the views of those affected, e.g. by creating negative externalities for them.

The regulation of financial markets mostly lay in the hands of non-inclusive institutions which served the interests of their constituencies, but not necessarily the interests of all those affected by their decisions. On the international level, organizations with limited membership and little transparency such as the Basel Committee or IOSCO have been responsible for a great deal of the regulation. Before 2009, the Basel Committee was an exclusive group of central bankers and bank supervisors from 13 developed economies.[75] Nevertheless, their standards affected people in many countries, thanks to integrated financial markets.

To the extent that financial regulation remained subject to the discretion of national legislatures and regulators, it enabled them to reduce regulatory requirements to create a competitive advantage for the institutions under their jurisdiction and incentivize regulatory arbitrage. That went as far as attracting institutions which did not unfold any substantial economic activity within the jurisdiction concerned. For example, Lehman Brothers channelled most of its non-retail products through its Swiss subsidiary Lehman International Finance AG, a multibillion company with only 14 employees. Under Swiss law, Lehman was not subject to any capital requirements because it did not engage in retail business in Switzerland.[76] This enabled higher leverage and increased the risks for market participants abroad, including the retail investors who eventually bought the securities. The example shows that fragmented regulators might take decisions which fail to meet Amartya Sen's standard of public reasoning because they exclude the views of those who might be affected.

---

[74] On the Canadian approach to regulation, *see* Konzelmann et al. (2010); on Canada's performance due to better quality capital, *see* Ratnovski and Huang (2009), p. 16.

[75] Until 2009, only Belgium, Canada, France, Germany, Italy, Japan, Luxembourg, the Netherlands, Spain, Sweden Switzerland, the UK, and the US were members of the Basel Committe.

[76] Severin (2010).

Mutual acceptance regimes constitute a similar case of deficient public reasoning caused by fragmented decision-making structures. They enable regulators to create externalities in another jurisdiction which serve their own industry and thus their own power interests. Examples from within the European Union abound. Lehman Brothers preferred the Irish supervisor for its light touch approach, but once the securities thus approved had received a "European passport",[77] they were marketable throughout the union. And the freedom of establishment required European supervisors to accept on their territory branches of banks sitting in other member states, even if they were insufficiently supervised, as in the case of Icelandic banks.[78] Outside mutual recognition regimes, the "equivalence" standard, by which supervisors in one jurisdiction recognize that an institution doing business in its jurisdiction is adequately supervised in another jurisdiction, had similar effects. The European Union eventually introduced the requirement that financial conglomerates are subject to consolidated supervision to be recognized as being under equivalent supervision.[79] But the requirement turned out to be rather undemanding. The "light-touch" approach of the Securities and Exchange Commission, which granted capital relief in exchange for voluntary supervision, sufficed to meet the "equivalence" standard and easily transformed unregulated investment banks into "consolidated supervised entity".[80] Mutual acceptance regimes and equivalence standards thus allowed supervisors to expand their reach over other jurisdictions without paying due regard to their legitimate public interests, resulting in deficient public reasoning.

Apart from regulatory arbitrage, the supervision of integrated global financial markets by a large number of dispersed, non-inclusive supervisors with limited competencies also led to a situation in which no-one had an overview of the entire system. It is by now well understood that the lack of systemic (or macroprudential) oversight, on the domestic as well as the global level, facilitated the breakout of the crisis. Supervisors focused on the microprudential supervision of individual firms, but they were neither required to take the perspective of the financial system as a whole and worry about its stability, nor did they have the requisite information.[81] In addition, the composition of pre-crisis supervisors was probably not inclusive enough to allow for successful systemic supervision and to avoid regulatory arbitrage and turf protection.

[77] Directive 2003/71/EC of the European Parliament and of the Council of 4 November 2003, OJ L 345/64, 31 December 2003.

[78] Financial Services Authority (2009), pp. 36 f.

[79] Art. 18, Directive 2002/87/EC of the European Parliament and of the Council of 16 December 2002, OJ L 35/1, 11 February 2003.

[80] "Alternative Net Capital Requirements for Broker-Dealers That Are Part of Consolidated Supervised Entities", SEC Release No. 34-49830, 20 August 2004.

[81] *See only* Squam Lake Working Group (2008); Scott (2010), pp. 763–778. This criticism is all but new. *Cf.* Tietmeyer (1999), p. 4.

4.3 Public Reasoning and the Sovereign Debt Crisis Since 2010

On the one hand, the sovereign debt crisis which has struck European states since the about 2010 was a direct consequence of the preceding banking crisis. On the other hand, it did not come out of the blue. Rather, it was fuelled by a preexisting high level of sovereign debt.[82] As in the case of the banking crisis, deficits in public reasoning may have contributed to the buildup of such debt and to unawareness of the looming risks.

4.3.1 Misleading Indicators for Sovereign Debt Management

From the beginning of the Euro, misleading indicators contributed to the accumulation of debt of an eventually unsustainable level in some European states. Since the European Monetary Union (EMU) was established on the premise that member states would not be liable for the debt of each other (Art. 125 TFEU), and given that exchange rates and interest rates as mechanisms for the absorption of macroeconomic imbalances are unavailable in a monetary union, the EMU presupposed (1) macroeconomic and fiscal convergence as an entry requirement,[83] and (2) effective mechanisms for the prevention and correction of imbalances arising after the introduction of, or accession to, the single currency.[84] However, the attainment of both these goals was hampered, amongst other causes, by a lack of public reasoning due to misleading indicators.

Regarding the convergence criteria, it appears that some member states of the EMU trimmed their figures prior to their accession with methods which could be characterized as doubtful. For example, among other measures, Italy introduced a special tax in 1997 in order to reduce its government debt. However, the tax merely advanced tax receipts from future years to 1997 and therefore did not substantially alleviate its debt burden. The effective functioning of the preventive and corrective mechanisms in the frame of the Growth and Stability Pact suffered from similar data problems. After the 2009 Greek elections, it turned out that the outgoing Greek government had dramatically understated its budget deficit, which eventually amounted to 15.4 % instead of 6–8 % as previously projec ted.[85] But even so, markets were slow at reacting to this news. It took Moody's until December 2009 to downgrade Greek government debt from A1, the fourth highest rating which classifies short-term debt into prime-1 tier, to grade A2.[86] Those examples

[82] The situation is different for Ireland and Spain, which had relatively low levels of sovereign debt before the crisis, but had to come to the rescue of banks at a time when their real economy was ailing.

[83] Art. 140 TFEU; Protocol No 13 on the Convergence Criteria, OJ C 115/281, 09.05.2008.

[84] Arts. 121, 126 TFEU.

[85] For a description of the statistical difficulties, *see* European Commission (2010).

[86] Moody's (2009).

are not trivial and reveal a structural transparency problem. As Reinhart and Rogoff observe, the intransparency of government debt or guarantees has been a serious, epidemic problem since long.[87] The problem does not stop with governments, but also extends over forecast errors on the part of the International Monetary Fund.[88] It is questionable whether government interventions such as prohibitions of covered short sales of sovereign debt fight speculation more effectively than they hamper price discovery.[89]

4.3.2 Non-inclusive Decision-Making

Apart from misleading indicators, the European sovereign debt crisis was spurred by non-inclusive decision-making. One aspect of this the fact that the economic policy coordination envisaged by Art. 121 TFEU, according to which governments should coordinate their economic policy through broad guidelines, did not work. That concerns both current account deficits and surpluses. For example, after the introduction of the Euro, Germany froze or even reduced the cost of labor, while it increased in other, less competitive states. In this way, domestic politics caused externalities for the entire Euro area. They took decisions without effective involvement of, and regard for, all those affected.

More serious is the intergenerational problem. It plays a role not only in the European Union, but in literally every state with a significant level of public debt. The problem consists in the fact that decisions on the assumption of public debt affect not only current tax payers, creditors, and recipients of government funds, but also future generations which need to pay it back. There is thus an intergenerational issue of inclusiveness. Metaphorically speaking, the assumption of sovereign debt amounts to a contract at the expense of a third party. Precautions taken to counterbalance the asymmetry and include the interests of future generations, such as balanced budget rules, were fraught with a lot of ideology and caused mixed practical effects.[90]

5 Conclusion

It seems that deficits in public reasoning played a role in the emergence of the 2007 banking crisis and the subsequent European sovereign debt crisis. Supervisors (as well as market participants) lulled in the belief that the system was sound due to misleading or lacking information. At the same time, they took decisions that were

---

[87] Reinhart and Rogoff (2009), pp. xxxi f.

[88] Blanchard and Leigh (2013).

[89] *Cf.* Brenner and Subrahmanyam (2009), pp. 269–275.

[90] On their ideological underpinnings, *see* Biebricher, chapter "Neoliberalism and Law: The Case of the Constitutional Balanced-Budget Amendment"; Wagschal (2011), pp. 352–382.

not sufficiently other-regarding and did not take into account the views of those negatively affected by them, who were often in another jurisdiction.

The analysis provided in this chapter is too limited to receive definitive, reliable results. It would be necessary to extend the analysis and to examine, for example, the South American debt crises of the 1980s and 1990s, taking especially into account the fact that the affected states had sometimes accumulated considerable debt before they turned into democracies. Nevertheless, the identified deficits in public reasoning concern some widely recognized causes of the crisis since 2007. Tentatively, one might therefore argue that the crisis is not necessarily the visible result of the incompatibility of democracy, market economies and globalization. Rather, it appears as the result of, amongst others, deficient public reasoning that was clearly remediable.

It should be added that the concept of public reasoning casts doubt on Lipscy's assumptions about the alleged correlation of financial crises and democratic government. The two explanatory hypotheses for which he finds empirical confirmation, liberalization and open markets, are not necessarily outstanding examples for advances in public reasoning. Rather, the liberalization and opening of markets in the 1980s and 1990s occurred in a rather undemocratic fashion. Lipscy rightly points to the pressure for liberalization exercised by Western states through, e.g., the Washington Consensus.[91] Interestingly, a full-scale democracy like Canada could resist this pressure better than some autocratic regimes. Also, the opening of financial markets led to regulatory and supervisory fragmentation, which gave regulators, supervisors and market participants the opportunity to produce negative externalities for those outside their respective jurisdiction. On the other hand, Lipscy's finding that increased transparency through democratic governance does not lead to a higher propensity for banking crises[92] is fully in line with the theory of public reasoning.

This tentative conclusion, if confirmed by further research, has immediate normative implications for the design and application of the regulatory framework to be adopted in order to confront the causes of the crisis. For example, it could be taken as a guideline for the regulation of credit rating agencies. Indeed, the European regulation on rating agencies aims at increasing transparency.[93] Also, supervisors should carefully examine the Canadian model and might be well-advised to adopt similar practices. Most importantly, however, the current regulatory and supervisory fragmentation needs to be overcome. The G20 has tried to function as an umbrella institution, but it is neither inclusive nor particularly transparent, and its success seems moderate so far.

Regarding the issue of sovereign debt, the above considerations emphasize the urgent need for greater transparency. Decisions to incur debt or extend credit should be taken on the basis of sound fiscal data, and by institutions representing the views of all those affected. The UNCTAD Principles on Promoting Responsible Sovereign

---

[91] Lipscy (2011), p. 23.

[92] *Id.*, p. 21.

[93] Regulation (EC) No. 1060/2009 of the European Parliament and of the Council of 16 September 2009 on Credit Rating Agencies, OJ L 302/1, 17 September 2009.

Lending and Borrowing emphasize the significance of transparency in the process of lending and the management of debt.[94] A number of states, especially in South America, have adopted fiscal responsibility laws for exactly this purpose.[95]

Beyond transparency, governments need to tackle the difficult issue of the inclusion of future generations. Since they cannot speak for themselves, one option is to implement substantive limits on sovereign borrowing. The UNCTAD Principles urge governments to weight the costs and benefits of borrowing.[96] On the domestic level, the debt crisis has spurred a lot of creativity regarding the design of deficit brakes which are strict enough to prevent excessive borrowing, and flexible enough to ensure that sudden shocks can be absorbed.[97] Should bad come to worse and a government need to reschedule its debt, this should be done in a fair and inclusive setting involving all those affected.[98]

Certainly, all these measures provide little reassurance as to whether crises will actually be prevented or their consequences mitigated. But there is even less reason to believe that non-public, self-interested, intransparent reasoning will yield better results and enhance the enjoyment of capabilities by large parts of the population.

Acknowledgements For helpful comments I am deeply indebted to Armin von Bogdandy, Philipp Dann, Kevin Davis, Christoph Engel, Martin Hellwig, Robert Howse, Silvia Steininger, and the late Sarah P. Woo†.

References

Acharya VV, Schnabl P (2009) How banks played the leverage game. In: Acharya VV, Richardson M (eds) Restoring financial stability, pp 83–100. John Wiley & Sons, Hoboken, NY

Acharya VV, Philippon T, Richardson M, Roubini N (2009) A bird's-eye view – the financial crisis of 2007–2009: causes and remedies. In: Acharya VV, Richardson M (eds) Restoring financial stability, pp 1–56. John Wiley & Sons, Hoboken, NY

Albert H (1991) Traktat über kritische Vernunft, 5th edn. UTB, Stuttgart

Altman EI, Sabri Öncü T, Richardson M, Schmeits A, White LJ (2011) Regulation of rating agencies. In: Acharia VV, Cooley TF, Richardson M, Walter I (eds) Regulating wall street, pp 443–467. John Wiley & Sons, Hoboken, NY

Aragonés JR, Blanco C, Dowd K (2001) Incorporating stress tests into market risk modeling. Deriv Q 7(3): 44–49

Bach S, Beznoska M, Steiner V (2011) A wealth tax on the rich to bring down public debt? Revenue and distributional effects of a capital levy, SOEP Paper No. 397, p 11

Basel Committee (2006) International convergence of capital measurement and capital standards. Comprehensive Version, June 2006. https://www.bis.org/publ/bcbs128.pdf. Accessed 12 March 2018

---

[94] Principles 10, 11, and 13, UNCTAD (2012).

[95] *Cf.* Lienert (2010).

[96] Principle 14, UNCTAD (2012).

[97] Goldmann (2012a), pp. 25 f.

[98] *Cf.* Principles 7 and 15, UNCTAD (2012); *see also* Bogdandy and Goldmann (2013), pp. 39–70.

Basel Committee (2009) Principles for sound stress testing practices and supervision, January 2009. https://www.bis.org/publ/bcbs155.pdf. Accessed 12 March 2018
Basel Committee (2011) Revisions to the Basel II market risk framework. February 2011. https://www.bis.org/publ/bcbs193.pdf. Accessed 12 March 2018
Bentham J (1823 [repr. 1907]) An introduction to the principles of morals and legislation, 2nd edn p 2. W. Pickering, London
Biebricher T (2016) Neoliberalism and law: the case of the constitutional balanced-budget amendment. German LJ 17:835–856
Biondo F (2012) Comparative vs. transcendental approaches to justice: a misleading dichotomy in sen's the idea of justice. Ratio Juris 25:555–577
Black J (2000) Proceduralizing regulation: Part I. Oxf J Leg Stud 20:597–614
Black J (2001) Proceduralizing regulation: Part II. Oxf J Leg Stud 21:33–58
Blanchard O, Leigh D (2013) Growth forecast errors and fiscal multipliers. IMF Working Paper No. 1
Bogdandy AV, Goldmann M (2013) Sovereign debt restructurings as exercises of public authority: towards a decentralized sovereign insolvency law. In: Esposito C, Li Y, Bohoslavsky JP (eds) Sovereign debt restructurings as exercises of public authority: towards a decentralized sovereign insolvency law, pp 39–70. Oxford University Press, Oxford
Brenner M, Subrahmanyam MG (2009) Short selling. In: Acharya VV, Richardson M (eds) Restoring financial stability, pp 269–275. John Wiley & Sons, Hoboken, NJ
Bureau of Labor Statistics (2017) Labor force statistics from the current population survey, 13 May 2017. https://data.bls.gov/timeseries/LNS14000000. Accessed 12 March 2018
Cagetti M, De Nardi M (2008) Wealth inequality: data and models. Macroecon Dyn 12:285–313
Crouch C (2004) Post-democracy. John Wiley & Sons, Hoboken, NJ
Da Silva M (2012) Book review – Amartya Sen's the idea of justice (2009). German LJ 13:54–66
Davies JB, Sandstrom S, Shorrocks A, Wolff EN (2006) The world distribution of household wealth, p 50. World Institute for Developement Economics Research, Helsinki
European Commission (2010) Methodological issues, COM(2010) 1 final Annex 1. http://ec.europa.eu/eurostat/documents/4187653/6404656/COM_2010_report_greek_annex_1/4b10d-2ba-7a93-4c18-b50f-957f2ad3af8a. Accessed 9 Jan 2018
Eurostat (2017) Unemployment by sex and age. http://appsso.eurostat.ec.europa.eu/nui/show.do?query=BOOKMARK_DS-055418_QID_-2627F2CD_UID_-3F171EB0&layout=-TIME,C,X,0;GEO,L,Y,0;AGE,L,Z,0;UNIT,L,Z,1;SEX,L,Z,2;INDICATORS,C,Z,3;&zSelection=DS-055418INDICATORS,OBS_FLAG;DS-055418AGE,TOTAL;DS-055418SEX-,T;DS-055418UNIT,PC_ACT;&rankName1=TIME_1_0_0_0&rankName2=UNIT_1_2_-1_2&rankName3=GEO_1_2_0_1&rankName4=AGE_1_2_-1_2&rankName5=INDICATORS_1_2_-1_2&rankName6=SEX_1_2_-1_2&sortC=ASC_-1_FIRST&rStp=&cStp=&rDCh=&cDCh=&rDM=true&cDM=true&footnes=false&empty=false&wai=-false&time_mode=ROLLING&time_most_recent=false&lang=EN&cfo=%23%23%23%2C%23%23%23.%23%23%23. Accessed 9 Jan 2018
Financial Services Authority (2009) The turner review, March 2009
Goldmann M (2012a) Responsible sovereign lending and borrowing: the view from domestic jurisdictions. Comparative Survey Written for the United Nations Conference on Trade and Development. http://unctad.org/en/PublicationsLibrary/gdsddf2012misc3_en.pdf. Accessed 12 March 2018
Goldmann M (2012b) Stress testing stress tests: challenging the authority of indicators. Paper Presented at the VIIIth GAL Conference, 14–15 June 2012, Rome. Available at SSRN http://ssrn.com/abstract=2083594. Accessed 9 Jan 2018
Goldmann M, Steininger S (2016) A discourse theoretical approach to sovereign debt restructuring: towards a democratic financial order. German LJ 17:709–746
Habermas J (1981) Theorie des kommunikativen Handelns, vol 1, p 384. Suhrkamp, Frankfurt a. M.
Habermas J (1996) Between facts and norms, pp 1–3. MIT Press, Cambridge, MA
Hanson S, Kashyap AK, Stein J (2011) A macroprudential approach to financial regulation. J Econ Perspect 25:3–28

Hayek FA (1979 [ed. 2003]) Recht, Gesetz und Freiheit, p 404. Mohr Siebeck, Tübingen
Heller H (1930) Rechtsstaat oder Diktatur? In: Heller H (ed) Gesammelte Schriften, vol. 2, pp 443–462. Mohr Siebeck, Tübingen
Hourani GF (1956) Ethical value. University of Michigan Press, Ann Arbour, MI
Iversen T (2006) Democracy and capitalism. In: Weingast BR, Wittmann DA (eds) The Oxford handbook of political economy, pp 601–623. Oxford University Press, Oxford
Jolls C (2007) Behavioral law and economics. National Bureau of Economic Research Working Paper No. 12879
Kant I (1797) Metaphysik der Sitten. Ripol Classic, Moskau
Konzelmann S, Fovargue-Davies M, Schnyder G (2010) Varieties of liberalism: anglo-saxon capitalism in crisis? Centre for Business Research Working Paper No. 403
Krugman P (2007) The conscience of a liberal p 21. Norton, New York
Lienert I (2010) Should advanced countries adopt a fiscal responsibility law? IMF Working Paper WP/10/254
Lipscy PY (2011) Democracy and the financial crisis. Paper Presented at the Annual Meeting of the International Political Economy Society, 12 Nov 2011. https://ssrn.com/abstract=1900126. Accessed 9 Jan 2018
Macdonald T (2008) Global stakeholder democracy. Power and representation beyond liberal states, p 139. Oxford University Press, Oxford
Marx K (1887) Capital, vol. 1. Swan Sonnenschein, London
Mill JS (1859 [2006]) On liberty, p 71. Parker, London
Möllers C (2008) Demokratie – Zumutungen und Versprechen, p 22. Wagenbach, Berlin
Moody's (2009) Moody's downgrades Greece to A2 from A1, 22 Dec 2009. http://www.moodys.com/research/Moodys-downgrades-Greece-to-A2-from-A1--PR_192460. Accessed 9 Jan 2018
National Commission on the Causes of the Financial and Economic Crisis in the United States (2011) Financial crisis inquiry report
Nussbaum M (2004) Beyond the social contract: capabilities and global justice. Oxford Dev Stud 32:3–18
OECD (2014) Income inequality update, June 2014. http://www.oecd.org/els/soc/OECD2014-Income-Inequality-Update.pdf. Accessed 9 Jan 2018
Piketty T (2014) Capital in the twenty-first century. Belknap Press of Harvard University Press, Cambridge, MA
Polity IV Project (2016) Dataset users manual, p 13. http://www.systemicpeace.org/inscr/p4manualv2016.pdf. Accessed 9 Jan 2018
Posner R (1979) Utilitarianism, economics, and legal theory. J Leg Stud 8:103–140
Ratnovski L, Huang R (2009) Why are canadian banks more resilient? IMF Working Paper No. WP/09/152
Rawls J (1972) A theory of justice. Harvard University Press, Cambridge, MA
Rawls J (1993) Political liberalism. Columbia University Press, New York
Rawls J (1997) The idea of public reason revisited. Univ Chicago Law Rev 64:765–807
Reinhart CM, Reinhart VR (2010) After the fall. National Bureau of Economic Research Working Paper No. 16334
Reinhart CM, Rogoff KS (2009) This time is different. p xxxi. Princeton University Press, Princeton, NJ
Richardson M, Ronen J, Subrahmanyam MG (2011) Securitization reform. In: Acharya VV et al (ed) Regulating Wall Street: the Dodd-Frank Act and the new architecture of global finance, pp 469–489. John Wiley & Sons, Hoboken, NJ
Rousseau J-J (1762) Du contrat social. Rieder, Paris
Schäfer A, Streeck W (eds) (2013) Politics in the age of austerity. John Wiley & Sons, Hoboken, NJ
Scott HS (2010) Reducing systemic risk through the reform of capital regulation. J Int Econ Law 13:763–778
Sen AK (2005) Human rights and capabilities. J Hum Dev 6:151–166
Sen AK (2009) The idea of justice. Harvard University Press, Cambridge, MA
Severin C (2010) Lehman's langes Begräbnis, 8 July 2010. Neue Züricher Zeitung. http://www.nzz.ch/finanzen/nachrichten/lehmans_langes_begraebnis_1.6472110.html. Accessed 9 Jan 2018

Skopek N, Buchholz S, Blossfeld H-P (2011) Wealth inequality in Europe and the delusive egalitarianism of Scandinaivan countries, MPRA Paper No. 35307
Squam Lake Working Group (2008) A systemic regulator for financial markets, Working Paper No. 4
Streeck W (2011a) The crises of democratic capitalism. New Left Rev 71:5–29
Streeck W (2011b) The crisis in context. Democratic capitalism and its contradictions, MPIfG Discussion Paper No. 15
Streeck W (2014) Buying time: the delayed crisis of democratic capitalism. Verso Books New York
Suttle O Debt, default, and two liberal theories of justice. German LJ 17(5):799–834
Taylor JB (2008) The financial crisis and the policy responses: an empirical analysis of what went wrong. In: Bank of Canada (ed) A festschrift in honour of David Dodge's contributions to Canadian public policy, pp 1–18. Bank of Cananda, Montreal
Tietmeyer H (1999) International cooperation and coordination in the area of financial market supervision and surveillance. Report to the G7 Finance Ministers and Central Bank Governors
UNCTAD (2012) Principles on promoting responsible sovereign lending and borrowing. http://unctad.org/en/PublicationsLibrary/gdsddf2012misc1_en.pdf. Accessed 9 Jan 2018
van Aaken A, List C, Luetge C (eds) (2004) Deliberation and decision. Economics, constitutional theory and deliberative democracy. Ashgate, Farnham
Wagschal U (2011) Allheilmittel oder Bugetmimikry: Wie wirksam sind Verschuldungsgrenzen zur Haushaltskonsolidierung? Zeitschrift für Staats- und Europawissenschaften 9(3):352–382
Wehler H-U (2012) Die neue Umverteilung. Soziale Ungleichheit in Deutschland, p 65. C. H. Beck, München

Matthias Goldmann is Junior Professor for International Public Law and Financial Law at Goethe University Frankfurt and Senior Research Affiliate at the Max Planck Institute for Comparative Public Law and International Law, Heidelberg.

Neoliberalism and Law: The Case of the Constitutional Balanced-Budget Amendment

Thomas Biebricher

Abstract This chapter discusses the significance of law in neoliberal theory and practice. Prefaced by a brief look at the role that law plays in the theories of the ordo- and neoliberal thinkers Franz Böhm and Friedrich August von Hayek, the subsequent sections focus on the work of James Buchanan and his brand of neoliberalism, which combines constitutional economics public choice theory. Buchanan's core demand is a balanced-budget amendment to the constitution. The following sections examine this measure in its various aspects before the final section switches to the world of "actually existing neoliberalism" with a discussion of the various reforms of the economic governance structure of the European Union in recent years, particularly the "Fiscal Compact", which amounts to the real world equivalent of a balanced-budget amendment.

Revised version of the original published article "Neoliberalism and Law: The Case of the Constitutional Balanced-Budget Amendment" by Thomas Biebricher, German Law Journal 17(5):835–856. A version of this article was presented at the workshop on *The Politics of Legality in a Neo-Liberal Age* at the University of New South Wales in Sydney in August 2014. Ben Golder and Daniel McLoughlin, the organizers of the workshop, commissioned the piece to be published as Thomas Biebricher, The Rise of Juridical Neoliberalism. In: Ben Golder, Daniel McLoughlin (eds), The Politics of Legality in a Neoliberal Age, Routledge 2018, forthcoming. The author would like to thank the publisher for granting permission to publish the chapter in this edited volume.

T. Biebricher (✉)
Goethe University Frankfurt, Frankfurt a.M., Germany
e-mail: thomas.biebricher@normativeorders.net

M. Goldmann, S. Steininger (Eds.), *Democracy and Financial Order: Legal Perspectives*, Beiträge zum ausländischen öffentlichen Recht und Völkerrecht,
https://doi.org/10.1007/978-3-662-55568-2_8

1 Introduction

This chapter seeks to elucidate the significance of law for both neoliberal theory and practice, or what could be termed "juridical neoliberalism". Conventionally, neoliberalism is understood as a set of economic doctrines that give rise to the unfettered dominance of markets in social life. Accordingly, one may doubt that there is a legal dimension to neoliberal theory and practice that is of any significance. Still, I will argue that neoliberal theory is a body of *politico-economic* thought that is not confined to purely economic reflections but is also—necessarily—interested in broadly political themes, among which law is particularly prominent. Furthermore, law is not just a matter of neoliberal theory; juridical norms are a key instrument used in the neoliberal restructuring of economic governance.

This contribution begins with Sect. 2 defining neoliberalism. Before engaging questions related to neoliberalism, it is essential to clarify the term, not the least because one of the few things commentators can agree on is the highly contested nature of neoliberalism. My starting point in developing a working definition of neoliberalism will be a reconstruction of the context of the emergence of the term and the intellectual current it refers to.

Sect. 3 examines the significance of law in neoliberal thought, which is not a homogeneous current despite considerable commonalities between the various thinkers. Given this undeniable heterogeneity, it is useful to distinguish varieties of neoliberal thought and a more encompassing analysis of juridical neoliberalism would require an examination of all those varieties and the respective role(s) that law plays in each of them. This chapter focuses on the commentary of James Buchanan, whose work represents a variety of neoliberal thought that draws heavily on public choice theory and is often referred to as constitutional economics, indicating the importance of constitutional law for its agenda. This will be the subject of Sect. 3. Rather than attempting to summarize Buchanan's immense oeuvre in its entirety and the various ways juridical norms figure in it, Sect. 4 focuses on one particular aspect crucial to the normative dimension of constitutional economics—the call for a constitutional balanced-budget amendment (BBA) that requires public expenditures be matched by public revenue.

Sect. 6 explores actually-existing neoliberalism in the context of the aftermath of the European financial crisis. In response to the sovereign debt crisis triggered by the original financial crisis, the European Union (EU) passed a series of reforms to curtail potentially unsustainable economic and fiscal policies pursued by member states. Among them is the Treaty on Stability, Coordination, and Governance (TSCG) dubbed the Fiscal Compact in public discourse, which is essentially the equivalent of Buchanan's balanced-budget amendment (BBA). The discussion and critique of the TSCG will reference some of the theoretical concerns raised in the preceding sections. Additionally, this chapter will place the TSCG in the context of Stephen Gill's widely discussed criticisms of what one might consider an earlier incarnation of the TSCG, namely the Stability and Growth Pact (SGP) of 1997 that Gill considered an integral part of the "new constitutionalism".

In conclusion, Sect. 7 reflects on the role of juridical neoliberalism in Europe at the current conjuncture, which is characterized by a somewhat contradictory constellation. On the one hand, we witness what I consider a moralization of juridical norms regarding economic and fiscal policy intended to buttress the legal facticity of those norms, i. e. breaking these rules would not only be illegal but also immoral. On the other hand, this fixation on rules that must never be broken exists in an overall context of legal insecurity with regard to EU law or, more specifically, what commentators refer to as the EU's economic constitution. The legal validity of almost every aspect of the politics of the sovereign debt crisis, from the Fiscal Compact to the European Stability Mechanism (ESM) and the Outright Monetary Transactions (OMT) program by the European Central Bank (ECB), remains contested. Thus, the overall picture is paradoxical. Juridical norms are morally charged to make them almost sacrosanct, but they developed extra-legally during states of emergency.

2 What Is Neoliberalism?

Terms used to group together intellectual and political traditions are inherently difficult to define. First, it is difficult to pin down the essence or the core of any tradition that includes a variety of thinkers, either because they are considered to be a part of this tradition by others and/or they themselves located their work within it. Second, the political stakes involved in defining a tradition as including or excluding certain elements and thinkers add to the difficulty. The question of what constitutes conservatism, to choose but one example, and who can or should count as a legitimate representative of this intellectual current, is far from purely academic. Referring to someone as conservative, let alone as socialist, is a highly political act of signification. The political stakes rise exponentially in the case of the intellectual tradition of neoliberalism.

Not only is liberalism a notoriously diverse tradition, at least in political discourse being a liberal in Europe has come to mean almost the complete opposite of being a liberal in North America. This is one of the reasons why neoliberalism is almost absent from political discourse in the United States,[1] although it shows no sign of disappearing from academic discourse in Europe. But even in European political discourse—and to some degree academic discourse—the term has become somewhat toxic because it is hardly ever put to non-polemical use. Consequently, no one refers to themselves as neoliberal because characterizing a position as neoliberal immediately raises the suspicion that this characterization is just an oblique way of discrediting that position instead of engaging it substantively. Thus, there is a reluctance to apply the term to others' position because doing so may disqualify one's own position.

[1] Libertarianism is more prevalent in the United States, while it is rarely even mentioned in political discourse in Europe.

Given the complications associated with the term and its heavy political charge—at least in certain geographical areas—the most promising way to give it content is to reconstruct its emergence and study the project pursued by those who referred to themselves as neoliberals.[2] This requires going back to the interwar years of the last century, specifically the so-called *Colloquium Walter Lippmann* that took place in Paris in 1938. In the records of this meeting, attended by several first generation neoliberals, the term is first used to label of a common intellectual and political project.[3] The context from which this project arose was what appeared to the participants—as well as many other observers at the time—as an existential crisis of liberalism which manifested itself in phenomena ranging from the Great Depression and the ascent of Keynesianism to the rise of deeply illiberal political forces from Soviet Communism, to Fascism and National Socialism. Neoliberalism must be understood as a response to this crisis, the underlying roots of which the early neoliberals detected in the self-incurred decline of liberalism dating to the second half of the nineteenth century. According to the neoliberal diagnosis, liberalism unraveled into a quasi-social democratic strand on the one hand and a quasi-libertarian one on the other.[4]

Thus, the neoliberal project can be summed up in the following formula: It aims to revive liberal ideas against the illiberal *Zeitgeist* which requires critically revising the liberal agenda in order to clear it of both overly social democratic and libertarian elements—the twin legacies of the nineteenth century, so to speak. Neoliberalism is opposed to the merger of liberalism and progressivism but it is also adamant about the fallacies of a simplistic call for *laissez-faire*.[5]

Still, while these and many other views are shared among virtually all neoliberals—such as Friedrich August von Hayek, James Buchanan, Milton Friedman, Walter Eucken and Wilhelm Röpke—share these and many other views, this group does not form a homogeneous intellectual current. The neoliberal "formula" already implies inevitable controversy because, even at the outset, the exact combination of revitalizations and revisions remains a matter of dispute. While it is useful to introduce the notion of varieties" of neoliberal thought in order to capture the irreducible heterogeneity built into neoliberalism, it is possible to sharpen the substantive contours of neoliberalism beyond this rather thin formula. The common denominator among all varieties of neoliberalism can be expressed in the following way. It is uncontroversial that neoliberal thought accords crucial societal importance to the economic sphere or, more precisely, functioning markets. It is important to note, though, that it is not a body of economistic thought that exhausts itself in exclusively economic reflections by implicitly detaching the economic sphere from its context. Rather, neoliberalism is explicitly concerned with the variable conditions of functioning markets. If the *laissez-faire* approach is no longer a satisfactory answer to this question, then neoliberalism must address questions about how states

[2] *See generally* Peck (2008), p. 3; Jackson (2010), pp. 53, 129.

[3] Peck (2010), p. 51.

[4] *See* von Hayek (2002), pp. 88–119.

[5] von Hayek (1944), p. 18; Buchanan and Musgrave (1999), p. 83.

should be constituted so that they can engage in market-creating or market-maintaining politics, what actions they must abstain from, what public goods they have to provide, and how all of this might be complicated by the democratic character of a state. Neoliberalism is thus a body of thought engaged in political economy. Given this intersection of economics and the political structure, an inquiry into the significance of law in all of these matters is part and parcel of the neoliberal agenda, as further explained in the next Section.

3 Neoliberalism and Law: Von Hayek and Böhm

Although the discussion of the relevance of law to neoliberalism mainly focuses on James Buchanan's constitutional economics, the ideas of two other neoliberal thinkers, Franz Böhm and Friedrich August von Hayek, also provide important context for better understanding the role of law in neoliberalism.

Franz Böhm was a law professor in Freiburg and the inventor of a crucial element in ordoliberal thought, namely the "economic constitution" that would provide the fundamental legal framework for the economy. Böhm, together with Walter Eucken and Hans Grossmann-Doerth, formed the core of the so-called Freiburg School which in turn constituted the nucleus of a variety of neoliberalism called ordoliberalism. Thinkers such as Wilhelm Röpke and Alexander Rüstow are also counted among the ordoliberals. The *Ordo Manifesto*, authored by Böhm, Eucken, and Grossmann-Doerth, that entails something like a mission statement for ordoliberalism, displays the crucial importance of legal thought for this tradition. The authors deplore the decline of the societal influence of both jurisprudence and political economy and set themselves the task of reversing this trend:

> [I]t is true that in Germany these two sciences no longer exercise any appreciable influence on fundamental decisions of a politico-legal and economic nature.... Accordingly, the authors consider that the most urgent task for the representatives of law and political economy, is to work together in an effort to ensure that both disciplines regain their proper place in the life of the nation.[6]

But what exactly is the task of these "representatives of law and political economy"? "Men of science, by virtue of their profession and position being independent of economic interests, are the only objective, independent advisers capable of providing true insight into the intricate interrelationships of economic activity and therefore also providing the basis upon which economic judgments can be made."[7] Thus, law and political economy should provide scientific policy advice for political decision-makers, and the core project that they should be engaged in is the constitution of a market system: "[W]e wish to bring scientific reasoning, as displayed in jurisprudence and political economy, into effect for the purpose of constructing and

[6] Böhm et al. (1989), pp. 15–16.

[7] *Id.*

reorganizing the economic system."[8] In other words, at the heart of the ordoliberal variety of neoliberal thought lies the assumption that the economic sphere in general—and markets specifically—are constituted through law. According to this theory, the most fundamental and encompassing set of legal rules in this regard is called the economic constitution, which encompasses "[t]he treatment of all practical politico-legal and politico-economic questions…."[9] The economic constitution entails "a general political decision as to how the economic life of the nation is to be structured."[10]

One aspect of the economic constitution to which the ordoliberals must pay close attention is competition law. According to the ordoliberals, functioning markets are characterized by effective competition, and since market actors have an incentive to circumvent the respective pressures of competition, competition law—as part of the economic order enforced by the state—must prevent market actors from avoiding these pressures, thus ensuring "favorable conditions for the emergence of effective competition."[11] Especially in Böhm's later work, the benefits of effective competition, safeguarded through a legal "competitive order," are not only found in the minimization of the economic power derived from institutions such as monopolies,[12] leading to the dependence of some market actors on others, but also in the proper, undistorted functioning of the price mechanisms. Böhm believed that only on the basis of price mechanisms could a non-coercive coordination of societal activities be possible.[13] Prices, he believed, "coordinate the partial plans of all participants on the basis of decisions which are made by these participants,"[14] and these partial plans formed important aspects of what he referred to as a "private law society",[15] i. e. a "plurality of people who are subject to a uniform order, indeed, to be more precise, a legal order."[16] Importantly, this legal system, although established and enforced by the state, is not one of public but private law.

Friedrich August von Hayek, the neoliberal with arguably the strongest interest in matters of law, expressed a preference for private over public law as the medium for the economic sphere of society and was also concerned about the increasing entanglement of both kinds of law. Von Hayek believed that the rule of law, correctly interpreted, was the key factor in ensuring what he called a catallaxy—a functioning market economy.[17] His position is informed by a narrative of the decline of the

---

[8] *Id.*, p. 23.

[9] *Id.*

[10] *Id.*

[11] Böhm (1989), p. 57.

[12] Böhm (2008), pp. 49–67.

[13] Böhm (1989), p. 53.

[14] *Id.*

[15] *Id.*, p. 49.

[16] *Id.*

[17] *See* von Hayek (1973), pp. 94–144. A more encompassing exposition would also have to address the distinction between *thesis* and *nomos* that von Hayek discussed at length in *Law, Legislation and Liberty*. *Nomos* concerns the rules of conduct and is often equated with private law by von Hayek, while thesis is public law explicitly set by legislatures. In his diagnosis of the decline of the rule of law, the problem is clearly thesis and not *nomos*.

principle of the rule of law, the core elements of which are two interrelated notions. According to von Hayek, the first element is the separation of power between legislative, executive, and the judiciary branches of government, including the stipulation that the executive branch's ability to coerce is bound by the legislative branch.[18] Closely related to that is the second element that concerns the criteria that have to be met for a juridical norm to be considered a law in the proper sense. In his *magnum opus* titled *The Constitution of Liberty*, von Hayek wrote that "[l]aws in the substantive sense"—adhering to the principle of the rule of law—are "essentially long-term measures, referring to yet unknown cases and containing no references to particular persons, places, or objects."[19] Part of the decline of the rule of law, according to von Hayek, is a tendency, fueled by radical republican thought and/or legal positivism, to consider juridical norms as laws as long as the legislature has passed them, largely irrespective of their form and content.

The rationale behind von Hayek's position resonated with many other thinkers in the liberal tradition and their concern about a legalized tyranny of the majority that could result in the legal discrimination against minorities. Von Hayek was particularly worried about the interventionist potential that the erosion of the rule of law opened up with regard to the economic sphere. As a *neo*liberal thinker, von Hayek's approach to the restoration of the rule of law in both of its key aspects, the separation of powers and the generality of law, was not aimed at establishing a *laissez-faire* system, but at limiting economic policy to a certain quality or kind of action—to laws in the substantive sense:

> The range and variety of government action that is, at least in principle, reconcilable with a free system is thus considerable. The old formulae of laissez faire or non-intervention do not provide us with an adequate criterion for distinguishing between what is and what is not permissible in a free system.[20]

Unfortunately, von Hayek has been unclear on how strictly the generality of law must be interpreted. To put it into context, consider the fact that liberal democracies routinely, and in line with most of our moral intuitions, discriminate between persons of a certain age—for example, such as with political rights. Von Hayek's lack of clarity on the matter leaves one wondering if he would be opposed to this discrimination. Yet, would a regulation that requires all car makers to meet certain exhaust standards be discriminatory because some manufacturers will find it costlier than others to comply with the regulation? If this were the case, states would be bereft of almost any steering capacity—economic or otherwise. Von Hayek, however, was clear about what would be impossible under the proper rule of law, namely any social policy that would aim at equality of opportunity and all other variants of social justice: "[T]hose who pursue distributive justice will in practice find themselves obstructed at every move by the rule of law."[21]

---

[18] Von Hayek (1960), p. 185.

[19] *Id.*, p. 182.

[20] *Id.*, p. 202.

[21] *Id.*, p. 203.

4 The Constitutional Economics of Rent-Seeking: James M. Buchanan

Just as there are parallels and overlaps between von Hayek and Böhm, shared understandings regarding the significance of the rule of law exist between von Hayek and Buchanan.[22] But just as von Hayek and Böhm differ in some important respects—for example, with regard to the way an economic constitution should be spelled out in detail, as well as their respective faith in the expertise of jurisprudence and political economy in advising political decision-makers—Buchanan and von Hayek ultimately part ways when it comes to some of the interconnections of law and politics. Buchanan could certainly agree with von Hayek on the general importance of non-discrimination for a meaningful rule of law, but his approach to avoiding a potential tyranny of the majority does not view the reconstruction of a proper understanding of law as the crucial lever in this endeavor. Instead, Buchanan focused on constitutions that he views as the basic legal framework of a society. He analyzed the differing effects that various constitutional arrangements would have on economic matters.

Shifting to constitutions enabled Buchanan, among other things, to reformulate the problem of a tyranny of the majority as a matter of constitutional consent. Buchanan hypothesized that to the degree that the level of required consent to constitutional rules—not legislated law—approximated unanimity, the danger of tyrannical majorities could be averted. More generally and importantly for the present context, Buchanan moved away from questions of economic policy choices or other related matters towards a broadly contractarian perspective emphasizing how constitutions—institutionally ingrained legal rules—frame and structure the possibilities open to ordinary politics. Buchanan's central and best-known constitutional demand is the BBA.[23]

He highlighted three core assumptions that underlie and inform his research agenda: Normative individualism, *homo oeconomicus*, and politics-as-exchange.[24] These assumptions separately are not original, but Buchanan's extension of the

---

[22] James Buchanan is a particularly interesting neoliberal thinker because of the unique combination of ingredients to his thought. He was trained as an economist at the University of Chicago but then went on to pursue an original research agenda that contributed to the establishment of public choice theory as well as constitutional economics. Both theories are key influences for some contemporary varieties of neoliberal thought. In the present context, his significance derives from his focus on public finance and his specific approach to reining in fiscally undisciplined states and governments.

[23] *See* Buchanan and Wagner (1978), pp. 79–100. Two prominent examples of countries, in which such amendments have been introduced, are Germany and Switzerland. The technical specifics differ in both cases. In Germany, the crucial parameter is net borrowing, which must remain below 0.35 per cent of GDP. In Switzerland, revenue and expenditure have to be kept in balance. Buchanan seems to have in mind the latter version: "With a balanced budget rule, any proposal for expenditure must be coupled with a proposal for taxation." *Id.* p. 89.

[24] Buchanan (1987), p. 243; *See* Hayek (2002), pp. 88–119.

behavioral assumptions of *homo oeconomicus* beyond the economic sphere to politics and bureaucracy is unique and innovative. Accordingly, political actors—among them democratically elected representatives—are not considered to be exclusively devoted to realizing what is best for a political community as a whole, such as general interest or general welfare. With this theoretical move, Buchanan distanced the so-called public choice approach, not only from welfare economics and its attempt to construct a social welfare function intended to guide well-meaning politicians, but also the ordoliberal trust in the willingness of decision-makers to be informed by scientific expertise from jurisprudence and political economy. Buchanan assumes that individual and collective actors from society will regularly ask their elected representatives for special treatment, whether it be the recognition of special rights, some form of economic protectionism, or some other form of what public choice theorists refer to as "rent-seeking."[25] What the extension of the *homo oeconomicus* model to politics yields is the assumption that in the democratic market for rents there is not just demand but also supply. After all, if politicians value their reelection, they have an incentive to participate in the rent-seeking interaction in hopes of securing the support of the particular actor or group as part of a winning alliance at the next election.

The charge against rent-seeking per se is not that it is an undemocratic practice; it is only undemocratic under certain assumptions about its general practice, what it means to represent a constituency, and how encompassing this constituency is. Nevertheless, Buchanan argues that rent-seeking's adverse effects as a generalized practice make it imperative to rein it in. And let us note, as an aside, that the uneasiness about some societal actors' undue influence on the democratic political process—through lobbying or financial donations particularly in the United States—causes uneasiness among observers with widely varying ideological backgrounds. For Buchanan, rent-seeking as a generalized practice is a self-defeating endeavor because rents can be considered positional goods. These goods are only valuable if not everybody can attain them. Any actor that strives to achieve some kind of improvement of their own position vis-à-vis others through political action must assume that others—if they heed the maxims of *homo oeconomicus*—will try to do the same, which means that on balance any actor is likely to experience a worsening of his or her position relative to others. More importantly for Buchanan, though, rents typically incur costs, at least in the realm of economic policy. To put this into context, a decrease in tax rates for home owners must be financed some way or another.

In principle, there are three ways of financing incurred costs: Increase revenue, decrease expenditures, or run deficits, possibly in a combination with a dosage of inflation. The first two are inauspicious from a rational and public choice perspective—at least under many, if not most, imaginable circumstances. Financing a rent given to one group by burdening the entire electorate through taxation makes little sense. Even if it is possible to finance the costs by burdening one other particular group, unless politicians can be certain there will be no electoral retaliation

[25] *See e.g.* Buchanan et al. (1980).

from that group, this is not a winning strategy. Similarly, cutting certain benefits for particular groups or threatening to take measures that would affect the entire electorate—and thus decrease expenditure—also offsets the electoral advantage that politicians may hope to gain through compliance with rent-seeking demands. This is true in the world of rational choice, whereas the real world of widespread austerity conveys a very different image.

Consequently, by far the most appealing and only remaining political strategy turns out to be running deficits. After all, under most circumstances, public debt is politically intangible and typically only becomes an issue when it has to be paid off—a prospect which is supposedly in the distant future. Thus, according to Buchanan, running deficits amounts to an externalization of costs onto people who cannot vote at the moment and who may not even be born yet. Furthermore, the chances are that those who run deficit after deficit will no longer be in office when the accumulated debt inevitably forces governments to resort to either or even both of the first two strategies in order to avoid insolvency. Given that future generations have no way of having their voices heard in this regard, let alone exercise any countervailing influence on political-decision makers, the only effective way of curtailing the tendency of democracies to run permanent deficits and accumulate debt—that they can no longer unilaterally shrink through fiercely independent central banks who reign supreme in Western monetary matters—is to introduce a BBA.

5 The Balanced-Budget Amendment, Democracy, and Depoliticization

The BBA presents two sets of questions for analysis: The first set concerns the theories of sovereignty and representation; the second set expounds on the challenges of the BBA.

5.1 Representation and Sovereignty

The first set concerns matters of popular sovereignty and representation. BBA advocates could put forward two arguments here: First, a BBA provides a more encompassing form of representation than democratic politics without BBA. Without a BBA, there appears to be a short-term bias to democratic politics that fails to give due consideration to the presumed interests of future generations.[26] This is not only the case with public debt but also includes, for example, environmental issues like climate change. Ensuring fiscal discipline through a BBA would preclude future generations having to pick up the tab for the current cohort's profligacy. A BBA

[26] Buchanan (1986), p. 217.

could be understood as a device that gives advocatory representation to those unrepresented—the unborn, those unable to vote, etc.—assuming that they have an interest not to be born into a political landscape in which servicing the public debt—for which they bear no responsibility—crowds out alternative political options. The second argument that advocates could make in favor of a BBA refers to the restoration or maintenance of popular sovereignty. A country that accumulates unsustainable levels of public debt *de facto* loses its sovereignty because it is incapable of pursuing political projects, even if a majority of the population were in favor of it, simply because it does not have the financial resources. At some point, servicing the debt's interest will consume up more and more resources and financial markets will require higher risk premiums in order to borrow money. Conversely, only a fiscally disciplined country can take on financially ambitious political projects that a majority of the population favors. Finally, Buchanan would probably add a point reminiscent of Rousseau we will revisit later. No matter what specific policies we favor as private persons or *bourgeois*, as *citoyens* faced with a constitutional choice, we want to avoid ever rising levels of public debt.[27]

In response to representation and popular sovereignty arguments, BBA opponents offer several rebuttals. With regard to representation, opponents believe that it is highly conjectural to attribute interests to not-yet-existing persons. One can assume that future generations will prefer a low public debt over high public debt, but this is only uncontroversial if it is *ceteris paribus*—other conditions remaining the same. If fiscal discipline in the present means that public infrastructure investments from bridges and roads to schools and water supply works is put off, it is arguable that society would choose debt over fiscal savings. It is plausible that future generations will not only have one overriding interest in fiscal prudence but a mix of interests that includes public investments even if it means running deficits. In addition, debt is a strictly relational concept. For someone to owe money, somebody else must own the respective obligation. In other words, if we assume a closed economy—or even economies like Germany or Japan where most of the sovereign bonds are held by their citizens—the public debt that must be repaid by future generations is being held by members of that same generation, which complicates the picture by creating relational conflicts.

With regard to the second argument on popular sovereignty, BBA proponents discuss the normative core of the issue of juridical neoliberalism. There is something intuitively appealing about the real—not just *de jure*—national sovereignty of a country that is supposedly restored through a BBA. It remains questionable, however, whether this is a chimerical goal to be pursued. After all, national sovereignty—let alone popular sovereignty—has always been as much fact as fiction, notwithstanding that it has powerfully captured and inspired political passions.[28] Today, at a time when commentators speak of a Post-Westphalian society,

[27] As an aside, the formulation of a constitutional choice designates the dividing line between Buchanan and von Hayek on the link between politics and law. The legal evolutionist von Hayek would have held strong reservations against such "rationalist constructivism" and the critique vice versa can be found in Buchanan (1975), p. 167.

[28] *See generally* Krasner (1999).

sovereignty seems more fictional than ever, despite all the qualifications that need to be added depending on the country and the policy field. Globalization has significantly reduced national sovereignty in many aspects of economic policy. The loss of "boundary control"[29] has been immense and, in an increasingly interdependent world, the option of going it alone—economically, politically, and militarily—is highly circumscribed. Finally, even inter-governmentalist scholars of European integration, who insist that sovereignty has only been delegated and not transferred to the supranational level of the EU, would acknowledge that the only realistic ways to regain national sovereignty are either withdrawal from the Union or the Union's collapse. Whether factual sovereignty would really increase in any of these scenarios must be viewed with great skepticism.

These considerations aside, the more important issue is whether the BBA can legitimately restore popular sovereignty, or whether it is either not capable of doing so or bound to achieve the very opposite. A radical republican will have to be weary of the sovereign's will being tied down to rules of strict fiscal discipline. This is in effect a circumscription of possibilities in economic policy; some options are taken off the political table irrespective of the considerable support they might enjoy in some segments of the electorate. I will not delve into the paradoxes of self-binding rules for sovereigns that are often spelt out with reference to Odysseus having himself tied to the mast of his ship so he could listen to the Sirens' song—and still survive.[30] My point is not that a sovereign can never effectively tie itself and be circumscribed juridically. The concern, however, is that the nature of this rule is such that it should not be written into a constitution. Whether fiscal prudence or deficit-financed investment is the better political strategy in a given conjuncture should not be a matter of constitutional fiat. The choices and trade-offs in this question are inherently political in the sense that they have inevitably redistributive effects because this re-shifting of burdens produces both winners and losers.

In a widely-discussed argument for the legitimacy of delegating certain tasks to regulatory authorities, Giandomenico Majone distinguishes between the political modes of regulation and redistribution.[31] Regulation is aimed at the realization of Pareto-efficiency, which benefits at least one of those affected by the regulation and does not put anyone at a disadvantage. Therefore, the requirements of democratic accountability and legitimation can and should be relaxed for these regulatory authorities. Or, to put it more strongly: Some matters are better kept out of the hands of parliamentary majorities. Aside from the fact that critics have rightly stressed that few examples fit this description of regulatory politics,[32] the effects of BBA can hardly be described in terms of Pareto-efficiency. I therefore assume that Majone would be opposed to leaving this matter to a regulatory authority[33] and, by analogy I would argue that such a political issue—after all, the requirements of the BBA

[29] Scharpf (1999), p. 121.

[30] *See generally* Biebricher (2014), p. 77 (providing reflections on the paradox of sovereignty).

[31] Majone (1994), p. 77.

[32] *See* Follesdal and Hix (2006), pp. 542–544.

[33] Majone (2014), p. 1222.

may trigger politics of austerity—should not be a matter of constitutional rules. Despite the concerns about the lack of a long-term sense of responsibility on behalf of elected politicians, it is for those politicians and the public at large to debate these issues and for parliament to decide on it. The pernicious effect of juridical neoliberalism lies in precluding the possibility of this debate and a more or less informed choice that results from it.

5.2 *Challenges of the BBA*

The second set of questions deals not with BBA's normative justifiability but with whether Buchanan's theory can explain how to best implement a BBA. The two challenges that exist in implementing a BBA are whether it has practical applicability and who is best qualified to implement it. This point is not particularly original—even Buchanan himself acknowledged the theoretical difficulties. Still, the implications are worth considering.

Recall that politicians are supposedly rational utility-maximizers, if not satisfiers/optimizers. Therefore, securing their re-election looms large in their considerations and the ability to grant rents to groups and/or individuals supposedly contributes to this goal. If this is an adequate way of describing the incentive structure, then it is highly improbable that these politicians will pass a BBA, depriving themselves of one crucial strategy of shoring up their chances of re-election. This is inconvenient for Buchanan's brand of neoliberalism because there is no easy way to escape the theoretical corner he has backed himself into with the extension of the *homo oeconomicus* assumption. Buchanan's call for a "constitutional revolution,"[34] flounders on the lack of a revolutionary subject.

There are three arguments that have been introduced to overcome this impasse in Buchanan's agenda: First, there is the appeal to a "veil of uncertainty" reminiscent of Rawls' veil of ignorance.[35] Due to their general and abstract nature, the impact of constitutional norms on any given individual or group over time is difficult to ascertain. Whether it is overall beneficial or detrimental to someone's plans cannot be determined *a priori*.[36] While this may mitigate the problems of explaining constitutional reform in general, it is less convincing in the case of the BBA. The effect the BBA has on politicians who want the possibility of offering costly rents seems straightforward enough. Second, what if politicians could be assumed to acquire a truly constitutional mindset? What this is can be inferred *ex negativo* from Buchanan's characterization of those who are constitutionally illiterate: "It becomes impossible to ask such persons to think of their long-term interest, and certainly it remains folly to ask them to think of the interests of the more inclusive community."[37] But

[34] Brennan and Buchanan (1985), p. 134.

[35] *Id.*, p. 31.

[36] *Id.*, p. 140.

[37] Buchanan (1986), p. 56.

if politicians could be assumed to broaden their considerations and inculcate the presumed interests of the more inclusive community, including future generations, why could they not be trusted to pursue a prudential fiscal policy without the BBA? Finally, Buchanan suggested the possibility of passing the BBA by circumventing what might be seen as a cartel of elected politicians through direct democratic channels; through referenda that would mandate the BBA.[38] But it seems that this way out is blocked as well. If citizens' mindsets were more constitutional and future-oriented, then pursuing a frugal fiscal policy would be a winning electoral ticket. Most public choice theories, however, suggest the contrary; hence, there is a need for the BBA. "Fiscal prudence simply cannot be made to pay off in democracy."[39] Furthermore, Buchanan himself has conceded that ordinary citizens do not systematically differ from elected politicians in their being torn between constitutional considerations and the incentive to engage in rent-seeking.[40] Consequently, Buchanan has to hope that something might happen that his own theoretical assumptions suggest could never happen: "To hold out hope for reform in the basic rules describing the sociopolitical game, we must introduce elements that violate the self-interest postulate."[41]

Rather than pursuing the eschatological motives of a *deus ex machina* underpinning that statement, it is necessary to explore one more option that will segue to the next Section. After all, despite the explanatory difficulties of public choice neoliberalism explained above, the empirical fact remains that various versions of a BBA have been passed. The only explanation available for this seems to be that the rule may have been passed but it is either watered down or ignored whenever political expediency necessitates. The Stability and Growth Pact (SGP) and what Stephen Gill has called the new constitutionalism.

6 Juridical Neoliberalism in Practice: From the Stability and Growth Pact to the Treaty on Stability, Coordination, and Governance

If someone unfamiliar with Stephen Gill's widely cited "European Governance and New Constitutionalism" read it today, they would probably be surprised that it was published back in 1998. This observation tells us two things: First, we must be careful not to overstate the uniqueness of the present transformations of EU governance, significant as they are, and second, we must not overstate the originality of the diagnosis to follow. All existing differences notwithstanding, the aspects and effects of juridical neoliberalism are not entirely dissimilar from what Gill attributed to the new constitutionalism:

[38] *See* Buchanan (1979), pp. 693–696.

[39] Buchanan (1986), p. 217.

[40] Buchanan and Musgrave (1999), p. 126.

[41] Brennan and Buchanan (1985), p. 146.

> New constitutionalism is an international governance framework. It seeks to separate economic policies from broad political accountability in order to make governments more responsive to the discipline of market forces and correspondingly less responsive to popular-democratic forces and processes. New constitutionalism is the politico-legal dimension of the wider discourse of disciplinary neoliberalism.[42]

Gill's primary examples of the new constitutionalism are the European Economic and Monetary Union and the SGP passed in 1997. Their aim sounds familiar to contemporary ears as "[t]hey seek to institutionalize the new currency and mandate a strict fiscal discipline as part of new practices of economic governance that will give credibility to governments and confidence to investors."[43] The four main aspects of the new constitutionalism are listed as a monetary policy of sound money: (1) Low inflation with the ECB as the sole guardian, (2) debt sustainability to keep the Euro stable and preclude speculation against it, (3) surveillance mechanisms to ensure that member states honor their fiscal commitments in this regard and, (4) the attenuation of democracy as a consequence.[44] A skeptic might argue that this was a premature and overly alarmist account of the governance restructuring taking place over the course of the introduction of the Euro. After all, the SGP undoubtedly served to discipline Eurozone member states and aspiring candidates to a certain degree. But when push came to shove, the new constitutionalism turned out to be a fairly toothless.

In the early 2000s, both France and Germany, the economic and political heavyweights of the Eurozone, ran deficits in violation of the three per cent of the GDP rule of the SGP for consecutive years. The European Commission in charge of implementing and enforcing the SGP wanted to sanction both countries according to the procedures of the SGP, but the Council of European Economic and Finance Ministers (ECOFIN) voted against it. The Commission challenged the vote, but The European Court of Justice (ECJ) confirmed its legality.[45] This scenario was exactly what the theoretical discussion in the preceding section suggested. In the somewhat unlikely case that government entities adopt rules prohibiting "excessive" deficits and debt are passed, their more powerful addressees are bound to disregard the rules whenever they find it to be necessary or in their self-interest. This is an important part of the prelude to the reforms of 2011 to 2013 that are aimed at tightening the SGP in a number of ways as a response to the sovereign debt crisis that followed the financial one.

The reforms in question are the so-called Six-Pack (2011), the Two-Pack (2013), and the already mentioned TSCG (2012).[46] They aim to ensure that Eurozone member states achieve balanced budgets, avoid excessive deficits and prevent and/or correct macroeconomic imbalances. The instruments range from preventive ones—for example, states have to submit draft budgets to the Commission before national parliaments even deliberate over them—to corrective ones. In the case of excessive deficits or macroeconomic imbalances, the Commission issues rectifying

[42] Gill (1998), p. 5.

[43] *Id.*, p. 8.

[44] *Id.*, pp. 15–17.

[45] Hodson and Puetter (2013), p. 374.

[46] For concise explanations of the rationale and functioning of these reform measures, *see* European Council, http://www.consilium.europa.eu/en/policies/six-pack-two-pack-review/.

recommendations that become binding unless there is a qualified majority against it in ECOFIN. If states do not comply in due time, they may be fined up to 0.1 per cent of GDP. The core of these measures is the Fiscal Pact. Almost the exact equivalent of the BBA, the Fiscal Pact stipulates that its 25 EU signees—excluding the UK and the Czech Republic—pass the pact on a national, preferably constitutional, level. In a way, what could be considered the prime manifestation of juridical neoliberalism in practice—evidenced by the various reforms passed in recent years—amounts to new constitutionalism, similar in its aims but tightened in its implementation and enforcement procedures. This leads to an even greater attenuation of democracy—at least on the nation-state level. After all, the Commission and ECOFIN now wield considerable influence over what used to be considered a core competence of parliaments, namely fiscal policy. While inter-governmentalists are quick to point out the democratic legitimation of ECOFIN as members of national governments, the Commission has seen an increase in its power vis-à-vis ECOFIN, not the least through the already mentioned reverse majority principle.[47] It is not likely that a qualified majority of ECOFIN, which would have to include countries that might have to act as creditors for indebted countries, will form a majority against the Commission's recommendations.

Needless to say, the fate of the SGP should caution against overly alarmist diagnoses. The newness of the rules, the recent entanglement between the Commission and France over the draft budget, and the Commission's leniency towards Portugal and Spain clearly demonstrates political leeway. When the President of the Commission thinks of his apparatus as a "political Commission," as Jean-Claude Juncker has indicated at the very beginning of this tenure and confirmed in his State of the Union in September 2016, this leeway is even more apparent.[48] The concluding Section reflects on the current state of juridical neoliberalism in Europe.

7 Conclusion

This chapter ends with three diagnostic observations concerning juridical neoliberalism as it is on display in the reformed governance structures of the EU.

7.1 Depoliticization

National governments' overarching aim is to use various legal rules and regulations that circumscribe the more or less discretionary decision-making space in economic policy in order to depoliticize the respective policies. Once a BBA has been passed,

[47] Bauer and Becker (2014), pp. 161–163.

[48] Juncker (2016).

as stipulated in the Fiscal Compact, the question of whether it may be expedient or reasonable to run a deficit of four per cent to fund an anti-cyclical Keynesian economic policy is largely off the table because it is simply illegal.[49]

Still, this attempt at depoliticizing fiscal policy is likely to fail although it is a matter of speculation how exactly this will manifest itself. The reason is that the matters that are to be depoliticized are inherently political in a double sense. First of all, there is no scientific consensus about the causal connection between austerity, inflation, and economic growth, to name the more important variables underpinning the BBA. This makes it extremely problematic to treat these questions as purely technical ones to be decided exclusively based on scientific expertise. Secondly, these rules produce more or less clearly identifiable winners and losers. In this respect, they are the opposite of the regulatory politics that commentators like Majone considered appropriate for delegation to independent regulatory agencies. Majone himself has written that "the risk of a complete normative failure—a default rather than a simple deficit of democracy at the European level—is by now quite concrete."[50] Given the emphatically political nature of the matters at hand, from a purely functional perspective, it remains doubtful whether juridical norms can sustainably depoliticize them. Repoliticizations from the rise of Syriza and Podemos in Greece and Spain to the confrontations between member states and the Commission—such as in the case of France—will likely occur and are desirable to avoid an increasingly technocratic form of rule on the European level. Whether it is Syriza or alternative political forces—on the left or the right of the political spectrum—they are bound to continue to challenge the status quo. In addition, the European refugee crisis has led to some significant changes in European power relationships. For example, Greece's geopolitical position as a key entry point to Schengenland has given it new leverage within the European Union. The brief episode of German hegemony within the European Union may already be fading.

7.2 *Moralization*

The second observation is best understood when prefaced with a quick look at Wendy Brown's permutations of law's characterization under neoliberalism, albeit in the context of the United States around 2005.[51] Brown analyzed the interplay between neoliberalism and neoconservatism and wrote: "And, as law is tacticalized or instrumentalized, it is radically desacralized, producing the conditions of its routine suspension or abrogation, and paving the ground for what Agamben,

[49] To be precise, it is not entirely off the table because in cases of natural disasters or grave recessions exceptions to the BBA can be made.

[50] Majone (2014), pp. 1221–1222.

[51] *See generally* Brown (2006), p. 690; *see also* Biebricher (2014), pp. 100–103.

drawing on Schmitt, has formulated as sovereignty in the form of a permanent state of exception."[52] Thus, the second point is that the overall thrust of the discourse surrounding juridical neoliberalism in Europe about ten years after Brown's assessment points in the opposite direction.[53] Brown describes the desacralization of law and its bending for tactical purposes,[54] whereas the official discourse in Europe aims at maybe not a resacralization of law in a strictly religious sense but certainly a moralization that aims to immunize law against critique and to further deter potential violators. Not only will those breaking the law have to reckon with being sanctioned quite stringently, but they also have to bear the moral burden of a lack of solidarity vis-à-vis other EU countries that might eventually have to pay for bailouts through the European Stability Mechanism or other channels. Moreover, if one subscribes to the necessary link between the common currency and the EU as political project, then the moral burden is even more significant. Aside from solidarity requirements, a fiscal policy violating the BBA rules might be in itself immoral because it is the equivalent of "living beyond one's means" and burdening future generations with debt. This immoral practice is rightfully punished with economic calamities by anonymous but seemingly moral forces. "We have turned the politics of debt into a morality play," writes Mark Blyth,[55] and even someone as sympathetic to the Eurozone crisis management as Mario Monti famously remarked that economics was still considered a branch of moral philosophy in Germany.[56] Rather than discussing the role Germany is playing in the moralization of Europe's economic constitution in the (re-)making, let us focus on the relation between the two diagnostic theses formulated so far. If the aim of a juridification of economy policy is the latter's depoliticization, then what are the respective implications of a moralization of these juridical rules? This question, along with the relationship between morality and law, deserves a more thorough treatment than this contribution can provide. To address the ambivalence, one can argue that the moralization of law serves to immunize it even more from challenges but, at the same time, this moralization negates the strictly technocratic character of the BBA, which are supposedly merely an expression of pure and sober economic reason. Charging these rules with moral implications might inadvertently rekindle the flames of political passions that the strategy of juridification put out.

---

[52] *Id.*, p. 695. More recently, Brown has expanded upon her diagnosis with a critique of some landmark Supreme Court rulings, especially the now infamous *Citizens United* case. She highlights the neoliberal logic of markets and capital underlying the ruling. Still, the neoliberalization of law she describes in the contemporary American context remains different from the kind of juridical neoliberalism in the European context. *See* Brown (2015), pp. 151–174.

[53] Brown (2006), p. 696.

[54] Brown (2006), p. 695.

[55] Blyth (2013), p. 13.

[56] Monti (2012).

7.3 *Depoliticization v. Moralization*

The final observation concerns the overall context in which both the depoliticization of fiscal policy and the moralization of the respective juridical rules occurs. The EU has been in crisis mode ever since the outbreak of the financial crisis in 2008. Initially, however, it was mostly the nation states that dealt with the fallout, such as bailing out banks and stimulating faltering economies. Then, the sovereign debt crisis hit and put the common currency in jeopardy, triggering the barrage of reforms mentioned above. What is striking about almost every aspect of the ensuing politics of EU crisis management since 2011 is their ambiguous legal status. To be sure, national and European adjudication so far have confirmed the legality of the measures[57]—although one might suspect that political reasons played a significant role. Still, there is plenty of controversy surrounding European crisis management. Consider the following examples: (1) the Six-Pack is questioned with regard to the possibility of far-reaching recommendations to overcome deficits and imbalances and affect policy domains that are exclusive to nation states; (2) the Fiscal Pact's use of the Commission and European Court of Justice for implementation and enforcement—despite the fact that it is not part of EU law but an international treaty; and (3) the recently launched ECB's Outright Monetary Transaction Program that seriously pushes the envelope of the bank's mandate. Therefore, Europe is not just faced with an economic and political but also a legal-constitutional crisis.[58] Of course, this raises specters of extra-legal states of emergency and Wendy Brown's concerns mentioned above come to mind.

At this point, it is enough to simply note the contradictory tendencies in the politics of legality in Europe. There exists a potential tension between the attempt to depoliticize issues through a particular form of juridification and the moralization of the rules in question. Furthermore, the insistence on the inviolability of legal rules that are arguably further immunized by the moralization of their contents stands in stark contradiction to the embattled legal status of those very rules. Future research aiming at a critical understanding of juridical neoliberalism in theory and practice will have to take these tensions and contradictions into account.

References

Bauer M, Becker S (2014) From the front line to the back stage: how the financial crisis has quietly strengthened the European commission. Pub Money Mgmt 34:161–163

Biebricher T (2014) Sovereignty, norms, and exception in neoliberalism. Qui Parle 23:77

Blyth M (2013) Austerity: the history of a dangerous idea. Oxford University Press, New York

Böhm F (1989) Rule of law in a market economy. In: Peacock A, Willgerodt J (eds) Germany's social market economy: origins and evolution, pp 15–16. Palgrave Macmillan, New York

[57] When the Portuguese Supreme Court ruled against the implementation of reforms demanded by the Troika, lawmakers responded with a constitutional reform.

[58] *See* Wilkinson (2013), p. 527; Joerges (2014), p. 249.

Böhm F (2008) Das Problem der privaten Macht: Ein Beitrag zur Monopolfrage. In: Goldschmidt N, Wohlgemuth M (eds) Grundtexte zur Freiburger Tradition der Ordnungsökonomik, pp 49–67. Mohr Siebeck, Tübigen
Böhm F, Eucken W, Grossmann-Doerth H (1989) The ordo manifesto of 1936. In: Peacock A, Willgerodt J (eds) Germany's social market economy: origins and evolution, pp. 15–16. Palgrave Macmillan, New York
Brennan G, Buchanan J (1985) The reason of rules: constitutional political economy. Cambridge University Press, Cambridge
Brown W (2006) American nightmare: neoliberalism, neoconservatism, and de-democratization. Pol Theory 34:690
Brown W (2015) Undoing the demos: neoliberalism's stealth revolution. Zone Books, New York
Buchanan JM (1975) The limits of liberty: between anarchy and leviathan. University of Chicago Press, Chicago, IL
Buchanan JM (1979) The potential of taxpayer revolt in american democracy. Soc Sci Q 59:691
Buchanan JM (1986) Liberty, market and state: political economy in the 1980s. Harvester Press, Brighton
Buchanan JM (1987) The constitution of economic policy. Am Econ Rev 77:243
Buchanan JM, Musgrave RA (1999) Public finance and public choice: two contrasting visions of the state. MIT Press, Cambridge, MA
Buchanan JM, Wagner R (1978) The political biases of keynesian economics. In: Buchanan J, Wagner R (eds) Fiscal responsibility in constitutional democracy, pp 79–100. Springer, Berlin
Buchanan JM, Tollison R, Tullock G (1980) Towards a theory of the rent-seeking society. Texas A&M Press, College Station, TX
European Council (2017) European Semester: a guide to the main rules and documents. http://www.consilium.europa.eu/en/policies/european-semester/european-semester-key-rules-and-documents/. Accessed 15 Jan 2018
Follesdal A, Hix S (2006) Why there is a democratic deficit in the EU: a response to Majone and Moravcsik. J Common Mkt Stud 44:533
Gill S (1998) European governance and new constitutionalism economic and monetary union and alternatives to disciplinary neoliberalism in Europe. New Pol Econ 3:5
Hodson D, Puetter U (2013) The European Union and the economic crisis. In: Cini M, Pérez-Solórzano Borragán N (eds) European Union politics, 4th edn. Oxford University Press, Oxford
Jackson B (2010) At the origins of neo-liberalism: the free economy and the strong state. Hist J 53:129
Joerges C (2014) Law and politics in Europe's crisis: on the history of the impact of an unfortunate configuration. Constellations 21:249
Juncker J-C (2016) State of the union 2016: towards a better Europe: a Europe that protects, empowers and defends. http://europa.eu/rapid/press-release_SPEECH-16-3043_en.htm. Accessed 15 Jan 2018
Krasner SD (1999) Sovereignty: organized hypocrisy. Princeton University Press, Princeton, NJ
Majone G (1994) The rise of the regulatory state in Europe. West Eur Pol 17:77
Majone G (2014) From regulatory state to a democratic default. J Common Mkt Stud 52:1216
Monti M (2012) Charlemagne: the other moral hazard. The Economist, 29 Sept. http://www.economist.com/node/21563741. Accessed 15 Jan 2018
Peck J (2008) Remaking Laissez-Faire. Prog Hum Geog 32:3
Peck J (2010) Constructions of neoliberal reason. Oxford University Press, New York
Scharpf FW (1999) Governing in Europe: effective and democratic? Oxford University Press, Oxford
Von Hayek FA (1944) The road to serfdom. Routledge, New York
Von Hayek FA (1960) The constitution of liberty. Routledge, New York
Von Hayek FA (1973) Law, legislation, liberty: rules and order. Routledge, New York
Von Hayek FA (2002) Liberalismus. In: Vanberg V (ed) Grundsätze einer liberalen Gesellschaftsordnung: Aufsätze zur Politischen Philosophie und Theorie, pp 88–119. Mohr Siebeck, Tübingen

Wilkinson M (2013) The specter of authoritarian liberalism: reflections on the constitutional crisis of the European Union. German LJ 14:527

Thomas Biebricher is Temporary Professor of Political Theory and Philosophy at the Goethe University Frankfurt.

An Alert from the Left: The Endangered Connection Between Taxes and Solidarity at the Local and Global Levels

Francisco Saffie G.

Abstract Neoliberal tax policies at the local and the global levels risk democracy consolidating economic inequality by allowing and fostering capital accumulation. As a consequence capital owners have increased their political power to influence and decide on local and global tax policies for their own benefit. The Chilean income tax system and the international tax law system (including tax competition among states and tax havens) are analyzed as examples of neoliberal tax policies at the local and the global level, respectively. At the same time, neoliberalism as a normative order of reason has replaced the political aspect of taxation with economic concepts that tend to dissolve the connection between taxes and solidarity. In this scenario, taxes make no economic or political sense as they are not understood as duties of citizenship. In this chapter recent alternatives proposed to diminish global no taxation and inequality, as the OECD BEPS project and Thomas Piketty's proposal for a global tax on capital are analyzed and criticized.

1 Introduction

One of the consequences of economic globalization combined with local neoliberal policies has been an increasing takeover of the political by the market. This shift from politics to market economy has favored the economic dimension of life to the

---

Revised version of the original published article "An Alert from the Left: The Endangered Connection Between Taxes and Solidarity at the Local and Global Levels" by Francisco Saffie G., German Law Journal 17(5):857–874

F. Saffie G. (✉)
Universidad Adolfo Ibáñez, Santiago, Chile
e-mail: francisco.saffie@uai.cl

M. Goldmann, S. Steininger (Eds.), *Democracy and Financial Order: Legal Perspectives*, Beiträge zum ausländischen öffentlichen Recht und Völkerrecht,
https://doi.org/10.1007/978-3-662-55568-2_9

detriment of its political dimension. Arguably, the freedom to invest around the world guaranteed to multi-national corporations (MNCs) has improved our lives as economic agents because it allows for the creation of new jobs around the world; free trade enhances consumers' choices, and so on. At the same time, our lives as political equals, that is as citizens, worsen as economic inequality increases in ways such as the endangerment of welfare entitlements. This chapter examines the role that neoliberal tax policy and tax law have played in this process. The analysis develops on two levels: locally and globally. This two-level analysis is justified by the way local economic decisions are interwoven with global effects in a globalized economy. At the local level, the way neoliberal tax policies increase inequality over time by failing to provide a counterweight to market distributions is analyzed. For this purpose, the effects of the Chilean neoliberal income tax system adopted in the early 1980s are analyzed. At the global level, the way the combination of local neoliberal tax policies and an international tax system anchored in the principle of state sovereignty has enabled MNCs and global capital to avoid tax liabilities is analyzed. Thus, the legal and political divisions between the local and international spheres enable participants in global markets to escape taxation, thereby undermining solidarity and, ultimately, the fragile alliance between democracy and a capitalist mode of production. Even more, as argued in this chapter, the normative order of reason that characterizes neoliberalism has replaced the connection between solidarity and taxation with economic concepts that make no economic or political sense when applied to taxation. By the end of the chapter, the analysis turns to two alternatives to this state of affairs: (1) the Base Erosion and Profit Shifting (BEPS) action plan proposed by the Organization for Economic Cooperation and Development (OECD), and (2) Thomas Piketty's proposal for a global tax on capital. The conclusion is that even if there are good proposals for tax policies based on demands of fairness according to a particular conception of global distributive justice, there is still a need to find the legal, and institutional, means to implement them. This limitation could be understood as part of what global tax law should aspire to; it should strive to leave the current taxable event structure to create a new form of taxation able to implement a coordinated global tax policy and provide criteria according to which nation states share or allocate their taxing rights under a principle of distributive, and not commutative, justice.

2 Neoliberalism, Economic Globalization, and Taxation

There is not much novelty in pointing out that the world is going through what could be called a redefinition of the structure and function of the political institutions that characterize modern nation states. In a world characterized by a global neoliberal economic order, part of this redefinition is explained by the way the economic dimension of life has taken over its political dimension.[1] Though the exact moment

[1] On the concept of neoliberalism, *see* Biebricher, chapter "Neoliberalism and Law: The Case of the Constitutional Balanced-Budget Amendment".

in which this change started cannot be determined, the new world economic order in which we are living has been the result of neoliberal economic policies that started to be implemented around the world by the end of the 1970s.[2] These policies initially developed within nation states brought a global change when new international institutions, such as the World Trade Organization, and previously existing international institutions, such as the International Monetary Fund (IMF) and the OECD, adopted and reinforced the neoliberal agenda in the mid-1990s.

In *Buying Time*, Wolfgang Streeck provides a strong and convincing argument showing how this redefinition of the function of the nation state happened. Streeck argues that by the mid-1970s capital owners—profit-dependent owners and managers of capital—became relevant political actors, endangering the post-war political stability. Until then, capital, as a political actor, had agreed with and conveniently accepted the terms of the post-war social contract. This agreement, according to Streeck, explains the stability of Keynesian policies adopted by Western governments. That period was characterized by peace and the establishment of the welfare state. Nevertheless, by the end of the 1970s, capital began to dismiss the post-war social contract, conditioning the function of the state by deciding to not invest when labor expectations started to grow and became difficult to control. Capital claimed a bigger share of the social product. According to Streeck, the economic crisis of the late 1970s—and the crises that were to come—is better explained if we consider capital in this way. These new social arrangements between capital and the state explain policies that lowered taxes and the consequently lost revenue. Capital, now as a self-conscious political and economic actor, conditioned the way in which the state could finance its activities and was in position to cause economic crises whenever its economic benefits were lower than expected. In this way, it became more powerful than the capital-dependent population in setting the conditions of the state's economic constitution.[3] Governments first reacted by diminishing tax burdens on capital, and then implemented policies that enabled the liberalization of markets and capital by opening their frontiers and abolishing financial controls. This gave way to what Streeck calls the "debt state":[4] governments decided to continue with the welfare state, financing it this time not with tax revenue but with public debt. The third and final phase of this evolution of the state has led us to international "politics of the consolidation state" caused by the accumulated debt.[5] The politics of the consolidation state are characterized by a double movement: at the local level, governments cut public spending, continue to reduce tax burdens, especially on capital and financial markets, and privatize what used to be public

[2] Harvey (2005); Brown (2015), pp. 20–21; Raymond Plant (2010), Ch. 9. On the general characteristics of neoliberal political economy, *see* Jessop (2002), pp. 95–139. Leo Panitch, perhaps with extreme optimism considered that the initial regulation of markets after the 2008 subprime crisis meant the end of neoliberalism understood as the opposition between states and markets. *See* his "Introduction" to Miliband (2009).

[3] Streeck (2014), pp. 6–26.

[4] *Id.*, pp. 47–96.

[5] *Id.*, pp. 97–164.

services; at the global level, especially in Europe, states entered into structures of international integration which make democratic decisions even more difficult because they disproportionately empower capital to press for neoliberal economic policies. Streeck argues that this evolution of the state, which is causally dependent on the economic policies adopted, during the last thirty or forty years, has only delayed the crisis of democratic capitalism, increasing the power of capital to the detriment of democracy. Streeck is not optimistic about the future of the democratic state, as he believes that this "process of de-democratization of capitalism through the de-economization of democracy" will bring redistributive democracy to an end and will reduce it "to a combination of the rule of law and public entertainment."[6]

Nevertheless, there are those who argue that neoliberal policies have improved the quality of life of people around the world, especially in developing countries.[7] At least in material terms, they say, individuals now have access to products and goods, such as a refrigerator in the case of Chile, that thirty years ago were not available worldwide. This is the result of free markets working as the network of information that allows an efficient production and allocation of goods. Hence, the role of the state is to secure the conditions under which markets can operate. Colin Crouch calls those who defend this interpretation of neoliberalism "pure neoliberals."[8] This pure conception of neoliberalism, Crouch argues, is not to be found in existing polities. On the contrary, what we find when analyzing in detail the relation between the economic order and the political order that neoliberalism has produced is what Crouch calls "actually existing neoliberalism."[9] This kind of neoliberalism is characterized by the power of MNCs that are able to lobby their interests successfully and, more generally, by the power of private wealth in politics. According to Crouch, actually existing neoliberalism "produces a politicized economy very remote from what economists understand by a liberal market economy, and a polity so unbalanced by plutocratic power that it seriously compromises the idea of liberal democracy."[10] In this sense, actually existing neoliberalism secures the political position and privileges of those who are able to benefit from market interactions. Under actually existing neoliberalism, economic inequalities carry with them inequalities of political power. The function of the state under neoliberalism has been reduced to secure the distributional effects of the market, and, for this purpose, a particular conception of private property and the rule of law have been championed and legally protected. While neoliberal discourse tries to convince individuals that this is all that is needed from the state, because obtaining economic benefits depends exclusively on how well they do in market interactions, according to their effort and responsibility, neoliberals take political control of the state to secure that this promise is not fulfilled. Hence, what seems to be a promise open to all, is not.

[6] *Id.*, p. 5.

[7] For an argument showing how neoliberal policy brings economic growth, *see* Paus (1994), pp. 31–56.

[8] Crouch (2013), p. 23.

[9] *Id.*, p. 24.

[10] *Id.*

In this vein, David Harvey argues that neoliberalism has brought not the well-being of all, as it promises, but the "restoration of class power"[11] through a process of "accumulation by dispossession."[12] This process redistributes the social product to the owners of capital who benefit from low taxation and the privatization of all sorts of services that used to be provided by the state.[13]

By now, the neoliberalization of economic policy has gone global. What started as a shy policy of open markets became a sphere of power dominated by the global economic interests of capital. In this scenario, MNCs are the real citizens of the world, or, as Crouch puts it, global firms became the "key institution of the post-democratic world."[14] They benefit from free capital flows over the world, no restrictions to commerce, global instances of dispute resolution modeled to incentivize international commerce, and especially from low taxation. Following Crouch, MNCs obtained these benefits, as they became the survivors in a world in which the toughest take it all. Once these firms became global, they had enough power to condition their investment to preferential fiscal and labor regimes.[15] At the same time, states compete to obtain the resources from these firms making all kind of regulatory concessions to them. This is how special non-tax regimes have trended worldwide, for example tax benefits for capital gains such as deferrals or exemptions for the exchange of stocks and other benefits for financial market capital gains, such as bonds.

According to Harvey, one of the ways in which the neoliberal process of dispossession has been successful was the establishment of tax policies that permit the accumulation of capital, but do not take into account that capital accumulation endangers equality. This also explains why states have lost the democratic control of the economy, as Streeck argues. At the same time, states have had to continue financing part of their public expenditure through the tax system.[16] The middle class has had to carry an important part of the economic burden associated with the State. But it is easy to see how the tax system loses its legitimacy under actually existing neoliberal policies. First, direct taxation does not fulfill its traditional redistributive function because capital and profit can be easily shifted to low or no-tax jurisdictions if they do not receive preferential treatment. Secondly, the tax system relies heavily on indirect taxation to obtain revenue; hence, those who pay taxes are either those who obtain their income from labor or those that cannot easily move their source of income to a different jurisdiction. Finally, the tax system becomes oppressive, as the state does not give anything back to its citizens; the citizens have to pay

[11] Harvey (2006), p. 29. *See also* Harvey (2005).

[12] *See* Harvey (2006), p. 43.

[13] *See also* Crouch (2004), pp. 31–69; Crouch (2011).

[14] *See* Crouch (2004), p. 31.

[15] *Id.*, p. 32.

[16] Many countries finance their public expenditure with a combination of tax revenue and public debt. This is not the case of a consistent neoliberal country as Chile, where public debt has been strictly controlled through a structural balance rule. According to this rule public expenditure cannot exceed tax revenue. This rule, nevertheless, has not been constitutionally adopted.

for their own pensions, health, education, and so on, while at the same time they cannot accumulate capital. This can be called the economic nonsense of taxation under neoliberalism.[17]

The economic nonsense of taxation under neoliberalism is not the only way in which taxation has lost meaning. Taxation also lost its political meaning, namely as part of those duties of citizenship required by solidarity. According to Wendy Brown, neoliberalism is not only a set of economic policies but also a "normative order of reason" that "transmogrifies every human domain and endeavor, along with humans themselves, according to a specific image of the economic."[18] Brown argues that neoliberalism has extended the "model of the market to all domains and activities" and "configures human beings exhaustively as market actors, always, only, and everywhere as *homo oeconomicus*."[19] In this sense, neoliberalism is different from classical economic liberalism.[20] This normative idea that comes with neoliberalism pervades the political, pushing away the *homo politicus* from the political to exchange "democratic principles of justice into an economic idiom,"[21] with important consequences for democratic institutions. The normative idea of neoliberalism, according to which individuals that are part of a state are actually understood as units of human capital that compete with each other, or at most as economic agents who share the risks of economic life, as it happens in any firm, but receive no protection from even a liberal notion of the social contract,[22] has destroyed the notion of solidarity that justified taxation. Contrary to the normative logic of the market, one of the most important public goods of political communities is solidarity. It is a public, or collective, good in the sense that it is "indivisible and must be produced, or at least decided upon, by those who benefit from"[23] it. In this sense, solidarity is one of those goods that are part of political communities understood as "communities of fate."[24] Paying taxes is the paradigmatic way in which "citizenship demands that one provide generalized support to the community as a whole … which may be put to as yet undecided uses by a lawfully constituted government."[25] In this sense, taxes are part of those duties that constitute citizenship. Elsewhere I have developed in detail an argument in favor of this conception of taxation. It is argued that taxation and tax law should be understood as institutions of mutual recognition rather than as mere economic mechanisms for redistribution as which they have so

[17] For an exposition of the neoliberal argument, as an economic argument, according to which taxes "become inconsequential," *see* Kleinbard (2015), pp. 37–41.

[18] *See* Brown (2015), p. 9–10, Ch. 1.

[19] *Id.*, p. 31.

[20] *Id.*, p. 33.

[21] *Id.*, p. 35.

[22] *Id.*

[23] Streeck (2012), pp. 27, 41.

[24] *Id.*, p. 42.

[25] *Id.*

far been understood by liberal egalitarian and luck egalitarian justifications of progressive taxation.[26] The problem with those justifications is that they concentrate on providing a moral justification for redistribution but leave—neoliberal—institutions as they find them. Hence the duty to pay taxes is justified by the self-interest of those who interact in the market, and not by solidarity. But as said before, this is not of much help when taxation has lost its economic sense. Thus, liberal and luck egalitarian justifications for progressive tax systems have been fighting fire with fire. They have followed an economic rationale by showing that progressive taxation is in the interest of individual well-being, but they disregarded the political meaning of citizenship's duties and hence the importance of solidarity. In this sense they have assumed—perhaps rightly—that politics have become marketized.

This disconnection between taxation and solidarity had—and continues to have—consequences for both the design of tax policy and tax law. Regarding the former, beyond reducing tax rates, neoliberal policies are structured around rational choice theories, for example when arguing that the same tax rate should apply to capital and labor income and recommending a reduction of both tax rates, arguments in favor of fully integrated income tax systems—based on the idea that in the long run the incidence of corporate taxes is on individuals, hence they do not affect the owners of capital but individuals as consumers and laborers, and that corporate taxes combined with personal income taxes create double taxation[27]—and incentivizing through taxation, corporate equity finance and investment rather than debt. These ideas have led some to suggest a complete replacement of income tax by consumption taxes,[28] but the consequences for tax law have also been important. Tax law, as we actually know it, is a young and underdeveloped area of law.[29] The "unwelcome child of the law," as Johannes Popitz calls it,[30] became an independent legal branch in the early twentieth century. In Germany, for example, tax law began to be taught independently from budgetary law by Ludwig Waldecker at the University of Berlin after 1915.[31] In the UK, the evolution of tax law was not that different. According to Freedman, tax law "is a relative newcomer to the UK law degree curriculum." It has been taught as an independent legal discipline only since the 1950s when Wheatcroft started teaching and publishing in his role at the London School of Economics.[32] The problem is that tax law scholarship never fully developed a general theory able to explain the way in which tax duties are duties of citizenship—that is, public law duties. This theoretical underdevelopment contributed to the actual state of tax law and its appropriation by neoliberalism. In other words, the general theory

[26] *See* Saffie (2014), Ch. 3 (on file with author).

[27] *See generally* Harberger (1962), p. 3; Pomerleau (2015).

[28] *See generally* Goldberg (2013).

[29] This is not strange as progressive income taxes were only established around the beginning of the twentieth century. *See* Piketty (2014), pp. 498–508.

[30] Quoted in Stolleis and Dunlap (2004), p. 224.

[31] *Id.*, p. 219.

[32] Freedman (2004), p. 15.

of tax law adopted a structure that has left an enormous space for local and global tax avoidance, which is a different way of saying that tax law—the legal form of taxation—also contributed to taxes losing their grip as duties of solidarity.

According to the general theory of tax law, the legal duty to pay taxes has a correlative right, namely, the state's enforceable right to claim the tax. This relationship between the state and the taxpayer turns the tax duty into a legal relationship. According to the contemporary general theory of tax law, in this legal relationship, the taxable event represents the will of the state. The taxable event (TE) contains the description of the relevant facts and operative conditions (OC) according to which the taxpayer (T) will have a specific legal obligation to pay (P) a certain amount of tax. This is the way in which P by T, referred to above, is expressed and specified in tax law. Nevertheless, for T to P it is necessary that OC give way to TE.[33] The space left for tax avoidance, under this structure of P is big because as long as T does not cause TE to happen—for any reason, including the intention to avoid taxes—there is no duty to P. Even for theories that accept substantive interpretation in tax law, the structure of the general theory of tax law is a limit that restricts analogical reasoning or purposive interpretations of the law because without the satisfaction of TE there is no legal duty to pay taxes.[34] Under this structure, the protection of private property is in a privileged status compared with the public duty to pay taxes.

3 Neoliberal Tax Policies and Its Consequences: Locally and Globally

3.1 Neoliberal Tax Policy at the Local Level: The Chilean Case

Chile is probably the only country in the world where neoliberal policies were fully implemented. The process of radical neoliberalism could not have been as successful as it was had it not relied on military force. Not one of the new policies that were established by Pinochet's regime since 1973 was deflected by the democratic process as they did not need democratic legitimacy. Chile's neoliberalism was designed following the Chicago economic school of thought.[35] Public industries and health services were privatized, a private pension system was established, and

[33] According to Hensel, the legal duty to pay taxes is "born with the realization of the taxable event." Hensel (2005), p. 154.

[34] For further details of this argument, *see* Saffie (2014), Ch. 2. For another way of putting this point but from a different conception of tax law, Kleinbard argues that the structure of the legal duty to pay taxes raises avoidance as a moral and not a legal problem, even if he recognizes that "for every real-life action in the commercial sphere, one finds a tax description and a tax operator, that together yield a tax consequence." Kleinbard (2016), p. 132. For Kleinbard, therefore, there is no underlying substance to the artificiality upon which the legislature structures tax obligations.

[35] For details of this process, *see generally* Valdés (1995).

universities, schools, and any institution you name were left to private initiative. On top of the initial military force, neoliberal policies needed a supportive political discourse to survive. Presenting the new policies and the respective institutions as the only way to make the country prosper and free from Marxist totalitarianism was, at that moment, an easy and appealing discourse. It is a discourse that still echoes whenever social democratic reforms are presented in parliament. The force of the coup destroyed any other economic policy because the only alternatives that existed were a failed socialist project[36] and the new neoliberal policies that promised freedom and opportunities for all. The entire discourse was facilitated by the fact that Chileans had never experienced a welfare state, so politics had never represented that space of solidarity or common fate mentioned in the previous section. Since then, and especially after the economic success of the country during the 1980s and 1990s, neoliberalism has enjoyed a good life in Chile. Recently, neoliberalism has been at risk with the present government's proposals for tax, labor, educational and constitutional reforms, but the power of capital has shown how alive it is by threatening with less investment, capital flight and so on, a discourse that actually diminished popular support to the reforms. Be that as it may, the Chilean tax system that was established in 1983—that was recently reformed, though that reform is still debated and will be probably discussed again as part of the campaign for the next presidential election that will take place by the end of 2017 when there will be pressure to leave everything as it was before the reform (by the center right) or to push it further (by the center left)—was a solid example of neoliberal tax policies, and its consequences a solid example of the consequences of neoliberalism.

An important part of neoliberal tax policy is to give a privileged status to capital, taxing it as little as possible. This explains why the Chilean income tax was designed in the 1980s as a fully integrated income tax. In such a system, there is no distinction for income tax purposes between firms and their owners. In other words, following economic ideas about tax incidence, the only taxpayers for income tax purposes are natural persons.[37] At the same time, in its purest version, this system requires not to tax income as long as profit is not distributed to the firm's shareholders or partners.[38] This was the original design that changed a bit in 1990 when firms where obliged to pay on their accrued profits an advance of the personal income tax of their shareholders or partners—this rate reached a cap of 20 % on 2014 (before Bachelet's government tax reform), but started in 1990 at 10 %. This is not a real corporate income tax; it "is in reality a payment on account of" the owners of the firm's personal income taxes, "which are due when profits are distributed to them; at that time, they can fully credit against their tax liability the tax paid by the

[36] This is not the place to analyze why it failed, though there are good reasons to believe that the U.S. and Chilean capitalists had responsibility in the failure of the economic system by generating the economic crisis. What happened in Chile is a dramatic case that illustrates Streeck's point about the way in which capital can control democracy.

[37] Harberger (1962), was particularly influential on this issue.

[38] In the words of IMF No. 14/219, "Chile's full integration system is probably one of the purest in design." International Monetary Fund (2014).

company."[39] The fully integrated system, hence, allows shareholders or partners to get a refund if their personal income tax is lower than the advance payment made by the firm. Workers do not receive such a privilege treatment, as they are subject to a progressive income payroll tax with a top tax rate of 40 %. Employers directly pay this tax to the administration. Mainly the working middle class pays this tax, because nearly 82 % of the working population is exempt from the payroll income tax because they receive low salaries. This different tax treatment of capital and labor created an incentive to avoid the payroll tax by disguising work income as capital income through the creation of firm and incentivizing entrepreneurial innovation rather than work subject to labor law. This tax system therefore destroys taxes as citizens' duties by presenting them as economic costs that the citizen as an economic agent should avoid. Hence, the remaining 18 % of the working, or middle, class not exempt from income tax was probably paying less than what they should have because most of them paid for the profit they withdrew or that was distributed to them from the firms through which they developed their professional activities.[40]

This understanding of the tax system, specifically an economic one devoid of political meaning, is corroborated by an analysis of the composition of Chilean tax revenue. Actually, it is coherent with neoliberal tax principles as it is principally composed by indirect taxation. A value added tax (VAT) with no exemptions and with one proportional rate for all kinds of products represents a bit more than 50 % of the total tax revenue. This is problematic when combined with low public expenditure, because in those cases VAT tends to be a regressive tax.[41] Hence, the Chilean tax system does not make a redistributive difference. This explains why Chile, an extremely fiscally disciplined country, is the most unequal country of the OECD considering the Gini coefficient.[42] Over the years, this tax system financed a minimum state that destroyed solidarity bonds among citizens. It is a system that increased the power of economic elites and, at the same time, that explains why it has been so hard to reform.[43]

The tax reform bill presented to parliament by President Bachelet[44] by the end of march 2013 was designed to change part of this unfair income tax structure by

[39] *Id.*

[40] In Chile there is no corporate tax. As I explain in the main text, the income tax is fully integrated so that tax paid by firms is nothing but an advance of the shareholders or partners' income tax.

[41] Generally, it is understood that a tax is regressive when those who have less income end up paying proportionally more taxes than those who have more income. For an argument according to which saying of a particular tax that it is progressive or regressive is myopic for not considering public expenditure, *see generally* Murphy and Nagel (2004).

[42] Fairfield and Jorrat (2016), p. 1. The Gini coefficient "is a way of comparing how distribution of income in a society compares with a similar society in which everyone earned exactly the same account. Inequality on the Gini scale is measured between 0, where everybody is equal, and 1, where all the country's income is earned by a single person" (http://www.bbc.com/news/blogs-magazine-monitor-31847943).

[43] *See generally* Fairfield (2010), p. 2; *see also* Fairfield (2015).

[44] According to the Chilean constitution the President has exclusive powers in fiscal policy, hence is the only authority that can propose any change in tax law.

changing the income tax structure from a consumption base to an income base and, therefore, giving the same tax treatment to capital and labor income. But, because it was designed by economists it did not change what they understand to be a kind of technical orthodoxy that reigns in Chile (that could be understood to be nothing but neoliberal ideology) and maintained the fully integrated corporation income tax. Hence the proposal was to establish a system in which any legal entity (be it a partnership, a corporation, etc) would be considered as a pass-through entity for tax purposes at the end of each year; the system, however, required these same entities to pay an income tax on their income of 25 % (proportional tax rate) that was fully credited against the personal income tax of the owners of those entities (taxable with the same progressive personal income tax with maximum tax rate of 35 % as laborers).[45] One of the aims of this reform was to give capital and labor income the same tax treatment.[46] With this, capital owners would have had to pay income tax for all the income they produced yearly (even if profits were not withdrew or distributed from the firms they own[47]) without having a special deferral treatment as the neoliberal tax system provided them.

Though the tax reform was passed on September 2014, the bill was hardly criticized during parliamentary debate and the final result was different from what the executive proposed. Opposition came mainly from capital owners and their tax lawyers who used media for their purposes. The economic arguments against the tax reform were the same that are globally heard in these cases: that economic activity will be disincentivized, that capital will flow to lower tax jurisdictions, that employment was going to fall, that the cost of taxes would be transferred to consumers, and so on and so forth. Tax lawyers were working for their clients and argued that the income tax system imposed by the reform was technically defective because corporations could not be considered pass-through entities and that personal income tax required to be based on the realization principle (that is, capital owners could only be taxed when they withdrew or received distributed profits). All these arguments were based on the idea that there is something as a right way of designing an income tax system as if law was intrinsically connected with reason and not as an act of will.[48] Even more, it could be said that it was an argument oriented to maintain the existing privileges for capital. And what shows the power of capital is that these efforts were in part successful.

The pressure exerted by capital as a class—in the terms described by Streeck—during the legislative process led to an income tax law with two different systems to tax capital. The first one is the one according to which entities will be considered

[45] Because of the effect of the proportional tax rate credited against a progressive tax rate, the first will result in most cases in an excess tax paid that could be claimed back by taxpayers.

[46] An economic aim was to increase revenue in 3.1 % of the GDP to finance public expenditure, particularly, the education reform porposed by the government.

[47] Of course, because of what was said in note 45 above, only the very rich would have had effectively to pay personal income tax at the end of the year (as the credit of the tax advanced by the legal entity would not be enough to satisfy the personal tax).

[48] Detmold (1989), p. 2.

pass-through entities; the second one, allows for differal of personal income tax (just as the neoliberal income tax law system used to do) but with a higher tax rate paid at the entity level (27 %) and an attenuated integration at the personal income tax (instead of fully credit only a 65 % credit of the income tax paid at the level of the entity can be used). Taxpayers can choose the income tax system according to which they want to pay income taxes. This seems to me an excellent example of the way in which the economic use of taxes trumps over their political meaning and also as a vivid image of the stalemate between capital and democracy—following Streeck's arguments—as it brought the establishment of two income tax systems, in which one is still favoring capital.

3.2 *Neoliberal Tax Policy at the Global Level: International Tax Policy and Tax Competition*

International tax law is another example of how tax policy has drifted under the influence of neoliberalism. At the global level, MNCs and financial institutions have been able to shape "the structural features of the existing global economic and financial order"[49] benefiting from their indirect influence on the design of international tax policy, such as international policy recommendations and tax treaties, and pressing for tax competition with governments that have endorsed neoliberal economic policies. This diagnosis stands even if it were true that no international administrative coordination for the purposes of pursuing neoliberal economic tax policies at the global level existed, precisely because of the reasons given before in this contribution, specifically the influence and power of economic interests that reach the global level without any need to take part in representative political structures.[50] Following is an analysis of the two aspects here mentioned, that is, of the way in which international tax law and tax competition have been instrumental for neoliberalism at the global level.

The network of bilateral tax treaties could, arguably, be said to constitute international tax law.[51] Reuven Avi-Yonah has argued that international tax law is constituted by two principles to which every country would agree with: (1) the single tax principle, according to which "income from cross-border transactions should be subject to tax once … at the rate determined by the benefits principle"; and (2) the benefits principle, that "allocates the right to tax active business income primarily to the source jurisdiction and the right to passive investment income primarily to the residence jurisdiction."[52] Bilateral tax treaties have expanded through the world,

[49] Kleinbard (2016), p. 3.

[50] For a particularly interesting argument on these lines, *see* Dietsch (2015), pp. 23–25.

[51] *See generally* Avi-Yonah (2007).

[52] *Id.*, p. 3.

mainly following the OECD model.[53] Nevertheless, rather "than preventing 'double taxation' [this] has, in practice, led to a world of widespread double non-taxation."[54] This has happened because treaty tax rates are very low, while at the same time they give strategic alternatives to an MNC to establish its activities worldwide according to the best treaty network combination available to it. This movement has also been part of what could be considered a neoliberal policy agenda known as the "Washington Consensus" that has influenced economic policy worldwide.[55] This is particularly relevant when it comes to analyzing the way in which capital has benefited from investments in developing countries. As Mehta and Dayle Siu have argued, tax treaties diminish the revenue base of these countries and "often protect MNCs at the expense of developing countries" without improving foreign direct investment as initially expected.[56] In this sense, it seems that a lot needs to be done to find a middle ground between double taxation and no international taxation when it comes to MNCs as they can use international tax law at their will, as long as there is no abuse to diminish their taxes.

Even more, the combination between international tax law and local tax law influenced by the neoliberal ethos creates an explosive mix that is very productive for base erosion and profit shifting (BEPS). Corrick explains this problem very clearly:

> BEPS relates chiefly to instances where the interaction of different tax rules leads to double non-taxation or less than single taxation. It also relates to arrangements that achieve no or low taxation by shifting profits away from the jurisdictions where the activities creating those profits take place … In other words, what creates tax policy concerns is that, due to gaps in the interaction of different tax systems, and in some cases because of the application of bilateral tax treaties, income from cross-border activities may go untaxed anywhere, or be only unduly lowly taxed.[57]

It is a worrying consequence of the application of the combination of international and local tax law that income from "cross-border activities may go untaxed anywhere, or be unduly lowly taxed" as Corrick points out. Even more it is a major problem that tax law, the rules of which are designed to tax income, is legally used to not pay tax. This practice has led to what Kleinbard calls "stateless income," consisting of

> income derived for tax purposes by a multinational group from business activities in a country other than the domicile of the group's ultimate parent company, but which is subject to tax only in a jurisdiction that is neither the source of the factors of production through which the income was derived, nor the domicile of the group's parent company.[58]

---

[53] Owens and Bennett (2008) (showing more than 3000). *ICAEW* (showing over 1300). According to Rixen, "in 2004, 90.6 per cent of all possible bilateral treaties among OECD members were in place." *See* Rixen (2008), p. 115.

[54] Tax Justice Network, http://www.taxjustice.net/topics/corporate-tax/tax-treaties/. *See also* the description of the political resistance of the initial proposals for a financial tax before the 2008 financial crisis in Wahl (2016), pp. 205–207.

[55] Henry (2016), p. 37.

[56] Mehta and Dayle Siu (2016), p. 340.

[57] Corrick (2016), p. 175.

[58] Kleinbard (2016), p. 129.

The point here is that international tax planning allows to tax the income generated by the MNC group in a tax haven or a very low tax jurisdiction. Stateless income goes against the second principle of international tax law mentioned above, specifically, the benefits principle. In other words, the instrumental use of the law that makes stateless income possible shows how international tax law was designed around ideas that are not able to grasp the nature of global commerce and international capital as it exists today.[59]

At the same time that international tax policy and existing international tax law have been the downfall of the idea of international tax law, the problem only grows in dimension when combined with the ethos of neoliberalism at the local level. When it comes to attract foreign direct investment, local tax policy has been designed according to neoliberal principles, that is, tax rates are inversely proportional to foreign direct investment. The combination of all these factors brings what has been called "tax competition." According to Shaxson and Christensen:

> tax 'competition' occurs when jurisdictions—whether independent nations or states inside a federation—dangle tax incentives to tempt investment, hot money, financial activities, or even wealthy individuals away from other jurisdictions, often nearby. There are three main ways in which this happens: falling tax rates come down, the tax base (that is, what gets subjected to tax) shrinks, and enforcement gets weakened, often deliberately. Each move either directly takes a chunk out of other countries' tax systems, or puts pressure on them to follow suit and make their own cuts: in a 'race to the bottom.' This 'competition' goes way beyond tax: it is also found in the areas of financial secrecy, financial deregulation, tolerance for criminal money, and more.[60]

Shaxson and Christensen show that there is theoretical and empirical evidence to prove that the underlying economic assumptions for tax competition lack any rigor and do not actually explain foreign direct investment.

The analysis given in this Section shows that Streeck's and Crouch's arguments described in the first part of this chapter correlate highly—not only as the political will that may explain the implementation of neoliberal policies at the local level as in the Chilean case—with capital's interests as a class at the international level either in the design of tax policy or tax competition allowing capital owners to accumulate income by not paying taxes, increasing inequality worldwide.

All this explains why tax havens are such a problem for international tax law, as recently exemplified by the Panama papers leak. These countries benefit from attracting MNCs willing to be free of taxes. And MNCs benefit from tax havens even more if they can structure their business to combine local neoliberal tax policies in the countries where their economic activities take place—either by taking advantage of tax competition and ensuing low rates or by exploiting what are technically called "hybrid mismatch arrangements"—with the tax treaty network and

---

[59] Kleinbard makes a similar point, *see* Kleinbard (2016), p. 144. Nevertheless, I do not share his view that this is only, or mainly, a problem of the system being designed over non-commercial and noneconomic premises, *id.* p. 145, and hence of the connection principle to tax MNC—in his argument a "territorial tax model"—for the reasons given in the last Section of this chapter.

[60] Shaxson and Christensen (2016), p. 266.

tax havens. Well-known international cases are those of Amazon, Google, Apple, and Starbucks, companies that structure their business almost not to pay taxes at all, nowhere.[61]

It is not easy to suggest solutions to these problems. There are evident difficulties, starting from a common political will, to bring coordinated policy changes to local and international tax law and continuing with the inexistence of a global tax authority. This complex scenario, however, has not been a pretext for doing nothing at least at the level of proposals, as Wahl has argued.[62] The following Section evaluates some proposals to these problems.

4 Are There any Alternatives?

As argued in this chapter, local and global economic inequality caused by neoliberal tax policies and the consequent risk for democracy, are an important problem worldwide. Lately, political action to change this state of affairs has taken place at the local and global levels. At the local level, social movements have been urging for policy change[63] and tax policy reforms have been put forward for developing countries in order to increase "global tax fairness."[64] At the global level there has been political action and one interesting, and popular, policy suggestion. The former is the OECD BEPS action plan, and the latter, Thomas Piketty's proposal for a global tax on capital. The former only describes ways in which existing policies can be improved locally in developing countries and does not imply bigger changes to the global tax system.

The BEPS action plan is an effort in which OECD countries are trying to offer proposals to fight international tax avoidance. The first output of this project was delivered in 2014 and the final reports were delivered in 2015. At the same time, an implementation package has launched negotiations on a multilateral agreement to implement tax treaty-related BEPS measures, country-by-country report obligations, and "criteria to assess whether preferential treatment regimes for intellectual property (patent boxes) are harmful or not."[65] Needless to say this is an impressive and important effort to improve states' ability to tax MNCs by assuring that "profits are taxed where economic activities take place and value is created."[66] The final report includes

---

[61] Kleinbard (2016), p. 132. When finalizing this chapter the European Commission ruled that Apple has to pay €13 billion plus interest in taxes because of illegal tax benefits given by Ireland, as reported by Farrell and McDonald (2016).

[62] Wahl (2016), p. 208.

[63] In Chile, for example, a tax reform was recently passed to increase revenue to finance the public education reform. A reform that could be read as the triumph of the 2011 student movement. As the tax reform will only be put into effect in 2018, however, there has been space to increase the opposition to it and some are strongly lobbying to abolish it.

[64] *See* all the proposals contained in the recently published book edited by Pogge and Mehta (2016).

[65] OECD (2015).

[66] OECD/G20

policy recommendations divided in 15 actions, including measures to address the tax challenges of the digital economy, neutralize the effects of hybrid mismatch arrangements, strengthen controlled foreign company rules, limit base erosion via interest deductions and other financial payments, counter harmful tax practices more effectively, taking into account transparency and substance, prevent treaty abuse, prevent the artificial avoidance of permanent establishment status, assure that transfer pricing outcomes are in line with value creation, measuring and monitoring BEPS, require taxpayers to disclose their aggressive tax planning arrangements, re-examine transfer pricing documentation, make dispute resolution mechanisms more effective, and develop a multilateral instrument. As the OECD reports, the project is in development until 2020 and it is not difficult to predict that it will be under continued pressure by lobbyists trying to undermine the final implementation of these measures. Even more, according to the OECD, challenges have already risen as "some practitioners" "denounced" an "increasing uncertainty" derived from measures adopted unilaterally by certain states and the aggressiveness of some tax administrations.[67] The OECD, however, read these challenges not as a concern for capital's lobby but as a concern to maintain existing tax policies not to generate "global tax chaos marked by the massive re-emergence of double taxation."[68]

My concern, however, is a different one. Remember the two principles of international tax law identified by Avi-Yonah mentioned before in this contribution, specifically the single tax principle and the benefit principle. These two principles on which international tax law has been historically built are not changed by the OECD BEPS project. On the contrary, the measures proposed by the BEPS final report mean reinforcing those principles. This brings two consequences: (1) the BEPS project does not mean that we will have a new international tax system that assures democratic influence over tax policy, or; (2) new ways to tax MNCs, or a global project linking tax policy with global distributive justice and solidarity. In other words, the BEPS project reinforces principles of commutative justice among those states entitled to tax according to the traditional principles of international tax law and hence leaves plenty of space for the neoliberal ideology that characterizes current tax policy and tax law, and only tries to fix certain excesses of those policies. New measures, however, based on distributive justice seem to be needed when the combination between local tax law, tax treaties, and tax competition creates what was called, as previously mentioned, "stateless income."

A different alternative has been suggested by Thomas Piketty in his *Capital in the Twenty-First Century*. Piketty proposed a tax policy oriented to make democracy "regain control over the globalized financial capitalism of this century."[69] The "new tool" Piketty proposes is a global tax on capital combined with high levels of financial transparency. This tax should be progressive, annual, and applied to "individual

[67] *Id.*, p. 9.

[68] *Id.*

[69] Piketty (2014), p. 515.

wealth—that is, on the net value of assets each person controls."[70] The tax base should be individual net worth for the wealthiest and for the rest, the market value of all financial assets and nonfinancial assets net of debt.[71] The tax rate proposed by Piketty is progressive but not necessarily high. According to Piketty these two measures, the global tax on capital and fiscal transparency, will improve equality and democracy.

Piketty's arguments for taxing capital at a global level are convincing and the policy he proposes for that is sound. He may even be right about the benefits that his proposal will bring for diminishing inequality and improving democracy's future. Nevertheless, the problem is not only the obvious coordination problem among states that he admits, but that his ideas need global legal structures to work and a principle of distributive justice to allocate this revenue as if it was a real global tax—without a necessary identity between the state that collects the tax and the state that is entitled to the revenue.

To recap, the alternatives offered in opposition to neoliberal tax policies or the consequences they bring at the local and the global level have two commonalities and one difference. The first common aspect is that they have a political problem: Their advocates have lost political power to capital as a social and economic actor. The second common aspect is that they share a legal problem: Tax law theorists have no local or global alternative to the traditional general theory of tax law and hence, the way in which tax duties are born is not structured as a duty of local or global citizenship. The difference is that at the local level, state institutions are wounded but still alive, so they are still the place of distributive justice and solidarity as common fate; at the global level, there are no institutions based on shared political values and, therefore, there is no place for distributive justice but only for commutative justice. The aim of this contribution is not to propose solutions to these problems, but to provide orientation of where to look for them. It is in this sense that Streeck's and Crouch's concern for the domestic level is understood—but with a turn, because we do not need to abandon the global. What is needed before looking again, with renewed ideas, at the global, is a reaffirmation of the political concepts underlying domestic institutions. This is the only way in which to counteract the normative order imposed by neoliberalism and the power of capital to preserve democracy and its underlying values of liberty and equality to finally reach fraternity.

Acknowledgements I thank all those who took part in the workshop Democracy and Financial Order: Legal Perspectives at Goethe University Frankfurt on 2–3 September 2015, where I presented an early draft of this chapter, for their questions and comments, and to Fernando Atria for reading and commenting on a version of this chapter. I would like to give special thanks to Silvia Steininger and Matthias Goldmann, not only for organizing and inviting me to the workshop, but also for their very detailed comments and suggestions that helped me improve and clarify the argument.

---

[70] *Id.*, p. 516.

[71] *Id.*, p. 517.

References

Avi-Yonah R (2007) International tax as international law. Cambridge University Press, Cambridge
Brown W (2015) Undoing the demos. Neoliberalism's stealth revolution. Zone Books, New York
Corrick L (2016) The taxation of multinational enterprises. In: Pogge T, Mehta K (eds) Global tax fairness, p 175. Oxford University Press, Oxford
Crouch C (2004) Post-democracy. Polity Press, Cambridge
Crouch C (2011) The strange non-death of neoliberalism. Polity Press, Cambridge
Crouch C (2013) Making capitalism fit for society. Polity Press, Cambridge
Detmold M (1989) Law as practical reason. Camb Law J 48:2
Dietsch P (2015) Catching capital: the ethics of tax competition. Oxford University Press, Oxford
Fairfield TA (2010) Business power and tax reform: taxing income and profits in Chile and Argentina. Latin Am Pol Soc 52:2
Fairfield TA (2015) Private wealth and public revenue in Latin America: business power and tax politics. Cambridge University Press, Cambridge
Fairfield TA, Jorrat M (2016) Top income shares, business profits, and effective tax rates in contemporary Chile. Rev Income Wealth 62:1
Farrell S, McDonald H (2016) Apple ordered to pay €13bn after EU rules Ireland broke state aid laws. Guardian. https://www.theguardian.com/business/2016/aug/30/apple-pay-back-taxes-eu-ruling-ireland-state-aid. Accessed 24 Jan 2018
Freedman J (2004) Taxation as legal research. In: Lamb M, Lymer A, Freedman J, James S (eds) Taxation an interdisciplinary approach, p 15. Oxford University Press, Oxford
Goldberg DS (2013) The death of the income tax. Oxford University Press, Oxford
Harberger AC (1962) The incidence of the corporation income tax. J Political Econ 70:3
Harvey D (2005) A brief history of neoliberalism. Oxford University Press, Oxford
Harvey D (2006) Spaces of global capitalism. Verso, London
Henry JS (2016) Let's tax anonymous wealth. In: Pogge T, Mehta K (eds) Global tax fairness, p 37. Oxford University Press, Oxford
Hensel A (2005) Derecho Tributario. Marcial Pons, Madrid
ICAEW Double tax treaties. http://www.icaew.com/en/library/key-resources/double-tax-treaties. Accessed 24 Jan 2018
International Monetary Fund (2014) Chile: Selected Issues Paper, IMF Report No. 14/219, July 2014. https://www.imf.org/en/Publications/CR/Issues/2016/12/31/Chile-Selected-Issues-Paper-41772. Accessed 24 Jan 2018
Jessop B (2002) The future of the capitalist state. Polity Press, Cambridge
Kleinbard ED (2015) We are better than this. How government should spend our money. Oxford University Press, Oxford
Kleinbard ED (2016) Stateless income and its remedies. In: Pogge T, Mehta K (eds) Global tax fairness, p 132. Oxford University Press, Oxford
Mehta K, Dayle Siu E (2016) Ten ways developing countries can take control. In: Pogge T, Mehta K (eds) Global tax fairness, p 340. Oxford University Press, Oxford
Miliband R (2009) The state in capitalist society. Merlin Press, London
Murphy L, Nagel T (2004) The myth of ownership: taxes and justice. Oxford University Press, Oxford
OECD (2015) First steps towards implementation of OECD/G20 efforts against tax avoidance by multinationals, 6 Feb 2015. http://www.oecd.org/ctp/first-steps-towards-implementation-of-oecd-g20-efforts-against-tax-avoidance-by-multinationals.htm. Accessed 24 Jan 2018
OECD/G20 Base Erosion and Profit Shifting Project, Explanatory Statement 4. http://www.oecd.org/ctp/beps-explanatory-statement-2015.pdf. Accessed 24 Jan 2018
Owens J, Bennett M (2008) OECD model tax convention. OECD Observer (Oct 2008). http://www.oecdobserver.org/news/archivestory.php/aid/2756/OECD_Model_Tax_Convention.html. Accessed 24 Jan 2018
Paus EA (1994) Economic growth through neoliberal restructuring? Insights from the Chilean experience. J Devel Areas 28:31–56

Piketty T (2014) Capital in the twenty-first century. Belknap Press, Cambridge, MA
Plant R (2010) The neo-liberal state. Oxford University Press, Oxford
Pomerleau K (2015) Eliminating double taxation through corporate integration. Tax Found. (23 Feb 2015). https://taxfoundation.org/eliminating-double-taxation-through-corporate-integration/. Accessed 24 Jan 2018
Rixen T (2008) The political economy of international tax governance. Palgrave Macmillan, Hampshire
Saffie F (2014) Taxes as practices of mutual recognition: towards a general theory of tax law. Unpublished Ph.D. thesis, Edinburgh University, 2 July 2014
Shaxson N, Christensen J (2016) Tax competitiveness—a dangerous obsession. In: Pogge T, Mehta K (eds) Global tax fairness, p 266. Oxford University Press, Oxford
Stolleis M, Dunlap T (2004) A history of public law in Germany 1914–1945. Oxford University Press, Oxford
Streeck W (2012) Citizens as consumers. New Left Rev 76:27–41
Streeck W (2014) Buying time: the delayed crisis of democratic capitalism. Verso, London
Tax Justice Network Tax treaties. http://www.taxjustice.net/topics/corporate-tax/tax-treaties/. Accessed 24 Jan 2018
Valdés JG (1995) Pinochet's economists: the Chicago school in Chile. Cambridge University Press, Cambridge
Wahl P (2016) More than just another tax. In: Pogge T, Mehta K (eds) Global tax fairness, pp 205–207. Oxford University Press, Oxford

Francisco Saffie G. is Assistant Professor at the Universidad Adolfo Ibáñez, Chile.

Public Law's Rationalization of the Legal Architecture of Money: What Might Legal Analysis of Money Become?

Isabel Feichtner

Abstract Many of the ills afflicting democratic capitalism have their source in the current legal architecture of money and finance. At the same time the reimagination of institutions of money and finance promise an avenue for reform to democratize the economy and prevent the perpetuation of austerity politics. Such institutional reimagination requires a perspective that recognizes money as an institution linking state and civil society, politics and the economy. Economics in great part eschews such a perspective and perceives of money as a medium of exchange largely independent of government and politics. Legal analysis, by contrast, should be ideally suited for the endeavor to analyse the various ways in which the institutional design of money configures political economy.

To start paving the way for such analysis, I seek to clarify how German public law scholarship has been obstructing a reimagination of monetary design. It has adopted an understanding of money that is informed by economics and on this basis has rationalized the particular legal architecture of money in Germany and in the European Economic and Monetary Union as necessary to protect individual freedom and democratic constitutionalism. Recent practice of the European Central Bank reveals

Republication with slight revisions of "Public Law's Rationalization of the Legal Architecture of Money: What Might Legal Analysis of Money Become?" by Isabel Feichtner, German Law Journal 17(5):875–906

I. Feichtner (✉)
Julius-Maximilians-Universität Würzburg, Würzburg, Germany
e-mail: feichtner@jura.uni-wuerzburg.de

M. Goldmann, S. Steininger (Eds.), *Democracy and Financial Order: Legal Perspectives*, Beiträge zum ausländischen öffentlichen Recht und Völkerrecht, https://doi.org/10.1007/978-3-662-55568-2_10

that the strict separation between monetary and economic policy, between money and public finance that characterizes the European Economic and Monetary Union, and its rationalization by legal scholarship and case law cannot be maintained. I argue that a growing body of literature on the political economy of money can inspire a legal analysis that overcomes the current fetishization of the legal architecture of money. This literature provides a starting point for imagining institutions that operationalize monetary sovereignty to serve the public interest and that decrease the hold of private creditors on democratic politics.

1 Shifting Attention to Money as a Central Institution in Democratic Capitalism

Legal analysis seeking to identify institutions that may reform political economy to the effect of strengthening democracy should concentrate on money.[1] Focusing on money is promising, as the current institutional architecture of money and finance appears to be the source of many ills in the current formation of capitalism, such as financial instability, sovereign indebtedness, and accompanying austerity regimes, as well as increasing societal inequality.[2] Moreover, rethinking institutions of money and finance reveals opportunities for reform that may incrementally, but substantially, transform political economy to better reconcile sustainable prosperity with individual and collective self-determination.

Two characteristics of the current legal architecture of money pose specific dangers not only to the viability of the economy, but also to social cohesion and democracy: One is the extensive ability of commercial banks to create money; the other the conceptual and institutional separation of monetary policy and economic policy, in particular fiscal policy. As concerns money creation, monetary specialists agree that commercial banks are not mere intermediaries between savers and investors, but engage in money creation largely uncontrolled by central banks.[3] Commercial banks engage in money production through extending loans accompanied by the creation of bank deposits.[4] While commercial banks are required to hold a certain amount of reserves with the central bank, and this requirement is meant to limit the amount of loans they extend, in practice, reserve requirements do not determine the amount of loans, but rather reserve creation by central banks

[1] Subtitle and argument of this text are inspired by and build on Unger (1996).

[2] *See* Streeck (2011, 2013); Kennedy (2013); Sassen (2014).

[3] *See* McLeay et al. (2014); Kumhof and Jakab (2016); Mayer (2014), p. 32. For references to various views in the literature on whether or not central banks can effectively control the money supply, *see* Degens (2013), p. 7.

[4] Bank deposits by most accounts are considered money, as account transfers are today the preferred and widely accepted means of payment.

succeeds the decision of private banks to extend loans.[5] Central banks only have limited and indirect means to control the private process of money creation.[6] A number of economists identify the largely unchecked power of commercial banks to create money as an important source of financial instability, asset bubbles, and, eventually, economic crises, which in past years have enhanced social inequalities and severely limited governments' capacities to spend on social welfare.[7] Monetary theorists have responded with calls to reform monetary institutions. Proposals for sovereign money,[8] for plain, full, or positive money[9] share the aim of limiting the ability of commercial banks to create money; they differ with respect to the authority they would give to governmental institutions to create and allocate money, and the importance they accord to seigniorage as a side effect of governmental money creation and a means to increase public revenue.[10]

A second characteristic of the present legal architecture of money, and one which is particularly pronounced in the European Economic and Monetary Union, is the strict conceptual and institutional separation of monetary policy and economic policy, including fiscal policy. One consequence of this separation is the prohibition of monetary financing. According to this prohibition, governments may not exercise monetary sovereignty to generate the means to finance investments, public services, or social welfare. Rather governments need to rely on taxation and debt to finance their budgets. Dependence on taxation and debt has far reaching consequences for democracy and social cohesion. As governments become increasingly indebted to private creditors, the latter's influence on politics rises; Wolfgang Streeck identifies financial investors as a new constituency alongside, and outcompeting, the electorate.[11] Sovereign indebtedness has the further effect of undermining governments' power to tax. If tax income is mainly used to pay off debt, and not to improve living conditions, then the social acceptance of taxation wanes.[12] Restrictions on government spending on infrastructure, education, and social services—resulting from governments' efforts to reduce debt and balance budgets increasingly mandated by constitutional debt brakes or the conditionality accompanying financial

[5] Mayer (2014), p. 36.

[6] These indirect means include the setting of interest rates and purchase of sovereign and commercial bonds, *see* McLeay et al. (2014).

[7] Mayer (2014), pp. 51 f; Turner (2015); Ricks (2015); Kumhof and Jakab (2016); Huber (2013).

[8] Huber (2013); Sigurjonsson (2015) (report commissioned by the Prime Minister of Iceland).

[9] Benes and Kumhof (2012); Mayer (2014).

[10] Josef Huber, who subsumes his reform proposal under the label "New Currency Theory," focuses on public revenue generation from seigniorage, such as the income accruing from money creation, and sees herein a distinguishing factor from other reform proposals. *See* Huber (2014); the proposal for monetary reform in Iceland, which is mainly the work of Josef Huber, attributes the power to decide how much money to create to the central bank and the power to decide how this money is allocated to the political institutions of government, *see* Sigurjonsson (2015), p. 78.

[11] Streeck (2013); *see also* Tabb (2004), p. 121.

[12] Streeck and Mertens (2010).

assistance—threaten to erode the social cohesion necessary for a functioning democracy.[13] Today, even actors at the center of financial capitalism identify a lack of social cohesion and growing inequality as the breeding ground for the rise of populist movements that threaten not only peace and democracy, but also the capitalist economic system itself.[14] While most policy proposals on how to restore public finances and alleviate social inequality focus on taxation,[15] a number of heterodox economists seek to reform public finance through the reconceptualization and redesign of money as a source of public credit.[16]

In the remainder of this contribution I neither analyze the monetary causes of the crisis of democratic capitalism nor do I engage in depth with the various proposals to reform and redesign the legal architecture of money. Rather, I seek to make the case for legal scholarship to engage in research on money and the legal design of monetary institutions to better understand the current political economy and to identify institutions that may reconcile economic prosperity, individual freedom, and democracy. Other legal scholars have drawn attention to money before. Gunther Teubner recently, from a systems-theory perspective, identified money as the most promising locus of reform to contain destructive excesses of the economic system. As money constitutes the medium of the economic system, limiting money production through the legal reform of central banking, according to Teubner, may effectively transform the economic system from within.[17] In this contribution, by contrast, I propose that legal analysis should address money not as a medium exclusively of the economic system, not merely as a medium of exchange, store of value, or unit of account necessary for capitalist transactions. Rather, legal analysis should attempt to understand money as forging linkages between the economic activities of private actors and political collectives—as an institution that determines the relationship between civil society and the state, between the economy and politics.[18] Thus understood, money presents itself as a natural starting point for a reconfiguration of the political economy and bears the potential for a politicization and democratization of the economy.

---

[13] *See also* Chap. 8.

[14] *See* Interview by Shiv Malik with Mario Draghi on 18 Feb 2016 (published on 11 Mar 2016), https://www.ecb.europa.eu/press/inter/date/2016/html/sp160311.en.html.

[15] *See only* Piketty (2014).

[16] The most prominent proponents of so-called modern money theory are Randall Wray, William Mitchell, and Warren Mosler. *See* Wray (2015); Mitchell et al. (2016); Mosler (2010).

[17] Teubner (2011). Teubner refers to Joseph Huber's and Jaromir Benes and Michael Kumhof's proposals to reform monetary institutions *supra* notes 7 and 9.

[18] For legal scholarship that seeks to understand how different monetary designs shape political economy, *see* Desan (2014); for a brief summary and indication of the promise her research holds for reform oriented legal analysis, *see* Desan (2015); Streeck (2013), also seeks to clarify the role of money and finance in political economy and to derive from this understanding proposals for monetary reform. Streeck concentrates on the external dimension of money, namely the potential of exchange rate policy to address economic imbalances.

Building on the work of Roberto Unger, I argue that it should be the objective of legal analysis, informed by political economy research, to propose reforms of monetary institutions to enable democratic experimentalism.[19] Currently, one obstacle for such legal analysis lies in legal scholarship itself and more specifically in what Unger has termed rationalizing legal analysis.[20] Focusing on the conceptual and institutional separation of monetary policy and economic policy, in particular fiscal policy, I, first, set out how German public law scholarship and the Federal Constitutional Court[21] rationalize the separation of money and public finance not only with reference to economics, but also on the basis of constitutional principles. As a consequence of this rationalization, they come to "understand pieces of the law as a purposive social enterprise that reaches toward comprehensive schemes of welfare and right."[22] This rationalization, and its constitutionalization, consolidate a particular institutional design and shield it from critical analysis and change. Second, I critique public law's rationalization of the separation of money and public finance, of monetary and economic policy with reference to recent European Central Bank (ECB) practice. ECB practice not only calls into question this rationalization, but also reveals the close ties and interdependence between monetary and economic policy. Third, I contrast the conceptualization of money in public law scholarship with alternative understandings that emerge from research on the political economy of money. This research further demonstrates how the law's limited understanding of money and its rationalization of the current design of monetary institutions foreclose inquiries in the many different ways in which monetary institutions can shape state society relations. I conclude, fourth, that this research provides inspiration and guidance for a different legal analysis—namely legal analysis that aims at reimagining institutions of money and finance to overcome the current crisis of democratic capitalism and to foster democratic experimentation rather than a state of perpetual austerity.

2 The Separation of Monetary and Economic Policy and Its Rationalization and Constitutionalization in Legal Scholarship and Case Law

For legal analysis to recognize the potential of the institutional design of money to transform the political economy and strengthen democracy requires recognition of the contingency and variability of monetary institutions, and also of the intricate linkages that money forges between state and economy, between government and

[19] Unger (1996, 1998).

[20] Unger (1996), p. 34.

[21] I concentrate on German legal scholarship and jurisprudence because the separation was already very pronounced in Germany prior to the establishment of European Monetary Union and now is even more pronounced in the European Monetary Union in response to German demands for this particular institutional design.

[22] Unger (1996), p. 36.

civil society. In this section I seek to demonstrate how German public law scholarship and case law rationalize and constitutionalize a particular institutional design and thus immunize it from critique and politics. I begin by setting out the main institutional features which characterize the separation of monetary and economic policy in the current legal architecture of the European Economic and Monetary Union. I then lay out German public law scholarship's understanding of money, as the foundation of individual freedom and a precondition of modern statehood, that forms the conceptual basis of this separation. Finally, I reconstruct how, based on this understanding of money, scholarship and case law rationalize and the European Monetary Union constitutionalizes the legal architecture of money.

2.1 Separation of Monetary and Economic Policy in the Current Legal Architecture

The current legal architecture of the European Economic and Monetary Union[23] replicates and further consolidates the separation of monetary and economic policy, of money and public finance, that had characterized the legal architecture of money in Germany already prior to European monetary integration. In Germany the *Bundesbank*, since its establishment in 1957, has operated rather independently from other institutions of government in exercising its mandate to issue currency and conduct monetary policy.[24] The fiscal budget, by contrast, is the prerogative of the executive and parliament. German constitutional law specifies that taxation shall be the main source of public finance.[25] Apart from collecting taxes, and generating revenue in form of other dues, the state incurs debt to finance public investments, for example, by issuing sovereign bonds. The so-called debt brake, since its inclusion in the German Basic Law in 2011, quantitatively limits financing of the public budget through debt.[26]

The distinction between monetary policy and economic, including fiscal, policy is one of the defining features also of the European Economic and Monetary Union. It is reflected in Title VIII "Economic and Monetary Policy" of the Treaty on the Functioning of European Union (TFEU). Those member states which have

[23] It should be noted that while the treaties postulate that "[t]he Union shall establish an economic and monetary union" (Article 3:4 TEU), it would be more correct to speak just of monetary union as member states have not fully transferred their economic policy powers to the EU.

[24] On the objectives of the *Bundesbank's* monetary policy before monetary integration, which encompassed not only monetary stability, but arguably also full employment and economic growth, *see* Roth (2015).

[25] Public law scholarship and the Federal Constitutional Court speak of the principle of the tax state (*Prinzip des Steuerstaats*), Bundesverfassungsgericht [BVerfG] [Federal Constitution Court], Case No. 2 BvL 9/85 and 3/86, 78 Entscheidungen des Bundesverfassungsgerichts [BVerfGE] 249, 266 f.

[26] *See* Article 109:3 Basic Law, §4 Stabilitätsgesetz.

completed the final stage of monetary integration and form part of the euroarea have transferred their monetary policy powers to the EU. Monetary policy, with respect to these states, is the exclusive competence of the EU, to be exercised by the European System of Central Banks (ESCB), consisting of the ECB and the national central banks.[27] The basic tasks of the ESCB include the definition and implementation of the monetary policy of the Union.[28] In exercising its tasks, the ECB and the national central banks must as their primary objective pursue the maintenance of price stability.[29] A number of legal provisions seek to secure the independence of the ECB and national central banks from other institutions of government.[30]

While the EU has the exclusive competence for monetary policy with respect to member states whose currency is the euro, its competences in the realm of economic, including fiscal, policy are more limited. Member states shall regard their economic policies as a matter of common concern and shall coordinate them within the Council.[31] Furthermore, EU law intends to impose fiscal discipline on member states, in particular through the Stability and Growth Pact, which obliges member states to avoid excessive deficits[32] and provides for procedures for the enforcement of this obligation.[33] The so-called no-bailout clause prohibits the European Union and member states from assuming commitments of governments or other public authorities;[34] according to the prohibition of monetary financing[35] the ECB and central banks of the member states may not grant credit to governments and may not buy government bonds on the primary market.

2.2 *Money in German Public Law Scholarship: Foundation of Individual Freedom and Precondition of Modern Statehood*

Justifications of the institutional separation of monetary and economic policy, of money and public finance frequently draw on economic theory. While public law scholarship in Germany also takes its cues from economics, it has established its own understanding of money and its constitutional functions. On the basis of this

[27] Article 282:1 TFEU.

[28] Article 127:2 TFEU.

[29] Article 127:1 TFEU.

[30] According to Article 130 TFEU, neither ECB nor national central banks shall seek or take instructions from EU institutions or member state governments; Article 282:3 obliges the ECB to independently exercise its powers and manage its finances.

[31] Article 121:1 TFEU.

[32] Article 126 TFEU. The reference values are 3 % of GDP for government budget deficits and 60 % of GDP for government debt.

[33] In the course of the eurocrisis, the Stability and Growth Pact was reformed *inter alia* through the so-called 6-pack legislation.

[34] Article 125 TFEU.

[35] Article 123:1 TFEU.

understanding, German public law scholarship rationalizes the legal architecture of money and, in particular, the strict separation of monetary and fiscal policy that finds expression in the prohibition of monetary financing. The understanding of money and its constitutional functions that emerges from public law scholarship is a rather uniform one. Given the wide agreement in scholars' understanding of money, one may wonder at their choice of sources and references, which is rather eclectic, and their style of argumentation that appears impressionistic; at times, quotations or aphorisms—by Jean Bodin, Vladimir Iljitsch Lenin, Fyodor Dostoyevsky, Georg Friedrich Wilhelm Hegel and others—all but replace legal analysis.[36]

When establishing the constitutional functions of money, public law scholarship follows closely, but mostly only implicitly, standard economic accounts of money that ascribe to money the functions to serve as medium of exchange, unit of account, and store of value.[37] Yet, public law scholarship does not stop here. It regards money not simply as the facilitator of economic transactions and a necessary element in a capitalist economy. Rather, in public law's account money becomes the foundation of individual freedom. Money makes freedom possible for the citizen;[38] without money, the realization of individual freedom in today's world is hardly possible.[39] Dostoyevsky provides the quote of choice in this respect: "Money is minted freedom."[40]

Apart from conceiving of money as the foundation of individual freedom, public law scholarship attributes to money a second constitutional function: Money is a precondition of modern statehood. Favorite quotes to underline this finding stem from Bodin, "*Les finances sont les nerfs de l'Etat*"[41] and Lenin, "The most effective way to destroy a society is to destroy its money."[42] This understanding is derived from an observation of a change in state functions. As the tasks of the modern state have multiplied, government can no longer rely on tributes in kind. It needs to generate revenue in the form of money to pay for public expenditures such as military services.[43] Capacity for governmental action comes to depend on money.[44] Based on the finding that money is a precondition of the modern state, public law scholars

---

[36] My observations are mainly based on contributions to a prominent twelve volume treatise on German constitutional law, Josef Isensee and Paul Kirchhof (eds.), Handbuch des Staatsrechts der Bundesrepublik Deutschland, as well as on Herrmann (2010) and Ohler (2015).

[37] *See, e.g.*, Herrmann (2010), p. 149. It should be noted that the function of money to serve as means of payment frequently appears to be subsumed under the function as medium of exchange. This lack of distinction indicates that money is taken to have an existence as medium of exchange that is independent of the legal order that makes it into a means of payment by declaring it legal tender.

[38] Waldhoff (2007), para. 9.

[39] Herrmann (2010), p. 145.

[40] Dostoyevsky (1862).

[41] Quoted in Vogel (2004); Kloepfer (2014), p. 1.

[42] Quoted in Friedman (1962) and from there requoted in numerous legal treatises on money.

[43] Waldhoff (2007), para. 1.

[44] Vogel (2004), paras. 2, 3; Waldhoff (2007), para. 2.

take a further step and denote money as a precondition of the constitution.[45] Even though this account acknowledges the intricate linkage between money and the state,[46] the depiction of their relationship remains surprisingly thin. The intimate connection between money and public finance is reduced to identifying the existence of money as a precondition for public finance generated, mostly, by taxation. Public law scholar Christoph Herrmann, for example, writes:

> From the perspective of the state it may be added [to money functioning as medium of exchange, unit of account and store of value] that only the existence of money enables the state to provide public goods and to pursue economic and social policies according to democratic objectives; as these objectives depend on the state being able to reap part of the economic success of its citizens not in natural produce but as fiscal and tax state in the form of money to be used for its own purposes.[47]

What remains unexamined is to what extent political organization and government are a precondition for money. The account of money as a precondition of modern statehood neglects the process of money creation and the role of government therein. Money is depicted as preceding the modern state and the task of government in this depiction is reduced to providing, administering, and spending this preexistent money.[48]

The understanding of money as having an existence independent of the state, and of the state as depending on the existence of money, may be explained with an uncritical takeover by public law scholarship of economists' accounts that depict the evolution of money as a process driven by private economic actors seeking to minimize transaction costs.[49] A further explanation for adherence to this view may lie in the distinction between the state and civil society that is fundamental to the liberal constitutionalism informing much of public law scholarship. Money is regarded as

---

[45] Vogel (2004), para. 19.

[46] Vogel (2004), para. 2; Waldhoff (2007), para. 9; Herrmann (2010), p. 146.

[47] Herrmann (2010), p. 149 (author's translation); the original reads:

> Aus der Sicht des Staates tritt hinzu [zur Funktion des Geldes als Tauschmittel, Maßeinheit und Wertübertragungs- und Wertaufbewahrungsmittel], dass erst die Existenz von Geld ihm die Bereitstellung öffentlicher Güter sowie die weitläufigen Möglichkeiten wirtschaftlicher und sozialer Lenkung nach Maßgabe eigener, demokratisch gesetzter Ziel- und Zweckvorstellungen ermöglicht; hängen diese doch davon ab, dass der Staat den von ihm beanspruchten Teil des wirtschaftlichen Erfolgs seiner Bürger nicht in Naturalien sondern als Finanz- und Steuerstaat in Geld abschöpfen und dann für seine Zwecke verwenden kann.

Not only can money be used to discharge governments' fiscal obligations, the existence of money also makes possible the taxation of income, expenditures, and production of services. *See* Goodhart (1998), p. 416.

[48] Vogel (2004), para. 3; Waldhoff (2007), para. 1.

[49] *Cf.* also Streeck's observation of the adherence by recent German social theory to the economic concept of money as a politically neutral medium of exchange: Streeck (2015), pp. 9–10. On the account of the evolution of money in mainstream economics and an alternative, cartalist, account, which stresses the central role of the state, see Goodhart (1998). Regarding the success of economic accounts of money that explain its evolution independent of the state, Goodhart hypothesizes that it "may also reflect economists' normative preference for systems determined by private sector cost minimization rather than messier political factors." Goodhart (1998), p. 409.

belonging to the sphere of civil society; it is the medium through which civil society conducts its economic relations. Recognition of a political role of the state in the creation of money, beyond its role as neutral protector of money's value, might undermine the conceptualization of civil society as a sphere separate from politics and the state.[50] Liberal constitutionalism acknowledges taxation, not money, as the main link between state and civil society. As constitutional law scholar Klaus Vogel notes, it is a consequence of the separation of state and economy that the modern state is a tax state, meaning that it generates public revenue mainly through taxation and not through some direct participation in economic production.[51] Taxation not only provides government with the fiscal means, with the money, to pay for its expenditures; it is also understood as an instrument to mitigate harmful effects of the exercise of individual economic freedom through redistribution. According to Vogel, the taxing state is a welfare state, a state of tamed capitalism. In the words of Paul Kirchhof, taxation is the flipside of the medal which on its frontside shows the principle of freedom.[52]

Thus, even though public law scholarship identifies a strong connection between money and public finance, the way this connection is perceived ultimately results in their separation. It is a separation not only reflected in institutional design, but also in the treatment of money and public finance as the subjects of separate subfields in public law scholarship. German public law scholarship conceptually distinguishes between the constitution of money/currency (*Geld-/Währungsverfassung*) that addresses fundamental questions of the legal order of money on the one hand and the constitution of public finance (*Finanzverfassung*) that concerns fundamental questions of public finance on the other hand. This distinction is reflected in scholarly monographs and treatises, which usually deal either with the law of money or the law of public finance.[53] The subdivision of the discipline of public law with some scholars focusing on the constitution of money and others on the constitution of public finance further reinforces the conceptual separation. It results in a research gap as concerns the analysis of the interconnections between the institutions of money and public finance.[54]

---

[50] *Cf.* Charles Blankart's critique of Abba Lerner: Blankart (2011), p. 398. On Abba Lerner's theory of functional finance, *see* Sect. 4.3 below.

[51] Vogel (2004), para. 52.

[52] Vogel (2004), para. 58; Kirchhof (2007).

[53] Isensee and Kirchhof (eds.) (2007) contains separate chapters written by different authors on the constitution of finance and the constitution of money, including: Waldhoff (2007) and Schmidt (2007); on the constitution of money, *see* Herrmann (2010); Hahn and Häde (2010); on the constitution of finance, *see* Kloepfer (2014).

[54] *See also* Goodhart (1998), p. 416 (making a similar point with reference to economics and the lack of analysis of the linkages between money and taxation). The linkages between money and finance are manifold, including, but not limited to, the role of sovereign bonds in the money creation process, the impact of monetary policy on the interest yields of sovereign bonds and money creation by commercial banks. To close the research gap on these linkages collaboration with private lawyers is needed. The work of Christine Desan fills the lacuna as concerns money and finance in early modern England. Desan (2014, 2015); on the links between sovereign bonds and money creation by central banks, *see also* Ingham (2004), ch. 7.

2.3 *Rationalization and Constitutionalization of the Legal Architecture of Money*

Public law's understanding of money as the foundation of individual freedom and precondition not only of modern statehood, but also of the constitution, provides the conceptual basis for a rationalization and constitutionalization of the legal architecture of money. In a first argumentative step, public law scholarship derives from the constitutional functions of money the responsibility of the state to ensure a functioning monetary order, and to protect the value of money. In a second step, it rationalizes the given legal architecture of money—in particular, central bank independence and the prohibition of monetary financing—as necessary to meet this responsibility. With the European Monetary Union this legal architecture has become constitutionalized as it is enshrined in treaty law and thus no longer can be changed by simple legislation.

Given the way in which public law scholarship understands money as the foundation of individual freedom and the existential basis of modern statehood and its constitution, it is not surprising that public law scholarship derives from this understanding the primary responsibility of the state to guarantee a functioning monetary order.[55] Some scholars add that the state's responsibility for the monetary order stems from the fact that the state has assumed the authority to issue money and to conduct monetary policy[56]—a view that again points to the underlying assumption that money preexisted the state and owes its existence to private ordering and only subsequently was captured by the state.[57] In accordance with the understanding of money's functions as medium of exchange, unit of account and store of value, the responsibility to ensure a functioning monetary order is seen to mainly entail the protection of the value of money.

German public law scholarship locates the responsibility to protect the value of money in a number of constitutional provisions, neither of which expressly mentions it: Article 109:2 of the Basic Law (obligation to give due regard to the requirements of overall economic equilibrium), Article 20:1 of the Basic Law (social state principle), and Article 14 of the Basic Law (right to property).[58] According to the German Federal Constitutional Court, the right to property does not, as was argued by some legal scholars, entail an individual right to the protection of the value of money. The Court bases its reasoning mainly on the factual finding that the value of money depends on many different factors—including prices, wages, interest—and that due to these dependencies it is impossible for the state to guarantee the value of

[55] Waldhoff (2007), para. 9; Schmidt (2007), para. 6.

[56] Additional support for the state's responsibility to protect the value of money is derived from the private law principle of nominalism, according to which the value of money depends on its nominal value; put differently nominalism means that the extent of a payment obligation is generally determined nominally and not by the purchasing power of money, Hahn and Häde (2010), pp. 32 f.

[57] As was already indicated, the view that money "can do without the state" finds ample support in economics; Friedrich Hayek, for example, advocated a denationalization of money. *See* Hayek (1977).

[58] Schmidt (2007), paras. 21, 22, 23; Herrmann (2010), p. 185.

money.[59] Nonetheless, public law scholarship sees the constitutional property guarantee as establishing an objective responsibility of the state to provide for a functioning monetary order.[60] With the establishment of the European Monetary Union, it is no longer the German state alone which acts as the guarantor of a functioning monetary order, but rather the members of the Monetary Union and their economies have become the joint guarantors of money.[61]

Having established government's responsibility to provide for a functioning monetary order and to protect the value of money, public law scholarship then rationalizes the existing legal architecture of the monetary order as necessary to meet this responsibility. Public law scholars speak of the "constitution of money" to denote the fundamental legal norms—in particular the independence of central banks, their primary mandate to pursue price stability, and the prohibition of monetary financing—that shall secure the functioning of money as the foundation of the market economy and, thus, of individual freedom and the existence of the state.[62]

This "constitution of money" is based on the premise that the political institutions of government cannot be trusted to effectively protect money's value. Yet, trust is seen as crucial for the maintenance of money's value.[63] In a system of fiat money, democratically elected government officials, so the argument goes, may be tempted to misuse monetary power to pursue short term interests in reelection thus endangering the long term interest in monetary stability.[64] In particular monetary financing, the exercise of monetary sovereignty to generate public finance, is considered as a threat to the value of money as it may not only undermine trust in money's value, but also lead to inflation. To protect the value of money against the temptation of politicians "to start the money printing press," central banks need to be established that operate independently of political government institutions. Independence is to enable central banks to conduct credible monetary policy in pursuit of the objective to protect price stability as an indicator of the stability of money's value.[65] Government, in turn, may not issue money to finance the public budget, but must rely on taxation or debt financing through capital markets. The prohibition of monetary financing is regarded as necessary to ensure the neutrality of public finance.[66] The

[59] Bundesverfassungsgericht [BVerfG] [Federal Constitutional Court], Case No. 2 BvR 1877/97, 97 Entscheidungen des Bundesverfassungsgerichts [BVerfGE] 350 (31 March 1998).

[60] Schmidt (2007), para. 23.

[61] Bundesverfassungsgericht [BVerfG] [Federal Constitutional Court], Case No. 2 BvR 2134/92, 2 BvR 2159/92, 89 Entscheidungen des Bundesverfassungsgerichts [BVerfGE] 155, 174 (12 Oct. 1993).

[62] Herrmann (2010), p. 149; for such accounts of the constitution of money, apart from Christoph Herrmann's, *see* in particular Ohler (2015), and Schmidt (2007); on the prohibition of monetary financing, *see* Kämmerer (2013), para. 5.

[63] Ohler (2015), p. 2 (citing Milton Friedman and Anna Schwartz).

[64] In public choice terms, this situation is referred to as the time inconsistency problem.

[65] The link between the value of money and price stability is provided by purchasing power as a generally accepted expression of the value of money. *See* Ohler (2015), p. 8.

[66] *See* Schmidt (2007), para. 5.

public budget is treated analogously to private households and the conclusion drawn from this analogy is that a state should only be able to incur debt in capital markets according to its creditworthiness "like any other capital market participant."[67]

In the European Economic and Monetary Union, monetary and fiscal policy have been separated to an unprecedented extent and the fundamental norms of the "constitution of money" have indeed been constitutionalized as they have become part of treaty law and, thus, are withdrawn from legislative change. Independence of the ECB and the prohibition of monetary financing in Article 123 of the TFEU rank in the legal hierarchy above member state constitutions and can only be modified through the treaty amendment procedure.[68] Insulation of the ECB from democratic government is thus greater than the *Bundesbank's* insulation from other government institutions ever was.[69] While this institutional design feature of the European Monetary Union has been the subject of some severe criticism, the Federal Constitutional Court endorsed public law's rationalization of the constitution of money also in relation to the legal architecture of the European Monetary Union.

Some economists have long criticized the integration of monetary and economic policy at different speeds. They have warned that giving up monetary autonomy would deprive EU member states of important policy instruments to address economic imbalances in the euroarea. Such economic imbalances or asymmetric shocks, according to the critics, were likely to persist and not be absorbed by full labor mobility, wage flexibility or fiscal transfers—the characteristics usually required for "optimal currency areas"[70] yet not in place in the EU. Governments in the euroarea may no longer use monetary policy instruments—for example the lowering of interest rates to stimulate investment or devaluation of the currency to enhance exports—to counter such economic shocks.[71] While they may still adopt fiscal measures, here too their policy space is restricted by EU norms that seek to impose fiscal discipline. A more fundamental critique, formulated by Charles Goodhart, holds that the optimal currency area model itself is to be criticized as based on a deficient understanding of money—namely one that, ignoring history and empirical facts, accords to money an existence independent of, and prior to, government and public finance. To Goodhart, the European Monetary Union represents not only an unprecedented, but also undesirable divorce between monetary and fiscal competences.[72]

---

[67] *See* Kämmerer (2013), para. 5.

[68] The treaty amendment procedure is laid down in Article 48 TEU.

[69] Zioli and Selmayr (2001), pp. 32–35. In preparation of monetary integration, the German constitution was amended and Article 88, clause 2 Basic Law now expressly provides for a European Central Bank "committed to the overriding goal of assuring price stability."

[70] *See* Mundell (1961).

[71] *See* Eichengreen and Frieden (1993).

[72] Goodhart (1998). A further line of critique stresses how central banks and monetary policy play varying roles in different political economies and that a model of central banking that worked well for Germany could have detrimental effects on differing political economies of other EU member states, *see* Scharpf (2011).

Critics of the European Economic and Monetary Union have also formulated various *legal* objections. One of them, namely the critique that the institutional design of the Monetary Union violates the principle of democracy, poses a serious challenge to public law scholarship's rationalization of the strict separation of monetary policy from economic policy. It pits a high ranking constitutional principle, democratic government, against the function attributed to money as existential foundation of the constitutional state. Yet, in its *Maastricht* judgment, the Federal Constitutional Court in response to this challenge validated the rationalization of central bank independence put forward in public law scholarship. While on its face the decision presents central bank independence as an exception to the principle of democracy in need of justification, the decision can also be interpreted as arguing—closely following, and even going beyond, public law scholarship in this point—that central bank independence is a precondition of democracy.

The Court reformulated the democracy challenge as follows:

> A substantial political sphere which supports individual liberty by maintaining the value of the currency, and influences public finances and those areas of politics dependent on them by controlling the money supply, has been withdrawn from the authority of the holders of sovereign rights and (without an amendment of the Treaty) from legislative control over functions and procedures.[73]

This statement is obviously influenced by the *Bundesbank's* style of monetary policy, but it also reflects public law scholarship's rationalization of the constitutional order of money. It assumes that the primary objective of monetary policy is "maintaining the value of the currency" and adds that the way to achieve this objective is by "controlling the money supply." Given this particular conception of the affected "political sphere" then provides the basis for the Court to rebut the challenge that the principle of democracy is unduly impaired. Transferring competence to an independent ECB which is to give priority to monetary stability is justified according to the Court:

> because it takes account of the special factor, established in the German system and also *scientifically proven*, that an independent central bank is more likely to protect monetary value, and therefore the general economic basis for national budget policy and private planning and disposition, while maintaining economic liberty than are sovereign governmental institutions.[74]

---

[73] Bundesverfassungsgericht, *supra* note 61; the English translation is available at: http://www.judicialstudies.unr.edu/JS_Summer09/JSP_Week_1/German%20ConstCourt%20Maastricht.pdf (quote at 30).

[74] *Id.* p. 31 (emphasis added). The Court reiterated this finding in its ruling of 14 Jan 2014 on OMT:

> Nevetheless, this restriction [of democratic legitimation] is still compatible with democratic principles because it takes the tested and scientifically documented special character of monetary policy into account that an independent central bank is more likely to safeguard monetary stability, and thus the economic basis, for budgetary policies, than state bodies whose actions depend on money supply and value and which need to rely on short-term approval by political forces.

Bundesverfassungsgericht [BVerfG] [Federal Constitutional Court], Case No. 2 BvR 2728/13, 134 Entscheidungen des Bundesverfassungsgerichts [BVerfGE] 366 (14 Jan. 2014), para. 59 (note the weakening of "scientifically proven" into "scientifically documented").

The argument can be restated as follows: Mandating a central bank, which is insulated from politics, with the conduct of monetary policy to be aimed at monetary stability, rather than encroaching upon democratic self-government, in fact, protects the very bases of democracy—individual freedom and the material security required to exercise this freedom, as well as the national budget. In this reading, money is elevated from precondition of the modern state and its constitution to precondition of democracy to be protected by an independent central bank. Constitutionalization of central bank independence and of price stability as the overriding objective of monetary policy thus becomes an asset rather than a problem for democracy.

The Federal Constitutional Court in *Maastricht* also addressed the economic critique that it was unsustainable in the long run to allocate the power for monetary policy to the EU, while member states remained largely responsible for economic policy. It did so by deferring to the political process. In response to the complainants' fear that monetary union would introduce economic union through the backdoor, the Court conceded that:

> [t]here may be justifiable grounds for suggesting that, in political terms, the monetary union may be implemented practically only if it is supplemented immediately by an economic union which exceeds simple coordination of the economic policies of the Member States and the Community.[75]

Moreover, it referenced the *Bundesbank's* view that a monetary union among states with active economic and social policies could only be realized within a political union with all "essential functions of public finance."[76] Yet, while registering the doubts with respect to the feasibility of monetary union without economic and political union, the Court stated that to go ahead with monetary union was a political decision "for which the relevant governmental institutions must assume political responsibility."[77] Were monetary integration to fail, the treaty would need to be amended either to reverse monetary union or to complement it with economic and political union.

The latter alternative seems somewhat disingenuous in light of the Court's subsequent case law, which sets limits to fiscal integration derived from the constitutional identity as protected by Article 79:3 of the Basic Law. While the withdrawal of monetary policy from democratic government is rationalized in terms of individual freedom and the protection of democratic government, the Court considers public finance and budgetary authority to constitute core competences of democratic government. According to the Court, the right to approve the national budget lies at the heart of parliament's control functions with respect to the executive[78] and the power to tax also forms part of constitutional identity.[79] Thus, while the Court upholds the

[75] Bundesverfassungsgericht, *supra* note 61, p. 29.

[76] *Id.* p. 30.

[77] *Id.*

[78] Bundesverfassungsgericht [BVerfG] [Federal Constitutional Court], Case No. 2 BvR 987/10; 2 BvR 1485/10; 2 BvR 1099/10, 129 Entscheidungen des Bundesverfassungsgerichts [BVerfGE] 124 (7 Sept. 2011).

[79] Bundesverfassungsgericht [BVerfG] [Federal Constitutional Court], Case No. 2 BvE 2/08; 2 BvE 5/08; 2 BvR 1010/08; 2 BvR 1022/08; 2 BvR 1259/08; 2 BvR 182/09, 123 Entscheidungen des Bundesverfassungsgerichts [BVerfGE] 267 (30 June 2009) para. 252.

constitutionality of the transfer of monetary power to an independent ECB, it establishes constitutional hurdles for the transfer of substantial fiscal powers to the EU.[80]

To sum up, the following picture emerges of German public law's understanding and rationalization of money and its institutions: Public law's treatment of money is informed by the dominant economic model of money. According to this model, money constitutes a medium of exchange originally generated from within civil society. The state subsequently assumed authority over money; yet, despite this assumption of monetary authority the state can, and should, be neutral as regards the process of money creation. This model is being increasingly criticized from within and outside the economic discipline, *inter alia* because it ignores politics and state involvement in money creation.[81] Yet, public law scholarship unquestioningly, and sometimes it seems unconsciously, bases its understanding of money on this economic model. It further valorizes this understanding by linking it to constitutional values, positing that money constitutes the foundation of individual freedom and democratic constitutionalism. The German Federal Constitutional Court even elevates the connection between central bank independence and containment of inflation to a matter of scientific truth thus abstracting from the particularities and contexts of social arrangements.[82] Legal scholarship's rationalizing legal analysis and its validation by the Federal Constitutional Court have the effect of immunizing the legal architecture of money from critique and foreclosing imagination of institutional alternatives.[83] In the European Monetary Union then, the legal architecture of money has become fully constitutionalized. Central bank independence and mandate, as well as the prohibition of monetary financing have been enshrined in treaty law and, thus, been further insulated from politics. Even though the Federal Constitutional Court stresses the responsibility of politics in case of failure of the European Economic and Monetary Union it appears illusionary that politics live up to this responsibility—one reason being the power of facts, the other the constitutional hurdle towards fiscal integration that the Court itself put up in its case law.

3 Collapse of the Separation of Monetary and Economic Policy in ECB Practice: Experimental Expertise and Expertocratic Politics

Current developments in the European Economic and Monetary Union seem to be proving the sceptics right. Instead of convergence of the economies in the euroarea, disparities increase between center and periphery. At the same time, the assumption

[80] *Cf.* Herrmann (2012), p. 807.

[81] *See* Goodhart (1998); Graeber (2011); Desan (2014, 2015).

[82] *See* Bundesverfassungsgericht, *supra* note 74.

[83] *Cf.* Roberto Unger's critique of rationalizing legal analysis in Unger (1996), p. 8.

of political responsibility by either reversing monetary union or complementing it with economic and political union is not in sight. Instead the ECB appears as the driving force in a reconstitution of the European Economic and Monetary Union through the adoption of so-called "unconventional" or "non-standard monetary policy instruments" in combination with calls for structural adjustment and the negotiation and monitoring of such structural adjustment as part of the conditionality of financial assistance. As a consequence the ECB has been called a "policy-maker of last resort".[84]

The ECB's non-standard monetary policy might be only the most visible sign that one of the fundamental principles on which the European Economic and Monetary Union is built—the strict separation between monetary policy and economic policy—collapses. Unconventional monetary policy and its justification demonstrate that the ECB is not the neutral, rules-based expert institution that the Federal Constitutional Court and rationalizing legal scholarship want it to be, but rather engages in experimental policy-making in reaction to the crisis. While the ECB justifies its policies with the pursuit of monetary objectives, these policies have consequences going far beyond the protection of the value of money—including financial instability and upward redistribution of income. The ECB recognizes these dangers. In response, it calls on the political institutions of government to implement further structural adjustments in order to contain them. As concerns the content of structural adjustment, the ECB has concise views which it regularly expounds in its communications. Consequently, it appears from recent ECB practice that rules-based expert governance in the ECB is being replaced with an experimental approach that blurs the distinction between monetary and (other) economic policy. Concomitantly, the political institutions of government increasingly come under pressure to implement the structural adjustments demanded by economic experts at the ECB.

3.1 Experimental Monetary Policy

The ECB added so-called unconventional or non-standard instruments, such as the announcement of an Outright Monetary Transactions (OMT) Programme on September 6, 2012 or the Asset Purchase Programme, to its arsenal of standard interest rate instruments in the course of the eurocrisis.[85] These instruments have been criticized as lying outside the ECB's mandate for the conduct of monetary policy in pursuit of price stability—the most vocal critics being German central bankers

[84] Eichengreen (2012). Ironically, the current expansive policy of the ECB, the governmental institution furthest removed from the electorate, appears aimed not only at stimulating the economy, but increasingly also at protecting social stability in Europe.

[85] Roubini speaks of unconventional unconventional monetary policy. *See* Roubini (2016). The ECB's newest addition to its unconventional monetary policy arsenal is the program commenced in June 2016 under which the ECB purchases company bonds: Decision (EU) 2016/948 of the European Central Bank of 1 June 2016 on the implementation of the corporate sector purchase programme (ECB/2016/16), https://www.ecb.europa.eu/mopo/implement/omt/html/index.en.html.

and economists who demand a return to standard monetary policy.[86] The ECB itself presents its policies as falling squarely within its mandate. Yet, their justification in terms of the ECB's primary objective to maintain the value of money reveals how porous the dividing line is between monetary and economic policy and that the determination of (unconventional) monetary policy depends on the experimental judgment of ECB experts which is largely intractable for outsiders.

Jean-Claude Trichet—under whose presidency the ECB first endorsed unconventional, non-standard monetary policy measures, including quantitative easing, i. e. large scale asset purchases—put forward an elaborate justification for this new practice. He was the one who explained their objective to be the removal of obstacles in the transmission of conventional interest rate policy.[87] In the euroarea non-standard instruments, according to Trichet, are not only a continuation of standard monetary instruments to be employed once the capacity of interest rate policy to inject new liquidity into the economy has been exhausted; rather non-standard measures are to accompany standard measures where this is necessary to ensure the effectiveness of monetary policy, its effective transmission, throughout the whole euroarea. Such effective transmission is obstructed, for example, where sovereign bonds of individual, financially distressed, states yield much higher interest than those of other euroarea members. This justification advanced by the ECB for unconventional monetary policy played a crucial role in the OMT proceeding before the Court of Justice of the European Union. Its restatement by the Advocate General Cruz Villalón presents an illuminating outside view on central bank expertise in the conduct of monetary policy. In his opinion, Advocate General Cruz Villalón stresses the expert knowledge of the ECB which sets it apart from other institutions:

> In fact, the Treaties confer on the ECB sole responsibility for framing and implementing monetary policy, for which purpose it is given substantial resources with which to undertake its functions. On account of those resources the ECB also has access to knowledge and particularly valuable information, which permits it to perform its tasks more effectively whilst also, over time, bolstering its technical expertise and reputation.[88]

According to this view, it is due to its access to expert knowledge and information that the ECB can assess whether unconventional monetary policy measures are needed to "unblock" the Union's monetary transmission channels. Yet, the Advocate General may have been too optimistic in assuming that the ECB has privileged access to expert knowledge. Even though Mario Draghi does not tire of stressing that the ECB is not a political institution, but rather acts according to pre-existing rules,[89] its recent practice of employing non-standard policy measures reveals that

[86] Plickert (2013).

[87] Trichet (2010).

[88] Case C-62/14, Gauweiler v. Deutscher Bundestag, ECLI:EU:C:2015:7 (14 Jan. 2015), para. 110.

[89] *See, e.g.*, Draghi (2015a).

there exist neither clear rules nor undisputed scientific knowledge that determine the content of monetary policy or the dividing line between monetary and other economic policy.[90] As Trichet, Draghi's predecessor, himself freely admitted, the ECB in the eurocrisis was acting in the "absence of guidance from existing analytical frameworks" and instead judgment and experience played a key role.[91] Moreover, Trichet called for "input from various theoretical perspectives and from a range of empirical approaches" and formulated the view that an "open debate and a diversity of views must be cultivated—admittedly not always an easy task in an institution such as the ECB."[92]

3.2 *Expert-Led Structural Adjustment*

The impossibility of cabining off monetary policy in pursuit of the protection of money's value is most apparent if one looks at the effects of monetary policy that go beyond influencing price stability. In response to these effects, the ECB ever more strongly advocates for economic reform, so-called structural adjustment. On the one hand, structural adjustment, including the flexibilization of the labor market, the reduction of entry barriers to protected sectors, as well as of administrative burdens on entrepreneurs, shall increase the effectiveness of ECB policy. Structural adjustment shall complement the ECB's efforts to secure price stability by improving the economy's ability to adjust to shocks and ensure that ECB interest rate policy is effective throughout the whole euroarea.[93] On the other hand, regulatory reform shall contain the potentially harmful effects of unconventional monetary policy, in particular the asset purchase programs.

Large-scale asset purchases by central banks have two immediate effects: First, they enhance commercial bank reserves with the central bank, and second, they lower the interest yields of the assets that are being purchased. These effects shall stimulate the real economy by increasing bank loans and investments in riskier assets with higher interest yields. The mechanisms of quantitative easing may also, however, produce a number of secondary effects, including unequal distributional effects. The Bank of England found, in a study conducted on its own quantitative easing policy, that while the policy boosted households' wealth, the increase was distributed unevenly with 5 % of households holding 40 % of the financial assets of the household sector as a whole.[94] Moreover, quantitative easing may negatively affect revenue from investments by pension funds and insurers as these frequently

[90] *See* Goldmann (2014).

[91] Trichet (2010).

[92] *Id.*

[93] Mersch (2015).

[94] Bank of England (2012), p. 254.

face legal restrictions concerning their investments. If, by law, they are prevented from investing in the higher yielding, but riskier, assets while the interest rates of assets they are allowed to invest in drop, their income decreases. Finally, there are warnings that the money creation induced by quantitative easing may not stimulate the real economy, but rather lead to asset bubbles that increase the risk of repeated financial crisis.[95]

The ECB acknowledges these dangers. Yet, its current president, Draghi, defends the view that it is up to the political institutions to address such dangers—through, on the one hand, liberalizing the investment constraints of pension funds and insurers and, on the other hand, strengthening prudential regulation of the finance industry.[96] At the same time, the ECB rebuts calls for a more focused asset purchase program according to which the ECB would purchase specific assets with a view to strengthening particular economic sectors, such as the sustainable energy sector. In response to such suggestions, Draghi points to the ECB's mandate and interprets it as not allowing the ECB to purposefully promote any other economic objectives apart from price stability.[97] From the communications of the ECB there emerges, thus, a comprehensive plan for the monetary and economic order of the EU and ECB officials do not shy away from giving clear guidance to governments as to what in their view is needed to turn the European Economic and Monetary Union into a success. According to this plan, monetary and economic, including fiscal, policy complement each other—one cannot be successful without the other. It consequently implicates strict limitations on democratic choice.[98]

3.3 *How to Square ECB Practice with the Rationalization of the Legal Architecture of Money?*

Recent ECB practice proves public law's rationalization of the legal architecture of money to be untenable. It reveals how central bank policy is becoming increasingly experimental and puts democratic politics under pressure to adopt particular policies as advised by central bank experts. As a consequence, the main pillar of the argumentative support for the institutional arrangement collapses: Monetary policy is not a domain which can be easily isolated from the rest of economic policy in the interest of protecting individual freedom, the state, and democracy.

---

[95] Bank of International Settlements (2016), p. 63.

[96] Draghi (2015b).

[97] Transcript of the Hearing at the European Parliament's Economic and Monetary Affairs Committee (2015): "You asked also whether this [higher inflation] is the only reason we are actually doing this, and whether price stability is the only reason? Well, the answer is yes; we are bound by the mandate. The mandate speaks only of price stability." *Id.* p. 10.

[98] *Cf.* also Christian Joerges' assessment that in the course of the eurocrisis management an authoritarian executive managerialism has come to replace democratic processes, *see* Joerges (2014b).

The two general reactions adopted by lawyers to the ECB's monetary policy present no convincing answers to the mismatch between practice and theory. The Federal Constitutional Court, following the *Bundesbank*, criticized the ECB for overstepping its mandate.[99] Yet, this critique does not provide a positive answer to the question how the ECB may conduct monetary policy in a way that conforms to the ideal of a politically neutral central bank that merely protects the value of money. The other response is offered by a number of legal scholars who, in reaction to the Federal Constitutional Court's first OMT decision, called for judicial restraint and deference to central bankers' expertise. They point to the formulation of the ECB's mandate, which encompasses the pursuit of economic objectives other than price stability, and further treaty provisions which leave leeway to interpret ECB policy as being in conformity with the law.[100] This stance of public law scholars—while it may accord to doctrines of separation of powers and judicial review of administrative acts—tends to undermine the discipline's understanding of money and its rationalization of monetary institutions as politically neutral institutions, controlling the money supply to protect the value of money. It also raises the question how ECB practice, which turns the ECB into an agenda setter for democratic politics to be conducted in the shadow of the power of private creditors,[101] may be reconciled with the principle of democracy. At the very least, this situation calls for public law scholarship to revisit its understanding of money.[102]

4 Reconceptualizing Money

In the endeavor to reconceptualize money, public law scholarship can build on a number of recent—and not so recent—works in sociology, anthropology, legal history and heterodox economics[103] that seek to clarify the political economy of money, i. e. the interplay of economics and politics in the creation and workings of money. These works expose the fetishism inherent in public law scholarship's rationalizations of the separation of monetary and economic policy, of money and public finance and illustrate the contingency of the current institutional arrangement.

---

[99] Bundesverfassungsgericht [BVerfG] [Federal Constitutional Court], Case No. 2 BvR 2728/13, 134 Entscheidungen des Bundesverfassungsgerichts [BVerfGE] 366 (14 Jan 2014).

[100] Goldmann (2014); Herrmann (2012).

[101] This shadow may explain why in Germany high tax income currently does not lead to increased public investments. While expansive monetary policy results in low interest rates on sovereign bonds and thus a good budgetary situation this may change at the hand of the ECB and the budget may again be strained due to increased debt service.

[102] *Cf.* also the critique by Christian Joerges of a missing theoretical paradigm to inform the European Economic Constitution, *see* Joerges (2014a, 2016).

[103] Mitchell-Innes (1913), *reprinted in* Wray (2004); Goodhart (1998); Ingham (2004); Graeber (2011); Desan (2014, 2015); Wray (2015); Mitchell et al. (2016); Mosler (2010).

In the following, I contrast public law scholarship's understanding of money with a number of insights that are produced by this research. First, historical and anthropological research dispels the standard account in economics, on which public law scholarship builds, that money emerged as an exchange commodity with the purpose of reducing transaction costs in a barter economy. This research further supports a conceptualization of money as credit as opposed to a conceptualization of money as medium of exchange. Second, research on the political economy of money reveals how money is the outcome of an intricate interplay between economic and political actors, economic and political rationalities, and how it resists subsumption under theories of sovereignty or division between state and civil society. Third, Abba Lerner's theory of functional finance illustrates how a reconceptualization of money could lead to a very different institutional design.

4.1 The Myth of Money's Origination as Exchange Commodity—Money as Credit

Public law scholarship understands money as precondition of modern statehood. It presents money as having emerged independently of, and prior to, the state in the sphere of private economic transactions. This understanding—more often implicitly than explicitly—builds on and potentially reinforces standard accounts in economics on the evolution of money. Possibly the most famous of such accounts is rendered by Adam Smith who, like so many economists after him, explains money as a solution to the problem of transaction costs in a barter economy.[104] Once economic actors had agreed on a particular commodity as exchange commodity, for example cod, this commodity could be exchanged for all other commodities, and thus the problem of the double coincidence of wants could be overcome. The butcher who needed bread whilst the baker did not need meat could pay the baker with cod instead of having to find someone who would take his meat in exchange for a commodity that the baker needed. The story continues by laying out how, over time, precious metals constituted preferred exchange commodities due to their qualities, such as durability, measurability and fungibility.[105]

Scholars of money have forcefully pointed out how this account of the historical emergence of money has been disproven time and again. David Graeber refers to anthropological research that falsifies the assumption that barter economies preceded money economies.[106] More important for my argument is the finding by Alfred Mitchell-Innes—writing a century earlier than Graeber—that coins hardly ever functioned as an exchange commodity, either in the sense that

[104] Smith (1776); *see also* Menger (1892).

[105] *Cf.* Marx (1867), ch. 1.

[106] Graeber (2011), ch. 2.

they had real value equaling their purchasing value or that they represented such value by being exchangeable into gold or silver.[107] Rather, coins constituted mere tokens which could be used in economic transaction because, for example, they were made legal tender or refusal to accept them was criminalized.[108] Drawing on commercial history, numismatics and archeology, Mitchell-Innes concludes that economic theories on the emergence of money do not rest on historical proof and are simply false.[109]

On the empirical findings that "there never was, a monetary unit which depended on the value of a coin or on a weight of metal, that there never was, until quite modern days, any fixed relationship between the monetary unit and any metal,"[110] Mitchell-Innes builds his own theory of money. To him, money is credit and "credit alone is money."[111] Returning to Adam Smith he holds that a lack of a double coincidence of wants—say between butcher and baker—need not forfeit the transaction. The butcher might receive bread from the baker in exchange for an acknowledgment of debt—a transfer of credit on the baker. The baker now owns an IOU (I owe you) from the butcher. The value of this credit lies not so much in the fact that it can be presented to the butcher to demand payment of the debt, but rather that the holder can use it to liberate herself from a debt.[112] Money emerges when such IOUs are being linked to a unit of account and become transferable and acceptable as payment.

Thus understood, money originates in debt and signifies debt and its flipside credit. In economics, representatives of the so-called banking school agree with this concept of money in so far as they, too, see credit creation as the key link between money and the real economy.[113] With regard to today's monetary system, one may at first glance consider a debate about whether or not money represents credit to be obsolete. With the emergence of fiat money and fractional reserve banking, the understanding of money as credit has become even more plausible. Money is not convertible into gold or some other valuable commodity. Paper bills issued by the central bank constitute liabilities of the central bank which, however, can only be redeemed in kind: Central bank money can only be exchanged for central bank money.[114] The credit function of money is even clearer in relation to money creation by commercial banks. As stated in the introduction, commercial banks create money when they extend a loan and instead of paying out the loan in cash, register

---

[107] Mitchell-Innes (1913), p. 14.

[108] *Id.* p. 19.

[109] *Id.* p. 15.

[110] *Id.* p. 16.

[111] *Id.* p. 31; with this theory Mitchell-Innes also dispels the standard economic account that credit succeeds the emergence of money, *id.* p. 27.

[112] *Id.* p. 31.

[113] *See* Goodhart (2015).

[114] McLeay et al. (2014), p. 7.

a deposit. This deposit money represents not some real economic value, but credit which the bank extends based on the debtor's "promise of productivity."[115]

Yet, despite the purchase of the credit theory of money—not only in light of historical and anthropological research, but also current banking practice—the account of money as an exchange commodity lives on in economics and in public law scholarship. Representatives of the currency school—banking school's opponent—consider money to ideally be neutral concerning its effects on the real economy, to constitute not more than a veil behind which exchanges between goods and services take place. To achieve such neutrality, commercial banks should not engage in money creation, but merely in financial intermediation and the central bank should control the money supply in accordance with predefined rules.[116] When German public law scholarship depicts money as a medium of exchange (rather than a means of payment[117]), when public law scholar Reiner Schmidt writes that liquidity creation by commercial banks must be restricted and the Federal Constitutional Court describes the task of the central bank as controlling the money supply,[118] they appear to have in mind just such an understanding of money.

4.2 Money as Public Private Partnership

Historical and anthropological studies not only show how an account of money as exchange commodity emerging from barter misrepresents history and provide the basis for an understanding of money as credit. They also call into doubt whether money can ever exist independently of government or rather some political organization of society. While Mitchell-Innes expresses skepticism with regard to the view that money is always a function of government,[119] he does acknowledge that credit money depends on a recognition by society to make it transferable and thus turn it into a means of payment.[120] Graeber is more explicit in his finding that money depends on political organization for its existence.[121] The less an economy is based on codes of honor and trust, the more plausible it seems that for credit money to become a generally accepted means of payment, governmental authority is required. Governmental authority can take the form of legislation designating money as legal tender, tax legislation that requires that debts owed to the state be

---

[115] Desan (2015), p. 27.

[116] Goodhart (2015).

[117] *See* Herrmann (2010).

[118] Schmidt (2007), para. 5; Bundesverfassungsgericht, *supra* note 61, p. 31.

[119] *See* Mitchell-Innes (1913), p. 27.

[120] *Id.* p. 29.

[121] Graeber (2011), ch. 2.

redeemed in money or the criminalization of the refusal to accept money as a means of payment.[122] Accordingly, for Friedrich Knapp, money is a creature of the legal order.[123] Christine Desan, abstracting from her historical study of money in pre-modern and early modern England, defines money and points to its collective and political dimension in the following way:

> In both early and modern worlds, money arises in groups that draw on the contribution of members to support themselves or their activities. It is created when a stakeholder, acting for the group, uses its singular position to specify and entail value in a way that no individual or bargaining pair of individuals can do.[124]

Desan, too, with her definition points to the credit function of money as well as to political organization as essential for the emergence of money.

Yet, even though studies of the political economy of money clarify the significant role of political organization and government in premodern, as well as modern capitalist societies, they also caution against simple classifications. They reveal the intricate interplay of economic and political actors and rationalities which varies over time. Joseph Vogl points out how money and finance have always posed a great challenge for theories of sovereignty,[125] how questions of public revenue, sovereign debt, taxation and fiscal affairs resist resolution with the help of a unitary concept of the political.[126] For him, public finance and money constitute sites where political power, commercial operations and interactions between private citizens become linked.[127] Contrary to German public law scholarship, Vogl does not locate the foundation of modern statehood in an account of money, but rather in the relationship between fiscal needs, sovereign indebtedness to private creditors and taxation that required institutionalization.[128] Desan's study of the legal history of the Bank of England[129] supplements this story. For Desan, the novel institutional design represented by the Bank of England[130] marks the transition in political economy to a capitalist system. In this system, government's fiscal position depends on private bondholders, a class of creditors takes an interest in sufficient taxation as assurance that

---

[122] For examples, *see* Mitchell-Innes (1913), pp. 19, 26.

[123] Knapp (1905).

[124] Desan (2015), p. 24.

[125] *See* Vogl (2015).

[126] *Id.* p. 76.

[127] *Id.* p. 80.

[128] *Id.* p. 94.

[129] Desan (2014), ch. 8.

[130] The Bank of England was created when a group of private investors extended a loan to the government of England to be dispensed in the form of bank notes. These notes became acceptable as means of payment as they could be exchanged for species and could be used to redeem tax obligations to the government.

government can meet its debt obligations, and money to a large extent is produced by commercial banks making loans based on promises of profitability.[131] While both Vogl and Desan provide a wealth of material and argument for public law scholarship to refine its understanding of money and in particular the relationship between money and public finance, Abba Lerner's theory of functional finance gives us an idea how money and monetary design might be used for the purpose of reconfiguring political economy.

4.3 Abba Lerner's Theory of Functional Finance

From a conceptualization of money as credit, it is only a small step to see how money could serve as a direct source of public finance. The public finance function of money is the focus of Abba Lerner's theory of functional finance[132] and the more recent modern money theory.[133] I reference them here in order to illustrate how an alternative understanding of money can inform a very different institutional design of monetary institutions, one that might significantly lessen government's dependence on private creditors. While according to public law scholarship's understanding of money and public finance, the state should obtain credit according to its creditworthiness like any private household,[134] the theory of functional finance holds that the power to issue money can render the state independent from private creditors' assessment of its creditworthiness. Government spending on this account truly can become a function of democratic politics instead of capital market preferences.[135]

According to Lerner, building on Georg Friedrich Knapp,[136] the state can create money by denoting any thing as money if concurrently it creates liabilities, such as tax liabilities, owed to the state. The state brings this token money into circulation through paying with it for goods and services provided by society. It further creates a demand for this money by imposing taxes or other liabilities to be redeemed through payment of this money to the state. Thus, the state can generate public finance through the issuance of money. Note the difference to German public law

[131] Desan (2015), p. 27.

[132] Lerner (1943); Lerner (1947).

[133] *See* Wray (2014, 2015); Mitchell et al. (2016); Mosler (2010).

[134] *See* Kämmerer (2013), para. 5.

[135] *See* Mosler (2010). To be sure, the legal architecture of money in the European Union currently does not allow an implementation of Lerner's theory of functional finance. Implementation would require a different institutional design.

[136] Knapp (1905).

accounts of money and taxation: According to Lerner not taxation, but money is the primary source of public finance. The theory of functional finance also addresses the relationship between the public finance function of money and the value of money or inflation. According to Lerner, in order to keep the value of money stable and to ensure full employment, it should be the financial responsibility of government to "keep the total rate of spending in the country on goods and services neither greater nor less than that rate which at current prices would buy all the goods and services that it is possible to produce".[137] If government spends too much so that the optimal rate is exceeded, the result will be inflation; if it spends too little, the result is unemployment.[138] Taxation becomes an instrument to contain inflation by reducing the money that taxpayers can spend.[139]

The understanding of money and monetary sovereignty put forward by Lerner enables government to judge fiscal measures by their effects on the economy and not by any traditional doctrines of what constitutes sound or unsound budgetary policies.[140] Modern money theory builds on Lerner's theory of functional finance to argue, for example, that the state should exercise its monetary sovereignty to establish a job guarantee that would function like a buffer stock in the commodities sector, i. e. create jobs in times of high unemployment which would then be absorbed by the private sector in times of economic upswing.[141]

Lerner's theory of functional finance not only points towards an alternative institutional design of money and public finance, it also sheds light on the dark side of the rationalization of the separation of money and public finance in terms of individual economic freedom and democratic government. With the prohibition of monetary financing, public finance becomes dependent on capital markets and private investment driven by profit. With governments increasingly indebted to private capital, citizens compete with creditors to hold governments accountable. The competition is an unequal one and the latter—given their economic power—are likely to be more successful in getting governments to cater to their special interests. Reimagining money as a source of public credit might enable governments to tap a society's productive potential and to finance investments that generate value independent from a profit rationale.

---

[137] Lerner (1943), p. 39.

[138] Spending can be financed either by borrowing or issuing money. According to Lerner, governments should only borrow if they hold it desirable that the public has less money and more government bonds (Lerner's 2nd law of functional finance). *Id.* p. 40.

[139] *Id.*

[140] Lerner (1947).

[141] *See* Mitchell and Muysken (2008); Kaboub (2007); *see also* Wray (2015), p. 221.

5 Freeing Legal Analysis of Money for Institutional Imagination and Democratic Experimentation

> The one thing that's clear is that new ideas won't emerge without jettisoning of much of our accustomed categories of thought—which have become mostly sheer dead weight, if not intrinsic parts of the very apparatus of hopelessness—and formulating new ones.[142]

With this text I aimed to show how public law's understanding of money and its rationalization of the legal architecture of money fetishize current institutions—such as independent central banks and the prohibition of monetary financing—and thus stand in the way of new ideas. The recognition of legal scholarship's complicity in consolidating a political economy, perceived by many as unjust, can, of course, be but a preparation for the real work of legal analysis, one that aims at institutional imagination and democratic experimentation, to begin. This legal analysis finds inspiration and can build on a number of studies on the political economy of money, *inter alia* from historical and anthropological perspectives. These studies remind us that the separation of monetary and economic policy, of money and public finance, and its institutional implementation is neither a matter of scientific truth nor the only possible social arrangement. They challenge us to consider monetary policy as fiscal policy and inquire into ways to make public finance dependent on democratic choice instead of the preferences of capital markets. They form a valuable source to inform programmatic thinking on how to reconfigure political economy through monetary design and thus to address the crisis of democratic capitalism.[143]

Legal scholars should be ideally suited to take up the project of an institutional reimagination of money. Economists may have been eager to minimize the role of government in their conception of money, be it to establish economics as an independent discipline[144] or, for ideological reasons, to minimize interference of politics in their domain of competence.[145] But why would lawyers follow suit and not assert their competence over exactly the messy interplay of politics and economics, individual freedom and collective restraint? Legal scholarship can build on what Unger considers to be the "genius of contemporary law" which is that it seeks to realize "a binary system of rights of choice and of arrangements withdrawn from the scope of choice the better to make the exercise of choice real and effective"[146] without assuming—like 19th century legal thought—that particular sets of legal rights and institutions will automatically protect political and economic freedom.[147] Taking the contingency of sociolegal arrangements as a starting point, legal analysis must

142 Graeber (2011), p. 384.

143 *Cf.* Specht (2015).

144 Graeber (2011), p. 25.

145 Goodhart (1998), p. 409.

146 Unger (1996), p. 27.

147 *Id.*

probe more boldly whether our existing arrangements indeed achieve a reconciliation of individual freedom of choice with the protection of the material bases for effective choice.

In devising new institutions, experimentation must point the way. Experimentation already today characterizes much of monetary policy. If we acknowledge that current experimentation, though highly political, is not only devoid democratic accountability, but worse, is further undermining parliamentary democracy, we should be able to muster the courage to detach ourselves from the "the cross of our arrangements"[148] and start a different experiment.

References

Bank of England (2012) The distributional effects of asset purchases. Bank Engl Q Bull Q3:186

Bank of International Settlements (2016) 86th Annual Report. 1 April 2015–31 March 2016

Benes J, Kumhof M (2012) The Chicago plan revisited, IMF WP/12/202

Blankart CB (2011) Öffentliche Finanzen in der Demokratie: Eine Einführung in die Finanzwissenschaft, 8th edn. Vahlen, Munich

Degens P (2013) Alternative Geldkonzepte – ein Literaturbericht, MPIfG Discussion Paper 13/1

Desan C (2014) Making money: coins, currency, and the coming of capitalism. Oxford University Press, New York

Desan C (2015) Decoding the design of money. Eur Financ Rev 24, Feb–Mar 2015

Dostoyevsky F (1862) Notes from a dead house (2015, translated by Richard Pevear and Larissa Volokhonsky). Alfred A. Knopf, New York

Draghi M (2015a) Introductory statement, hearing at the European Parliament's economic and monetary affairs committee, 15 June 2015. https://www.ecb.europa.eu/press/key/date/2015/html/sp150615_1.en.html. Accessed 8 Feb 2018

Draghi M (2015b) Speech at the ECB and its watchers XVI conference, ECB, 11 Mar 2015. https://www.ecb.europa.eu/press/key/date/2015/html/sp150311.en.html. Accessed 8 Feb 2018

Eichengreen B (2012) European monetary integration with benefit of hindsight. J Common Mkt Stud 50:123

Eichengreen B, Frieden J (1993) The political economy of European monetary unification: an analytical introduction. Econ Pol 5:85

Friedman M (1962) Capitalism and freedom. University of Chicago Press, Chicago, IL

Goldmann M (2014) Adjudicating economics? Central bank independence and the appropriate standard of judicial review. German L J 15:265

Goodhart C (1998) The two concepts of money: implications for the analysis of optimal currency areas. Eur J Pol Econ 14:407

Goodhart C (2015) Currency school versus banking school: an ongoing confrontation. Econ Thought 4:20

Graeber D (2011) Debt: the first 5,000 years. Melville House, New York

Hahn HJ, Häde U (2010) Währungsrecht, 2nd edn. Beck, Munich

Hayek FA (1977) Entnationalisierung des Geldes. Eine Analyse der Theorie und Praxis konkurrierender Umlaufsmittel. Mohr Siebeck, Tuebingen

Herrmann C (2010) Währungshoheit, Währungsverfassung und subjektive Rechte. Mohr Siebeck, Tuebingen

[148] *Id.* p. 189.

Herrmann C (2012) Die Bewältigung der Euro-Staatsschulden-Krise an den Grenzen des deutschen und europäischen Währungsverfassungsrechts. EuZW 21:805
Huber J (2013) Monetäre Modernisierung. Zur Zukunft der Geldordnung: Vollgeld und Monetative, 3rd edn. Metropolis, Marburg
Huber J (2014) Modern money theory and new currency theory: a comparative discussion, including an assessment of their relevance to monetary reform. Real-World Econ Rev 38(66):50
Ingham G (2004) The nature of money. Polity, Cambridge
Isensee J, Kirchhof P (eds) (2007) 5 Handbuch des Staatsrechts der Bundesrepublik Deutschland, 3rd edn. C.F. Müller, Heidelberg
Joerges C (2014a) Brother, can you paradigm? ICON 12:769
Joerges C (2014b) Three transformations of Europe and the search for a way out of its crisis. In: Joerges C, Glinski C (eds) The European crisis and the transformation of transnational governance: authoritarian managerialism versus democratic governance, p 25. Hart Publishing, Oxford
Joerges C (2016) Pereat Iustitia, Fiat Mundus: what is left of the european economic constitution after the OMT litigation? MJ 23:99
Kaboub F (2007) Employment guarantee programs: a survey of theories and policy experiences. Levy Economics Institute Working Paper No. 498, May 2007
Kämmerer JA (2013) Art 123 AEUV. In: Siekmann H (ed) EWU. Kommentar zur Europäischen Währungsunion, p 150. Mohr Siebeck, Tuebingen
Kennedy D (2013) International legal theory: law and the political economy of the world. Leiden J Int Law 26:7
Kirchhof P (2007) Die Steuern. In: Isensee J, Kirchhof P (eds) 5 Handbuch des Staatsrechts der Bundesrepublik Deutschland, 3rd edn, p 959. C.F. Müller, Heidelberg
Kloepfer M (2014) Finanzverfassungsrecht mit Haushaltsverfassungsrecht. Beck, Munich
Knapp GF (1905) Staatliche Theorie des Geldes. Duncker & Humblot, Leipzig
Kumhof M, Jakab Z (2016) The truth about banks. Financ Dev 53(1), Mar 2016
Lerner AP (1943) Functional finance and the federal debt. Soc Res 10:38
Lerner AP (1947) Money as a creature of the state. Am Econ Rev 37:312
Marx K (1867) Das Kapital. Kritik der politischen Ökonomie, vol 1. Otto Meissners Verlag, Hamburg
Mayer T (2014) Die neue Ordnung des Geldes: Warum Wir eine Geldreform brauchen. FinanzBuch Verlag, Munich
McLeay M, Radia A, Thomas R (2014) Money creation in the modern economy: an introduction. Bank Engl Q Bull Q1:1
Menger C (1892) On the origin of money. Econ J 2:238 (trans: Foley CA)
Mersch Y (2015) On European unity: economic and institutional challenges facing Europe, ECB, 25 June 2015. https://www.ecb.europa.eu/press/key/date/2015/html/sp150625.en.html. Accessed 8 Feb 2018
Mitchell W, Muysken J (2008) Full employment abandoned: shifting sands and policy failures. Edward Elgar Publishing, Cheltenham
Mitchell W, Wray LR, Watts M (2016) Modern monetary theory and practice: an introductory text. CreateSpace Independent Publishing Platform
Mitchell-Innes A (1913) What is money? Banking Law J 361(5):377
Mosler W (2010) The seven deadly innocent frauds of economic policy. Valance Co. Inc., Christiansted
Mundell RA (1961) A theory of optimum currency areas. Am Econ Rev 51:657
Ohler C (2015) Bankenaufsicht und Geldpolitik in der Währungsunion. Beck, Munich
Piketty T (2014) Capital in the twenty-first century. Harvard University Press, Cambridge, MA
Plickert P (2013) Deutsche Ökonomen werfen der EZB Staatsfinanzierung vor, FAZ, 11 Sept 2013. http://www.faz.net/aktuell/wirtschaft/eurokrise/neuer-appell-deutsche-oekonomen-werfen-der-ezb-staatsfinanzierung-vor-12569316.html. Accessed 8 Feb 2018
Ricks M (2015) The money problem: rethinking financial regulation. University of Chicago Press, Chicago, IL

Roth M (2015) Beschäftigung als gelpolitisches Ziel der Europäischen Zentralbank. Soziales Recht 4:141

Roubini N (2016) Unconventional monetary policy on stilts, Social Europe, 5 Apr 2016. https://www.socialeurope.eu/2016/04/unconventional-monetary-policy-stilts/. Accessed 8 Feb 2018

Sassen S (2014) Expulsions: brutality and complexity in the global economy. Harvard University Press, Cambridge, MA

Scharpf FW (2011) Monetary union, fiscal crisis and the preemption of democracy. MPIfG Discussion Paper 11/11

Schmidt R (2007) Geld und Währung. In: Isensee J, Kirchhof P (eds) 5 Handbuch des Staatsrechts der Bundesrepublik Deutschland, 3rd edn, p 935. C.F. Müller, Heidelberg

Sigurjonsson F (2015) Monetary reform: a better monetary system for Iceland. Report commissioned by the Prime Minister of Iceland. https://www.stjornarradid.is/media/forsaetisraduneyti-media/media/Skyrslur/monetary-reform.pdf. Accessed 8 Feb 2018

Smith A (1776) The wealth of nations. W. Strahan and T. Cadell, London

Specht L (2015) Review of Christine Desan, making money. Coin, currency, and the coming of capitalism. ICON 13:774

Streeck W (2011) The crises of democratic capitalism. New Left Rev 71:5 (Sept–Oct 2011)

Streeck W (2013) Gekaufte Zeit: Die vertagte Krise des demokratischen Kapitalismus. Suhrkamp Verlag, Berlin

Streeck W (2015) Why the Euro divides Europe. New Left Rev 95(5):9–10, Sept–Oct 2015

Streeck W, Mertens D (2010) Politik im Defizit: Austerität als fiskalpolitisches Regime. Der moderne Staat 3:7

Tabb WK (2004) Economic governance in the age of globalization. Columbia University Press, New York

Teubner G (2011) A constitutional moment? – The logics of 'hit the bottom'. In: Kjaer P, Teubner G (eds) The financial crisis in constitutional perspective: the dark side of functional differentiation, pp 3–42. Hart Publishing, Oxford

Transcript of the Hearing at the European Parliament's Economic and Monetary Affairs Committee, 15 June 2015. https://www.ecb.europa.eu/press/key/date/2015/html/sp150615_1.en.html. Accessed 8 Feb 2018

Trichet JC (2010) Reflections on the nature of monetary policy non-standard measures and finance theory, ECB, 18 Nov 2010. https://www.ecb.europa.eu/press/key/date/2010/html/sp101118.en.html. Accessed 8 Feb 2018

Turner A (2015) Between debt and the devil: money, credit, and fixing global finance. Princeton University Press, Princeton, NJ

Unger R (1996) What should legal analysis become? Verso, London

Unger R (1998) Democracy realized: the progressive alternative. Verso, London

Vogel K (2004) Der Finanz – und Steuerstaat. In: Isensee J, Kirchhof P (eds) 2 Handbuch des Staatsrechts der Bundesrepublik Deutschland, 3rd edn, p 843. C.F. Müller, Heidelberg

Vogl J (2015) Der Souveränitätseffekt. Diaphanes Verlag, Zürich

Waldhoff C (2007) Grundzüge des Finanzrechts des Grundgesetzes. In: Isensee J, Kirchhof P (eds) 5 Handbuch des Staatsrechts der Bundesrepublik Deutschland, 3rd edn, p 813. C.F. Müller, Heidelberg

Wray LR (ed) (2004) Credit and state theories of money. The contributions of A. Mitchell-Innes. Edward Elgar Publishing, Cheltenham

Wray LR (2014) From the state theory of money to modern money theory: an alternative to economic orthodoxy. Levy Economics Institute Working Paper No 792, Mar 2014

Wray LR (2015) Modern money theory: a primer on macroeconomics for sovereign monetary systems, 2nd edn. Springer, Heidelberg

Zioli C, Selmayr M (2001) The law of the European central bank. Hart Publishing, Oxford

Isabel Feichtner is Professor for Public Law and International Economic Law at the Julius-Maximilians-Universität Würzburg.

Max-Planck-Institut für ausländisches öffentliches Recht und Völkerrecht

Beiträge zum ausländischen öffentlichen Recht und Völkerrecht

Hrsg.: A. von Bogdandy, A. Peters

Bde. 27–59 erschienen im Carl Heymanns Verlag KG Köln, Berlin (Bestellung an: Max-Planck-Institut für Völkerrecht, Im Neuenheimer Feld 535, 69120 Heidelberg); ab Band 60 im Springer-Verlag GmbH

---

243 Marianne *Klumpp*: **Schiedsgerichtsbarkeit und Ständiges Revisionsgericht des Mercosur.** 2013. XX, 512 Seiten. Geb. € 94,99

242 Karen *Kaiser* (Hrsg.): **Der Vertrag von Lissabon vor dem Bundesverfassungsgericht.** 2013. XX, 1635 Seiten. Geb. € 199,99

241 Dominik *Steiger*: **Das völkerrechtliche Folterverbot und der "Krieg gegen den Terror".** 2013. XXX, 821 Seiten. Geb. € 139,99

240 Silja *Vöneky*, Britta *Beylage-Haarmann*, Anja *Höfelmeier*, Anna-Katharina *Hübler* (Hrsg.): **Ethik und Recht - Die Ethisierung des Rechts/Ethics and Law - The Ethicalization of Law.** 2013. XVIII, 456 Seiten. Geb. € 94,99

239 Rüdiger *Wolfrum*, Ina *Gätzschmann* (eds.): **International Dispute Settlement: Room for Innovations?** 2013. XIV, 445 Seiten. Geb. € 94,95 zzgl. landesüblicher MwSt.

238 Isabel *Röcker*: **Die Pflicht zur rahmenbeschlusskonformen Auslegung nationalen Rechts.** 2013. XXIII, 410 Seiten. Geb. € 89,95

237 Maike *Kuhn*: **Die Europäische Sicherheits- und Verteidigungspolitik im Mehrebenensystem.** 2012. XIII, 325 Seiten. Geb. € 79,95

236 Armin *von Bogdandy*, Ingo *Venzke* (eds.): **International Judicial Lawmaking.** 2012. XVII, 509 Seiten. Geb. € 94,95 zzgl. landesüblicher MwSt.

235 Susanne *Wasum-Rainer*, Ingo *Winkelmann*, Katrin *Tiroch* (eds.): **Arctic Science, International Law and Climate Change.** 2012. XIX, 374 Seiten. Geb. € 84,95 zzgl. landesüblicher MwSt.

234 Mirja A. *Trilsch*: **Die Justiziabilität wirtschaftlicher, sozialer und kultureller Rechte im innerstaatlichen Recht.** 2012. XIX, 559 Seiten. Geb. € 99,95

233 Anja *Seibert-Fohr* (ed.): **Judicial Independence in Transition.** 2012. XIII, 1378 Seiten. Geb. € 169,95 zzgl. landesüblicher MwSt.

232 Sandra *Stahl*: **Schutzpflichten im Völkerrecht - Ansatz einer Dogmatik.** 2012. XXX, 505 Seiten. Geb. € 94,95

231 Thomas *Kleinlein*: **Konstitutionalisierung im Völkerrecht.** 2012. XLII, 940 Seiten. Geb. € 149,95

230 Roland *Otto*: **Targeted Killings and International Law.** 2012. XVIII, 661 Seiten. Geb. € 109,95 zzgl. landesüblicher MwSt.

229 Nele *Matz-Lück*, Mathias *Hong* (Hrsg.): **Grundrechte und Grundfreiheiten im Mehrebenensystem - Konkurrenzen und Interferenzen.** 2012. VIII, 394 Seiten. Geb. € 89,95

228 Matthias *Ruffert*, Sebastian *Steinecke*: **The Global Administrative Law of Science,** 2011. IX, 140 Seiten. Geb. € 59,95 zzgl. landesüblicher MwSt.

227 Sebastian *Pritzkow*: **Das völkerrechtliche Verhältnis zwischen der EU und Russland im Energiesektor.** 2011. XXIV, 304 Seiten. Geb. € 79,95

226 Sarah *Wolf*: **Unterseeische Rohrleitungen und Meeresumweltschutz.** 2011. XXIII, 442 Seiten. Geb. € 94,95

225 Clemens *Feinäugle*: **Hoheitsgewalt im Völkerrecht.** 2011. XXVI, 418 Seiten. Geb. € 89,95

224 David *Barthel*: **Die neue Sicherheits- und Verteidigungsarchitektur der Afrikanischen Union.** 2011. XXV, 443 Seiten. Geb. € 94,95

223 Tilmann *Altwicker*: **Menschenrechtlicher Gleichheitsschutz.** 2011. XXX, 549 Seiten. Geb. € 99,95

222 Stephan *Bitter*: **Die Sanktion im Recht der Europäischen Union.** 2011. XV, 351 Seiten. Geb. € 84,95

221 Holger *Hestermeyer*, Nele *Matz-Lück*, Anja *Seibert-Fohr*, Silja *Vöneky* (eds.): **Law of the Sea in Dialogue.** 2011. XII, 189 Seiten. Geb. € 69,95 zzgl. landesüblicher MwSt.

220 Jan *Scheffler*: **Die Europäische Union als rechtlich-institutioneller Akteur im System der Vereinten Nationen.** 2011. XXXV, 918 Seiten. Geb. € 149,95

219 Mehrdad *Payandeh*: **Internationales Gemeinschaftsrecht.** 2010. XXXV, 629 Seiten. Geb. € 99,95

218 Jakob *Pichon*: **Internationaler Strafgerichtshof und Sicherheitsrat der Vereinten Nationen.** 2011. XXVI, 399 Seiten. Geb. € 89,95

217 Michael *Duchstein*: **Das internationale Benchmarkingverfahren und seine Bedeutung für den gewerblichen Rechtsschutz.** 2010. XXVI, 528 Seiten. Geb. € 99,95

216 Tobias *Darge*: **Kriegsverbrechen im nationalen und internationalen Recht.** 2010. XXXV, 499 Seiten. Geb. € 94,95

Lightning Source UK Ltd.
Milton Keynes UK
UKHW04n0906300818
327974UK00011B/557/P

9 783662 555675